CINEMATOGRAPHY

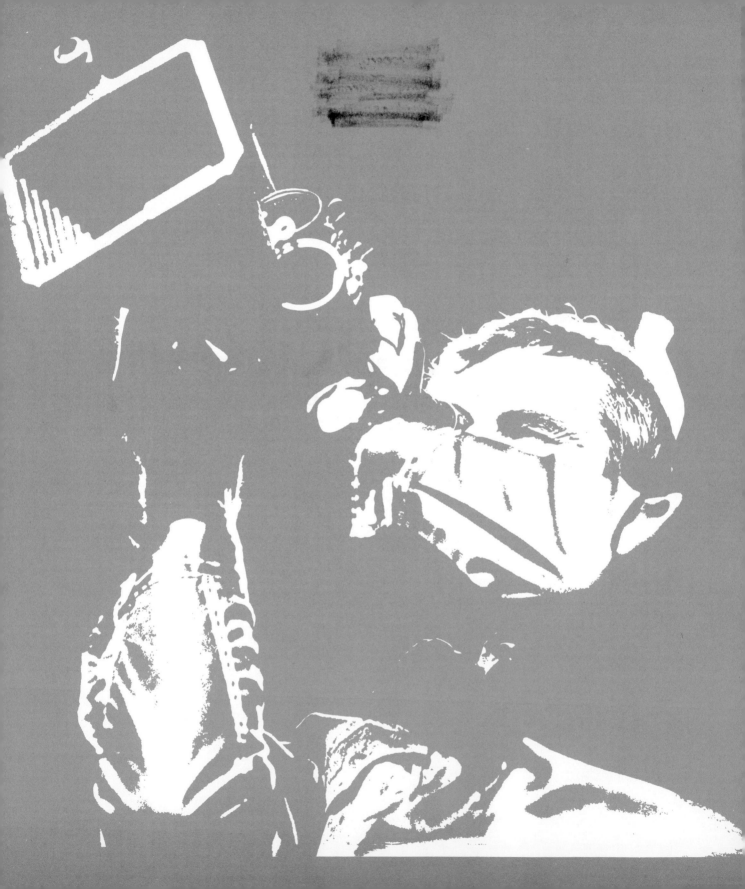

CINEMATOGRAPHY
A Guide for Film Makers and Film Teachers

Revised Edition

J. KRIS MALKIEWICZ
assisted by Robert E. Rogers

LINE DRAWINGS BY JIM FLETCHER

VNR VAN NOSTRAND REINHOLD COMPANY
NEW YORK CINCINNATI TORONTO LONDON MELBOURNE

Van Nostrand Reinhold Company Regional Offices:
New York Cincinnati Chicago Millbrae Dallas
Van Nostrand Reinhold Company International Offices:
London   Toronto   Melbourne

Copyright © 1973 by Litton Educational Publishing, Inc.
Library of Congress Catalog Card Number: 77-183487
ISBN 0 442 25079 7 cl.
ISBN 0 442 25080 0 pb.

Designed by Visuality

Published by Van Nostrand Reinhold Company
450 West 33rd Street, New York, N.Y. 10001
Published simultaneously in Canada by
Van Nostrand Reinhold Company Ltd.

16 15 14 13 12 11 10 9 8 7 6 5 4

to Judith

Contents

Preface

When a person is asked to explain something that he knows best in practical application, he often has to rethink the whole process and all the principles involved before he can communicate what he knows clearly and logically. I was fortunate enough to learn this basic fact of teaching before I attempted to write this book. I have taught film making, and my students' questions have both helped me learn how to teach the subject and forced me to clarify in my own mind many aspects of it. I hope that the reader, who cannot just raise his hand if he is puzzled, will benefit from this.

One difficulty in teaching cinematography is that whenever the teacher explains one technical aspect, there seems to be a need to explain many others as well. I have tried to avoid too many digressions. This book concentrates on the work of the cinematographer — the man behind the camera or in charge of the shooting. It does touch briefly on techniques of sound recording, cutting, and production logistics, because some knowledge in these areas is necessary for the serious cameraman, especially in view of the increasing trend toward personal film making, where a single creative individual performs the multiple functions of a film crew. Equipment miniaturization makes one-man film making more and more practical, opening the door to an era of "auteurs" in the true sense. But this is a technical book, and therefore it does not venture into film directing.

Nevertheless, I cordially invite film makers who direct their own films but know little of camera techniques to read it, if for no other reason than to make the lives of their cameramen much easier. In the quest for more innovative, experimental techniques, it is extremely useful to know the existing principles before one tries to break them. The only really important outcome of film making is what happens in the heads of the audience. That is what counts. But the long and painstaking route to the audience leads through the lens and film in a camera. This book will try to help you take that route and record your creative vision with fewer frustrating disappointments and more competency and joy.

I wish to express my thanks to Bob Rogers, whose collaboration was fundamental in the realization of this book. I would also like to thank several friends for their advice and encouragement — Brian Moore, Pat O'Neill, Haskell Wexler, Don Worthen, Frank Stokes, David Smith, Roy Findlon, and Milan Chupurdija. I am greatly indebted to my editor, Ted Johnson, for his expert help in shaping the text and to Myron S. Hall 3rd of Visuality for the visual layout of this book.

Finally, I am grateful to the manufacturers, suppliers, and laboratories that contributed photographs, charts, and information.

CHAPTER 1
CAMERAS

The cinematographer's most basic tool is the motion-picture camera. This piece of precision machinery comprises scores of coordinated functions, each of which demands understanding and care if the camera is to produce the best and most consistent results. The beginning cameraman's goal should be to become thoroughly familiar and comfortable with the camera's operation, so that he can concentrate on the more creative aspects of cinematography.

This chapter must cover many isolated bits of practical information. However, once the reader has become familiar with camera operation he will be able to move on to the substance of the cinematographer's art in subsequent chapters. In the meantime the reader is well advised to try to absorb each operation-oriented detail presented in this chapter, because operating a camera is *all* details. If any detail is neglected, the quality of the work can be impaired.

PRINCIPLE OF INTERMITTENT MOVEMENT

The film-movement mechanism is what really distinguishes a cinema camera from a still camera. The illusion of image motion is created by a rapid succession of still photographs. To arrest every frame for the time of exposure, the principle of an intermittent mechanism was borrowed from clocks and sewing machines. Almost all general-purpose motion-picture cameras employ the intermittent principle.

Intermittent mechanisms vary in design. All have a pull-down claw and pressure plate. Some have a registration pin as well. The pull-down claw engages the film perforation and moves the film down one frame. It then disengages and goes back up to pull down the next frame. While the claw is disengaged, the pressure plate holds the film steady for the period of exposure. Some cameras have a registration pin that enters the film perforation for extra steadiness while the exposure is made.

Whatever mechanism is employed, it requires the best materials and machining possible, which is one reason why good cameras are expensive. The film gate (the part of the camera where the pressure plate, pull-down claw, and registration pin engage the film) needs a good deal of attention when cleaning and threading. The film gate is never too clean. This is the area where the exposure takes place, so any emulsion deposits, dirt, or hair will show on the exposed

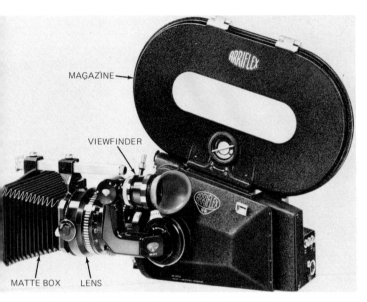

MAGAZINE→

VIEWFINDER

MATTE BOX   LENS

1-1 Arriflex 16 BL camera. (Courtesy of Arnold & Richter)

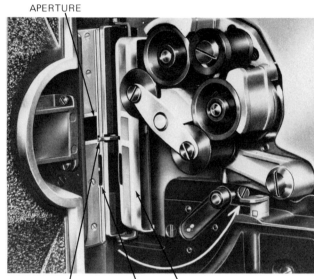

APERTURE

REGISTRATION PIN   PRESSURE PLATE

PULLDOWN CLAW

1-2 Arriflex camera gate. (Courtesy of Arnold & Richter)

1-3 Arriflex intermittent mechanism.
(Courtesy of Arnold & Richter)

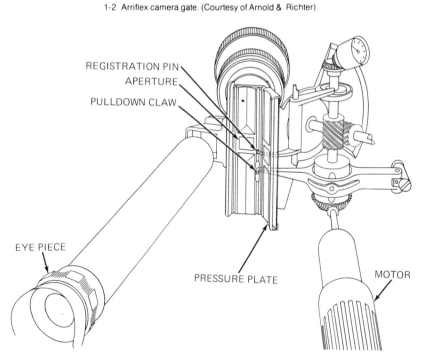

REGISTRATION PIN

APERTURE

PULLDOWN CLAW

EYE PIECE

PRESSURE PLATE

MOTOR

film and perhaps scratch it. This point is essential. On feature films, some assistant cameramen clean the gate after every shot. They know that one grain of sand or bit of emulsion can ruin a day's work. In addition to miscellaneous debris such as sand, hair, and dust, sometimes a small amount of emulsion comes off the passing film and collects in the gate. It must be removed.

The gate should first be cleaned with a rubber-bulb syringe to blow foreign particles away. (Many cameramen use compressed air supplied in cans; they must be used in an upright position or they will spray a gluey substance into the camera.) An orange stick, available wherever cosmetics are sold, can then be used to remove any sticky emulsion buildup. The gate and pressure plate should also be wiped with a clean chamois or cotton cloth — never with linen. Never use metal tools for cleaning the gate, or for that matter for cleaning any part of the film-movement mechanism, because they may cause abrasions, which in turn will scratch the passing film.

The gate should be cleaned every time the camera is reloaded. At the same time the surrounding camera interior and magazine should also be cleaned to ensure that no dirt will find its way to the gate while the camera is running.

The intermittent movement requires the film to be slack so that as it alternately stops and jerks ahead in one-frame advances, there will be no strain on it. Therefore, one or two sprocket rollers are provided to maintain two loops, one before and one after the gate. In some cameras (such as the Bolex and Canon Scoopic) a self-threading mechanism forms the loops automatically. In Super-8 cassettes and cartridges, the loops are already formed by the manufacturer. On manually threaded cameras, the film path showing loop size is usually marked.

Too small a loop will not absorb the jerks of the intermittent movement, resulting in picture unsteadiness, scratched film, broken perforations, and possibly a camera jam. An oversized loop may vibrate against the camera interior and also cause an unsteady picture and scratched film. Either too large or too small a loop will also contribute to camera noise.

Camera Speeds

The speed at which the intermittent movement advances the film is expressed in frames per second (fps). To reproduce movement on the screen faithfully, the film must be projected at the *same* speed as it was shot. Standard shooting and projection speeds for 16mm and 35mm are 24 fps for sound film and 16 fps for silent film; standard speeds for 8mm and Super-8 are 24 fps for sound and 18 fps for silent. Sound speed (24 fps) is the most common.

If both the camera and the projector are run at the *same* speeds, say 24 fps, then the action will be faithfully reproduced. However, if the camera runs *slower* than the projector, the action will appear to move *faster* on the screen than it did in real life. For example, an action takes place in four seconds (real time) and it is photographed at 12 fps. That means that the four seconds of action is recorded over 48 frames. If it is now projected at standard sound speed of 24 fps, it will take only two seconds to project. Therefore, the action that took four seconds in real life is sped up to two seconds on the screen because the camera ran slower than the projector.

The opposite is also true. If the camera runs *faster* than the projector, the action will be slowed down in projection. So to obtain slow motion, speed the camera up; to obtain fast motion, slow the camera down.

This variable-speed principle has several applications. Time-lapse photography can compress time and make very slow movement visible, such as the growth of a flower or the movement of clouds across the sky. Photographing slow-moving clouds at a rate of, say, one frame every three seconds will make them appear to be rushing through the screen when the film is projected at 24 frames per second. On the other hand, movements filmed at 36 fps or faster acquire a slow dreamy quality at 24 fps on the screen. Such effects can be used to create a mood or analyze a movement. A very practical use of slow motion is to smooth out a jerky camera movement such as a rough traveling shot. The jolts are less prominent in slow motion.

To protect the intermittent movement, never run the camera at high speeds when it is not loaded.

THE SHUTTER

A change in camera speed will cause a change in shutter speed.

In most cameras the shutter consists of a rotating disk with a 180° cutout. As it rotates it covers the aperture while the film advances into position. Rotating farther, the cutout portion allows the frame to be exposed and then covers it again for the next pull-down. The shutter rotates constantly, and therefore

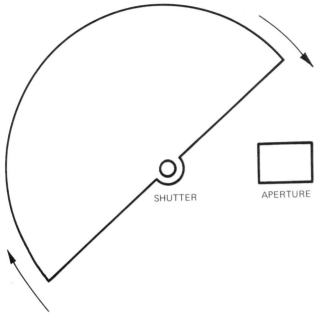

SHUTTER   APERTURE

1-4 180° rotating shutter.

Some cameras are equipped with a variable shutter. By varying the angle of the cutout we can regulate the exposure. For example, a 90° shutter opening transmits half as much light as a 180° opening. Some amateurs who do not intend to have prints made make fade-outs and fade-ins on their original film by using the variable shutter. Professionals have all such effects done in the lab.

1-5 Eclair NPR adjustable shutter. Notice the calibrations visible through the empty lens socket. (Courtesy of Eclair International)

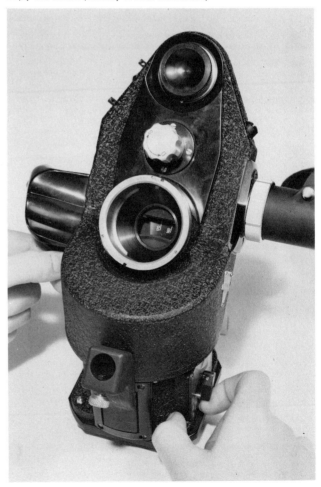

the film is exposed half the time and covered the other half. So when the camera is running at 24 fps, the actual period of exposure for each frame is 1/48 of a second (half of 1/24). Varying the speed of the camera also changes the exposure time. For example, by *slowing* the movement to half, or 12 fps, we *increase* the exposure period for each frame, to 1/24 of a second. Similarly, by *speeding up* the movement to double the normal 24 fps to 48 fps, we *reduce* the exposure period, to 1/96 of a second. Knowing these relationships, we can adjust the f-stop to compensate for the change in exposure time when filming fast or slow motion.

A change in the speed of film movement can be useful when filming at low light levels. For example, suppose you are filming a cityscape at dusk and there is not enough light. By reducing your speed to 12 fps, you can double the exposure period for each frame, giving you an extra stop of light that may save your shot. Of course this technique would be unacceptable if there were any pedestrians or moving cars in view; they would be unnaturally sped up when the film was projected.

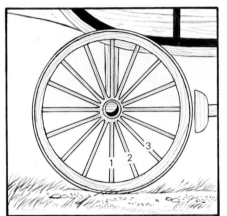 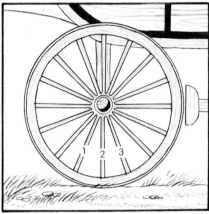 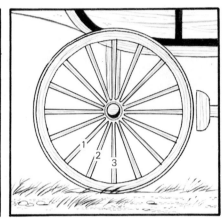

1-6 Stroboscopic effect.

1-7 Arriflex mirror shutter viewing system (Courtesy of Arnold & Richter)

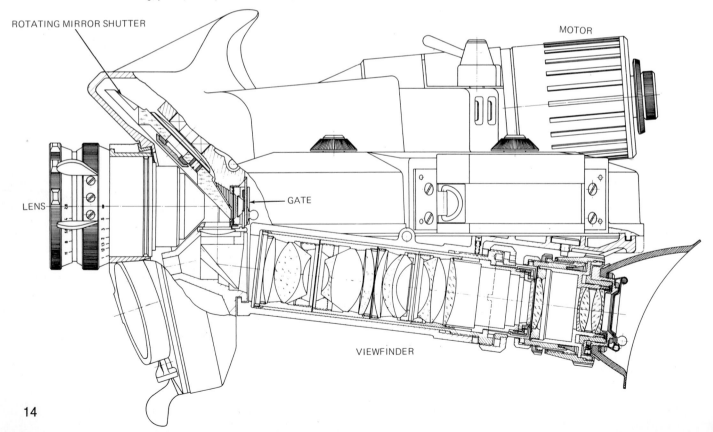

ROTATING MIRROR SHUTTER

MOTOR

LENS

GATE

VIEWFINDER

14

Shutter movement is directly responsible for the stroboscopic effect. Take the example of the spokes of a turning wheel. Our intermittent exposures may catch each *succeeding* spoke in the same place in the frame, making the spinning wheel appear to be motionless. Another variation, called skipping, results from movement past parallel lines or objects such as the railings of a fence. They may appear to be vibrating. These effects will increase with faster movement and with a narrower shutter angle.

VIEWING SYSTEMS

In many cameras (like the Arriflex and Eclair) the shutter performs a vital role in the viewing system. The front of the shutter has a mirror surface that reflects the image into the viewfinder when the shutter is closed. The great advantage of this system is that *all* the light goes alternately to the film and to the cameraman's eye, providing the brightest image possible. The surface of the mirror shutter should be cleaned only with an air syringe or other source of compressed air; nothing should be allowed to touch it.

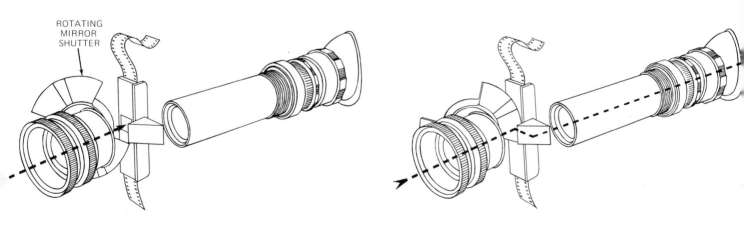

ROTATING
MIRROR
SHUTTER

1-8 Arriflex viewing system. *A:* Shutter open — all light passes to film. *B:* Shutter closed — all light passes to viewfinder. (Courtesy of Arnold & Richter)

Other systems (like the Bolex Reflex) use a prism between the lens and the shutter so that a certain percentage of the light is constantly diverted to the viewfinder. The disadvantage of this system is that it reduces the amount of light going both to the viewfinder and to the film, since the beam is split. An exposure compensation is required to allow for the light "stolen" from the film by the viewing system. It is usually very slight. For example, in the Bolex Rex-5 the loss is about a third of a stop. You should consult the operator's manual for the specific camera to learn the exact compensation.

The viewing systems discussed so far allow the cameraman to look through the taking lens. Many cameras of older design do not have this "reflexive" viewing system. As a result the camera may not see exactly what the viewfinder sees. Referred to as "parallax," this is especially a problem in closeups or with telephoto lenses. However, most nonreflex cameras have an adjustment that can partly correct for parallax.

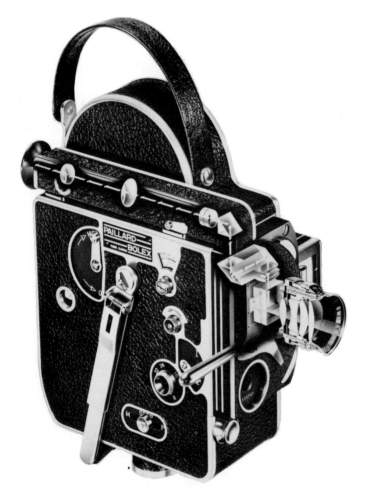

1-9 Bolex split-beam reflex viewing system. (Courtesy of Bolex/Paillard)

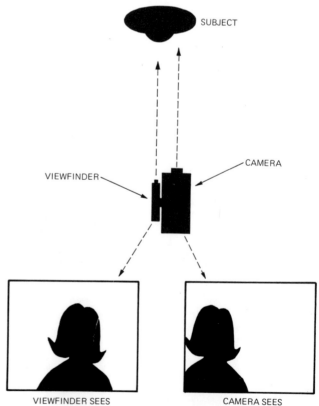

1-10 Parallax effect.

MOTORS

The film-transport mechanism, the shutter, and other moving camera parts are operated by the motor. There are two basic types of motors, spring-wound and electric. Spring-wound cameras run approximately 20 to 40 feet of film per wind. The advantages include a compact design and reliable performance under difficult conditions such as cold weather.

Electric motors are available in a wide variety of designs. The three most common types are wild, synchronous, and constant-speed motors. Wild, or variable-speed, motors have an adjustable speed control that may range from 2 to 64 fps or more. Synchronous motors are for sound-sync shooting and must be run from the same AC power source as the sound recorder. Since the introduction of the sync-tone sound system, the constant-speed motor has been replacing the synchronous motor for sound work, especially on location. Constant-speed motors always run at the one speed for which they are set.

The most advanced type of constant-speed motor is designed with a crystal control to regulate the speed with extreme precision. When the camera motor and the tape recorder are both equipped with crystal controls, you can film in-sync with no cables connecting the camera to the recorder. Furthermore, several crystal-control cameras can be held in-sync to one or more crystal recorders, allowing for multi-camera coverage with no cables to restrict the distances between them. Some crystal-control motors even combine several functions, allowing the operator to change from constant-speed crystal-sync to variable-speed or single-frame, at the touch of a switch.

Like all precise machinery, camera motors must be treated correctly. It is absolutely essential to learn all the characteristics of a specific motor before using it. Very expensive equipment is often seriously damaged by applying the wrong electric current or wrong polarity. Most 16mm and all 8mm electric motors operate on DC current, and any attempt to plug them into a wall socket (high AC voltage) without the proper rectifier (a device to change AC to DC) will result in disaster. Even *with* a rectifier it can be dangerous, and the manufacturer's literature should be consulted.

Many motors are transistorized and therefore will be badly damaged by incorrect polarity. Positive must go to positive and negative to negative. (A red marking on a terminal always means positive.) The wrong voltage or current will damage any camera motor. Always follow the manufacturer's recommendations.

For operating camera motors, properly wired batteries are the safest source of DC current. Nickel-cadmium batteries are best because they last a long time. Many batteries have a built-in charger to be operated either from 110-volt or 220-volt wall sockets. Always make sure the voltage setting on the charger matches the voltage of the outlet.

A few sophisticated batteries include meters indicating battery-charge level and sync tone (discussed in Chapter 6).

The battery belt consisting of built-in nickel-cadmium cells seems to be the most convenient power source for portable 16mm and 35mm cameras, especially when hand-held. All Super-8 cameras house the battery in the camera body, doing away with the cable connecting the battery as a separate unit. This trend is rapidly expanding into 16mm designs.

MAGAZINES

Most of the smaller 16mm cameras will house up to 100-foot loads (on daylight spools) inside the camera body. When loading 100-foot spools, one must remember the manufacturer's number punched into the roll about 6 feet from the beginning. The punched numbers will appear on the footage, perhaps ruining the first shot. This is avoided by running the film ahead 6 feet before filming on each new reel. (There will still be 100 feet of usable film remaining; the manufacturer includes extra footage on the roll to allow for this wastage.) To make sure you have passed the number you could remove the lens and watch the film advancing in the aperture until you see the numbers go by, though most cameramen merely run off 6 feet.

When considering magazines, the two decisive factors are the capacity and the design. Larger 16mm cameras are usually equipped with film magazines ranging in capacity from 200 to 1200 feet. The shape and placement of the magazine is sometimes important too. For most shooting situations it doesn't matter, but when you are shooting in cramped quarters, such as from the cockpit of a plane or from under a car, the bulkiness of the camera can make a difference. Here a cameraman may want a camera with magazines that are smaller or that mount to the back or bottom of the camera rather than the top.

At one time all magazines had to be loaded in total darkness. Today loads of 200 and 400 feet are available on daylight spools that require only subdued light when loading. Film not on daylight reels necessitates either a darkroom or a changing bag. The changing bag must be of adequate size and absolutely light-tight. It should be stored in a special case or cover to keep it spotlessly clean and dust-free. (Don't let your dog sleep on it.) Any hairs, dirt, or dust in the changing bag can easily enter the magazine being loaded and from there travel to the gate.

Before loading an unfamiliar magazine, practice loading it with a roll of waste film that you don't want, first in the light and then in the dark, to simulate the loading of unexposed stock.

Some magazines have their own take-up motors to wind up the film as it reenters the magazine after passing through the camera. Such motors should be tested with a waste roll before the magazine is loaded with unexposed film. Run this test with the battery to be used in filming. This test is advisable because a battery may sometimes have enough charge to run a camera with a 100-foot internal load or an empty magazine, but then fail to operate the magazine and camera when it is loaded.

Also, before loading, clean the magazine with your air syringe and camera brush to remove dust, film chips, hair, etc., and make sure the rollers are moving freely. (Never wear a fuzzy or hairy sweater when cleaning camera equipment or in the darkroom.)

After loading the magazine it is advisable to seal the lid with black camera tape. This is partly to prevent light leakage on old magazines, but mainly to prevent an accidental opening. When you are loading magazines in a hurry it is easy to confuse loaded ones and unloaded ones. Taping the loaded magazines immediately after loading will save you the annoyance of opening a supposedly empty magazine and ruining a roll of film.

It is also customary to tape a card onto each magazine. This card should provide space for various information: the type of film inside, the length of the roll and its number, the scene numbers shot, any special filters used, and other data that will be useful when you prepare a proper report sheet to accompany the film to the lab.

In spite of the greatest care in cleaning and loading, even the finest camera designs will occasionally jam. The film will stop advancing somewhere along its path and the oncoming film will continue to pile up at that point, creating a "salad" of twisted and folded film. If the camera jams, remove the film from the camera interior, checking carefully to see that chips of broken film are not stuck in the gate, around the registration pin, or anywhere else. Remove the magazine to a darkroom or put it in a changing bag. You will need a spare take-up core or spool (whichever you already have in the camera) and a can with a black paper bag to unload the exposed film and rethread the magazine.

Never spool up any film with broken sprocket holes. It may jam in the processing machine in the lab and ruin a considerable amount of footage, not only yours, but other customers' as well. If you suspect any damage inside your roll of film, write a warning clearly on the can to alert the lab technicians.

One simple procedure that helps prevent camera jams is to make sure there is no slack between the take-up roll and the sprocket roller. If there is, when the camera starts the take-up motor may snap the film taut, breaking it or causing the camera to "loose its loop" and become improperly threaded. There is usually some way of rotating the take-up roll to make it taut before you start to shoot.

Whenever unloading a magazine be sure to leave the center piece (on which the film core sits) on the spindle where it belongs, and do not send it to·the lab with your film. This is very important. If you send this costly little center piece to the lab, you will have trouble trying to reload the magazine without it.

Super-8 film comes in cartridges and cassettes. Not much can be done if a cassette jams, but you can prevent jamming to a great extent by making sure the cassette fits easily into the camera.

LENSES

Beginners in film making are quite often confused by the various aspects of camera lenses. They are intimidated by the mathematical formulas that appear in many photography books whenever lenses are under discussion. But today the film maker's life is easier. Readily available tables provide all the information that previously required mathematical computation. Common sense is all you need to understand lenses.

The basic function of a lens can be explained as a pinhole phenomenon. If you removed the lens from your camera and replaced it with a piece of black cardboard with a pinhole in it, you could take a picture, provided the exposure time was long enough. The picture on film would be upside down and the sides would be reversed. This is the first thing one should know about lenses: they produce images that are reversed both vertically and horizontally. The advantage of the lens over the pinhole is that where a pinhole allows only a very small amount of light to reach the film, the lens collects more

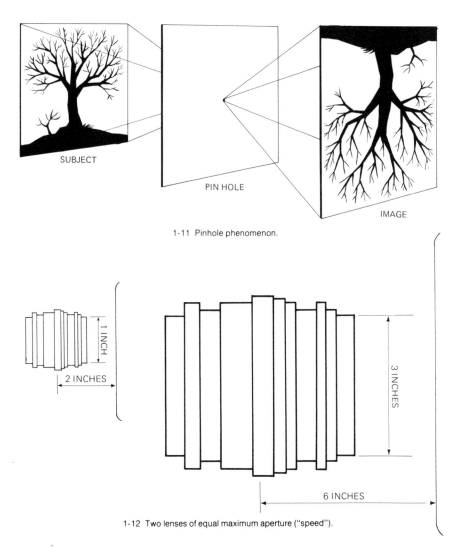

1-11 Pinhole phenomenon.

SUBJECT

PIN HOLE

IMAGE

1 INCH

2 INCHES

3 INCHES

6 INCHES

1-12 Two lenses of equal maximum aperture ("speed").

light and projects it onto the film. In this way shorter exposure and better pictures are achieved.

F-stops

The maximum amount of light a lens is capable of transmitting depends on the diameter of the lens and the focal length. By focal length we mean the distance from the optical center of the lens to the film plane when the lens is focused at infinity. The focal length divided by the diameter of the lens gives us a measure of the maximum aperture. It's quite simple. For example, a lens 1 inch in diameter with a focal length of 2 inches will pass the same amount of light as a lens 3 inches in diameter with a 6-inch focal length, because the maximum aperture, or f-stop, for both lenses is f/2. ($2 \div 1 = 2$; and $6 \div 3 = 2$ also.)

We can reduce the amount of light by means of an iris placed in the lens. By closing the iris we reduce the effective diameter of the lens, thus reducing the amount of light passing through the lens. Now, the f-stop equals the focal length divided by the *new* diameter created by the iris. Therefore, if a 2-inch-focal-length lens has an iris adjusted to a ⅛-inch opening, the f-stop is f/16, because 2 ÷ ⅛ = 16. A 4-inch lens with a ¼-inch iris opening would also be f/16, because 4 ÷ ¼ = 16.

So the f-stop calibration is not a measure of the mere iris opening, but instead expresses the relationship between focal length and iris.

It is important to note that the smaller the iris opening is, the more times it can be divided into the focal length. Therefore, as the iris opening becomes smaller, the f-stop number becomes higher. So a lower f-stop number means more light, and a higher f-stop number means less light.

F-stops are calibrated on the lens. They are commonly 1, 1.4, 2, 2.8, 4, 5.6, 8, 11, 16, and 22. *Each higher f-stop cuts the light by exactly half.* For example, f/11 allows half as much light as f/8. Conversely, f/8 allows twice as much light as f/11. If the difference is more than one stop, remember that the light doubles between each stop. So f/4 will yield 8 times as much light as f/11, because f/8 is twice f/11, f/5.6 is twice f/8, and f/4 is twice f/5.6. Therefore, f/4 is 8 times more light as f/11 because 2 x 2 x 2 = 8. It doubles with each step.

Lens Speed

The lowest (widest) f-stop setting will vary between lenses, depending on their focal lengths and diameters. For example, one lens may start at f/1.9 and another at f/3.5. (Often, as in these cases, the starting number is in between the usual calibrations.) "Lens speed" refers to the widest setting (lowest f-stop) a lens is capable of. For example, a lens that opens to 1.9 is a relatively fast lens, and one that opens only as far as 3.5 is a relatively slow lens. Because telephoto lenses are longer, their diameter will usually divide several times into their focal length, making their lowest f-stop high. Therefore, telephoto lenses tend to be slow, while wide-angle lenses tend to be fast.

T-stops

Some lenses have T-stops as well as f-stops. The two are almost equivalent. T-stops are more precise because they are calibrated for the individual lens. The lenses are individually tested with a light meter to determine how much light is transmitted at various settings, and the T-stops are marked on the barrel of the lens. F-stops, on the other hand, are determined by the mathematical formula and are not calculated for the individual lens. Therefore we should consider T-stops as very accurate f-stops. When calculating the exposure or consulting the tables, f-stops and T-stops can be considered equivalent.

Focusing

Apart from f-stops, nearly every lens has a calibrated ring representing focusing distances. The exceptions are some wide-angle lenses, such as 10mm and shorter, that have a "fixed focus" — that is, there is no need to adjust focus. With a well-adjusted reflex viewing system we can focus quickly and accurately by rotating the focus ring while looking through the lens. Another method, generally used in older cameras without reflexive viewing systems, is to measure the distance between the subject and film plane (marked on the camera by the symbol φ) and set the focus ring accordingly.

The settings achieved by focusing through a reflexive viewing system and by measuring and turning the focus ring may not agree. This may be due to a slight inaccuracy in the

1-13 Focal distances are measured from the subject to the film plane, sometimes indicated on the camera body by the mark φ.

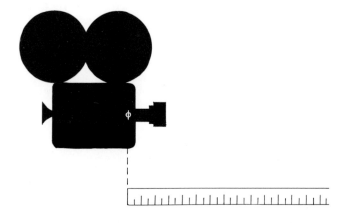

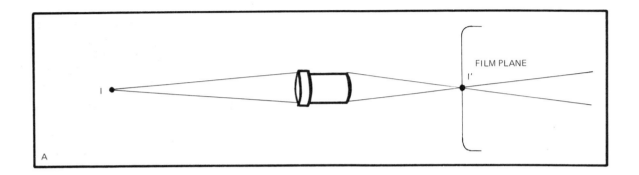

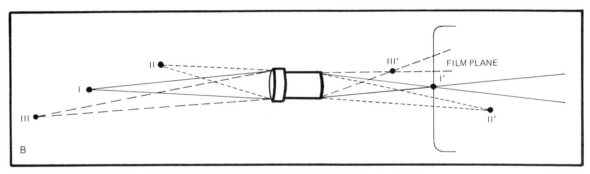

1-14 *A*: One point focused on the film plane. *B*: Lens focused on point I. Points II and III will appear out of focus.

focus ring adjustment. In such cases, *if the viewing system is accurate,* one should depend on it rather than on the focus-ring calibrations.

Depth of Field and Circle of Confusion

If we were to photograph only one distant point, such as a light, the lens would be in focus when it projects a point onto the film.

Because the lens can be focused for only one distance at a time, objects closer and farther away will be slightly out of focus. In the above example a second, closer light would have its image formed behind the film plane and be represented on the film as a circle. A third light, farther away, would form its image in front of the film plane and also appear on the film as a circle. These circles are called "circles of confusion," and they vary in size depending on how far out of focus they are. The "confusion" is that circles smaller than 1/1000 inch confuse our eye and are seen as points in focus. This allows us to see pictures of three-dimensional objects that appear in focus.

We have a range in which objects will appear sharp. It runs

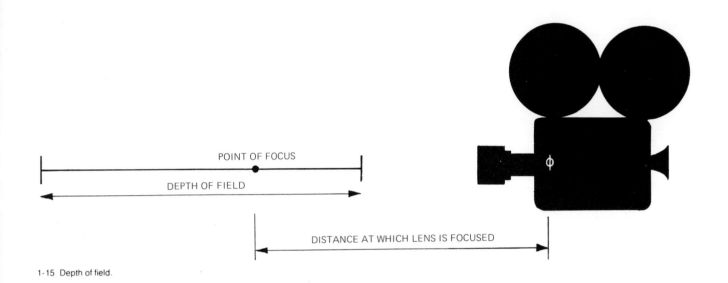

POINT OF FOCUS

DEPTH OF FIELD

DISTANCE AT WHICH LENS IS FOCUSED

1-15 Depth of field.

between the closest and farthest objects represented as circles of confusion smaller than 1/1000 inch. This range is called "depth of field" (and is sometimes incorrectly called "depth of focus").

The depth of field varies with the effective diameter of the lens opening and hence with the f-stop. By "effective diameter" we mean the actual size of the iris opening, not the f-stop number. If you want to change lenses without changing the depth of field, you must use the same iris opening, which will be a different f-stop. For example, an 8-inch lens shooting at f/4 has a 2-inch-diameter iris opening. If you now want to change to a 4-inch lens and retain the same depth of field, you must shoot with the same 2-inch-diameter iris, which for your 4-inch lens if f/2. This is a rare problem, and if it ever comes up, consult a depth-of-field chart. The example is offered here to illustrate that depth of field is dependent on the iris opening.

These general principles govern depth of field:

Greater Depth of Field	Less Depth of Field
Wide-angle lenses	Telephoto lenses
High f-stop (small aperture)	Low f-stop (wide aperture)
Subject far away from camera	Subject close to camera
Smaller format (such as 8mm)	Larger format (such as 35mm)

16mm CAMERA DEPTH-OF-FIELD, HYPERFOCAL DISTANCE & FIELD OF VIEW

LENS FOCAL LENGTH: 25mm   Circle of Confusion = .001" (1/1,000")
(Field of View is based on FULL 16mm Aperture: .402" x .292")

Hyperfocal Dist.	36'8"	28'10"	20'2"	14'5"	10'1"	7'4"	5'0"	3'8"	
	f/2	f/2.8	f/4	f/5.6	f/8	f/11	f/16	f/22	
LENS FOCUS (FEET)	NEAR / FAR	NEAR / FAR	NEAR / FAR	NEAR / FAR	NEAR / FAR	NEAR / FAR	NEAR / FAR	NEAR / FAR	FIELD OF VIEW
50	22'9" / INF.	19'6" / INF.	15'1" / INF.	11'8" / INF.	8'8" / INF.	6'6" / INF.	4'8" / INF.	3'6" / INF.	14'2"x18'9"
25	16'6" / 161'	14'9" / INF.	12'1" / INF.	9'9" / INF.	7'7" / INF.	5'11" / INF.	4'4" / INF.	3'3" / INF.	7'1"x9'5"
15	10'8" / 25'2"	9'11" / 30'11"	8'8" / 56'9"	7'5" / INF.	6'1" / INF.	5'0" / INF.	3'10" / INF.	3'0" / INF.	4'3"x5'8"
10	8'0" / 13'8"	7'5" / 15'2"	6'9" / 19'6"	5'11" / 31'6"	5'1" / INF.	4'3" / INF.	3'5" / INF.	2'8" / INF.	2'10"x3'9"
8	6'7" / 10'2"	6'3" / 11'0"	5'9" / 13'1"	5'2" / 17'6"	4'6" / 35'10"	3'10" / INF.	3'2" / INF.	2'6" / INF.	2'3"x3'0"
6	5'2" / 7'2"	5'0" / 7'6"	4'8" / 8'5"	4'3" / 10'1"	3'10" / 14'3"	3'4" / 29'4"	2'9" / INF.	2'4" / INF.	1'6"x2'0"
5	4'5" / 5'9"	4'3" / 6'0"	4'0" / 6'7"	3'9" / 7'6"	3'4" / 9'7"	3'0" / 14'8"	2'7" / INF.	2'2" / INF.	1'5"x1'10"
4	3'7" / 4'5"	3'6" / 4'7"	3'4" / 4'11"	3'2" / 5'5"	2'11" / 6'5"	2'8" / 8'5"	2'3" / 16'9"	1'11" / INF.	1'1"x1'6"
3	2'10" / 3'2"	2'9" / 3'4"	2'8" / 3'6"	2'6" / 3'9"	2'4" / 4'2"	2'2" / 5'0"	1'11" / 7'1"	1'9" / 8'2"	9"x12"
2	1'11" / 2'1"	1'11" / 2'2"	1'10" / 2'3"	1'9" / 2'4"	1'8" / 2'6"	1'7" / 2'9"	1'5" / 3'3"	1'3" / 3'10"	6"x8"

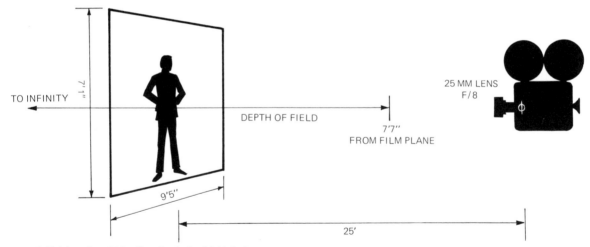

1-17 Information obtained from the depth-of-field chart.

TO INFINITY

7'1"

DEPTH OF FIELD

7'7"
FROM FILM PLANE

9'5"

25'

25 MM LENS
F/8

With greater depth of field more elements in the picture are in sharp focus. This causes the image to appear harder and of higher contrast. Therefore, using a higher f-stop number introduces apparently higher contrast.

Depth-of-field characteristics for lenses of various focal length under different conditions are available in many publications, such as the *American Cinematographer Manual*. Given the focal length and f-stop and the subject-to-film-plane distance, we can determine the range of the depth of field and the dimensions of the field of view at that distance.

For each lens and f-stop the chart also gives the hyperfocal distance. This is the point of greatest depth of field. It is a precalculated figure indicating that if the given lens at the given f-stop is focused at this hyperfocal distance, everything from half this distance to infinity will be in acceptable focus. For example, if for a given lens and f-stop the hyperfocal distance is 20 feet, by focusing at 20 feet we would obtain everything in focus from 10 feet to infinity.

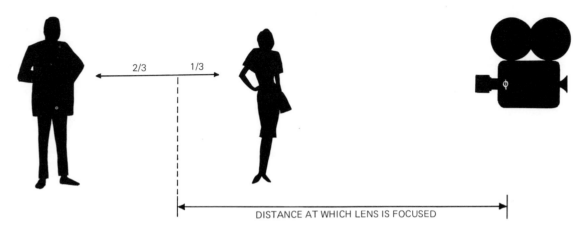

DISTANCE AT WHICH LENS IS FOCUSED

1-18 One-third-distance principle.

A similar principle is valuable when "splitting the focus" between two objects at different distances. They will both be equally sharp if we focus for a point not halfway between them, but a third of the separation distance from the closer object. For example, two objects at 10 and 16 feet respectively would both be equally in focus if you focus for 12 feet. This is often referred to as the one-third-distance principle.

Optimal Range

Every lens has an optimal range of f-stops that yield the sharpest image. This usually starts about two stops from the widest opening and runs to about f/11. Below and above this range the lens will tend to produce slightly less sharp images. Stopping down extends the depth of field, but beyond f/11 or 16 it also decreases the maximum resolution, thereby canceling out the increase in sharpness. This is especially true of wide-angle lenses. Most professionals when shooting indoors like to set the f-stop somewhere in the optimal range (for example, f/5.6) and then adjust the light levels for the proper exposure.

Zoom Lenses

The cinematographer uses a variety of focal lengths. Older camera designs accommodate three or four lenses on a rotating plate called a turret, which allows for quick changing between lenses. In newer cameras the turret is giving way to a one-lens design, the vari-focal lens (zoom lens). It contains not only the primary focal length but all the in-betweens as well as the zoom effect.

The first thing to be considered when describing a zoom lens is its range, for example, 12 to 120mm. We can also express it as a ratio, in this case one to ten (1:10).

The Angenieux 12 to 120mm achieved great popularity in the 16mm film industry. A 10mm lens became its customary companion. Newer zoom lenses like the Angenieux 9.5 to 95mm or the Zeiss Vario Sonnar 10 to 100mm represent a better choice to many cameramen, who are willing to sacrifice the telephoto end of the range in order to increase the wide-angle end. For Super-8 cameras the Schneider Variogon 7 to 68mm and the Angenieux 8 to 64mm are good choices.

Zooming smoothly is an art. There are many mechanical aids available. Zoom lenses come with either zoom levers or cranks or both. For smoother movement a lever can be extended, for example by taping a pencil to it. For very smooth zooming, several types of battery-powered motors are available with variable-speed controls. One type is operated by two buttons (in and out) with speed controlled by a dial. Another type features a "joy stick." The latter is preferable because the speed of zooming and the direction (in or out) are controlled by the one stick depending on which way and how hard you push it. Other combinations are available.

Some cameramen prefer to zoom by turning the zoom ring

with a full grip. If you use this method you must be careful not to move other rings on the lens, such as the f-stop and focus.

While zooming in or out a very slight horizontal panning movement may be needed to keep the subject centered. This is due to a "fault," called side-drift effect, that is inherent to most zoom-lens designs. Some lenses, like the Zeiss 1:10, are free of side-drift effect.

All zoom lenses require the same focusing procedure: you open the aperture fully, zoom all the way in on the subject, and closely examine the sharpness. After focusing, it is easy to forget to return the f-stop to its proper setting. This is a very common mistake among beginners.

Generally, zoom lenses do not focus closer than a few feet. For example, the Angenieux 12 to 120 will only focus as close as about 5 feet away. The exceptions are the "macro-zoom" lenses, such as the Canon Macro Zoom Lens Fluorite (12 to 120mm; f/2.2), or for Super-8 film, the Bolex 160 Macro-zoom (8.5 to 30mm; f/1.9).

For all practical purposes, the modern zoom lenses, when stopped between f/4 and f/16, are as optically perfect as primary lenses.

Optical Attachments and Close-up Work

For close-up work, "macro" lenses focus as close as a few centimeters away without the use of special attachments. Using macro lenses we can fill the screen with a cigarette pack. (In England they're called "pack" lenses.)

Regular lenses will require one of several types of attachments in order to focus closely.

Extension tubes or bellows can be used to focus practically as close as the front element of the lens. They are introduced between the lens and camera body. But because extension tubes and bellows upset the normal optics, they cannot be used with optically complicated lenses, including all zooms and many wide-angle lenses. When the subject is closer than 10 times the focal length of the lens, an exposure compensation is required and depends on the rate of extension. The correction can be found in tables supplied with the devices or in the *American Cinematographer Manual.*

A third way of dealing with this problem is through the use of close-up attachments called diopters. They are like small one-element lenses that attach to the front of the lens in use. Their convex side faces the subject. The small arrow on the rim should point away from the camera. Diopters come in series (+1, +2, and +3, etc.). Each higher number allows

for closer focusing. When diopters are combined, the higher number should be closest to the camera. No exposure compensation is required. Compared to extension tubes or bellows, diopters are the least satisfactory as far as optical quality. Yet unlike extension tubes or bellows, diopters can be used on zoom and wide-angle lenses.

A split-field diopter covers only half the lens, enabling the camera to be focused very close and far away simultaneously. It is frequently used in commercials where the soap package may be in the foreground with a housewife using it in the background. The one drawback is that the "soft" line at the split of the diopter must be hidden by lighting and composition. Also, zooming becomes difficult and panning impossible.

There are other optical attachments in current use. The magnification of a telephoto or zoom lens can be increased with a telephoto extender. For example, a 200mm lens may be made into a 400mm. Such attachments require two stops additional exposure each time the focal length is doubled. When a telephoto extender is used, the best resolution is usually obtained when the lens is stopped down (around f/11). The usual focal lengths of some zooms can also be shortened by retro-focus wide-angle attachments, and these do not require an exposure compensation. However, cameramen usually do not like either telephoto extenders or retro-focus attachments, as they soften the picture, decreasing the resolution.

Focal Lengths and Perspective

Perhaps the most important physical element related to creative lens use is perspective. A lens that is "normal" for a given film gauge will reproduce reality with perspective similar to that seen by our human eye. In the case of 16mm film, a 25mm lens is normal. In Super-8, a normal lens is about 12mm, and in 35mm film, a normal lens is 50mm.

Lenses shorter than normal for a given film gauge are considered wide-angle, and those two or more times longer are telephoto.

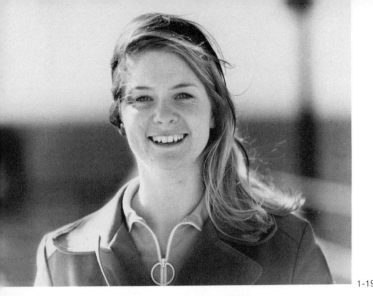

1-19

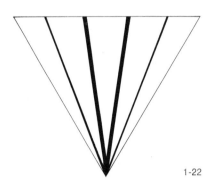

1-22

1-19—1-22 Long, medium, and wide-angle lenses used from the same position. Note that there is no change in perspective.

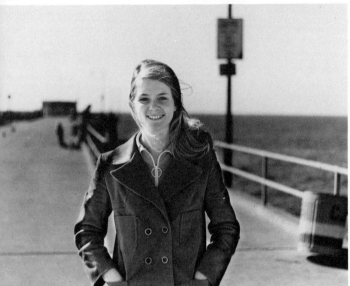

1-20

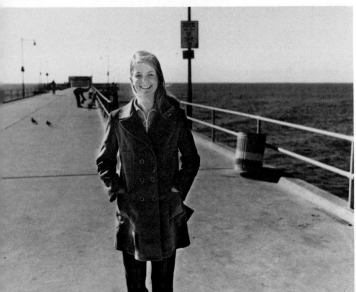

1-21

Picture perspective is frequently·misunderstood; it depends on the camera-to-subject distance—not on the lens. From the same distance, three different lenses (wide, normal, and telephoto) change the area of view but not the perspective. But using the same three lenses and changing the distances to the subject, we can retain the same field of view, but with different perspective.

One can see from figures 1-19 to 1-26 that a wide-angle lens exaggerates depth and a telephoto collapses it. For example, a person walking toward the camera will seem to approach faster with a wide-angle and slower with a telephoto. This is caused by the distance, not the lens. In a telephoto shot the person is almost always farther away than in a wide angle shot. When similarly framed, the person walking toward the telephoto may be 25 yards away, while the person moving toward the wide-angle lens is only 5 feet away. If the wide-angle approach is redone at 25 yards, the person (very small in the frame) will move just as slowly as with the telephoto. Therefore, remember that the degree of distortion is controlled by the distance, not the lens.

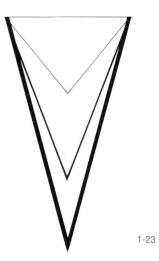

1-23

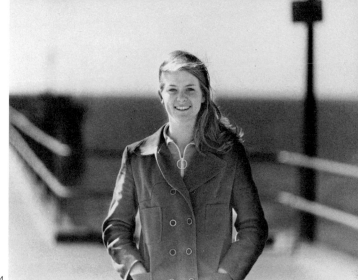

1-24

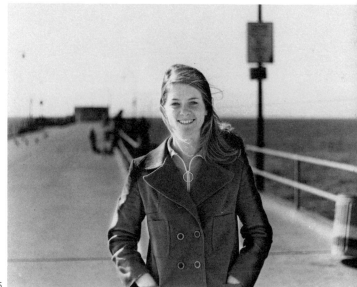

1-25

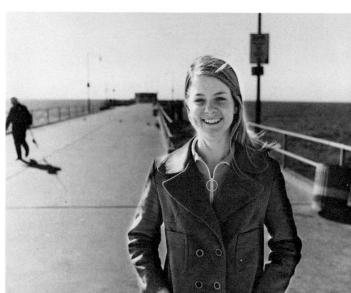

1-26

1-23—1-26 Long, medium, and wide-angle lenses used from different positions in order to obtain similar framing. Note that the perspective changes as the distance changes. Also, notice the depth of field diminishing with longer lenses. (Photos by Bob Rogers)

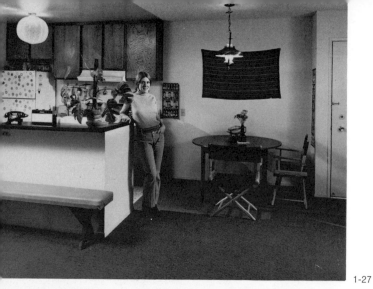

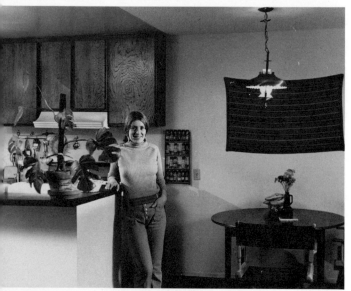

1-27

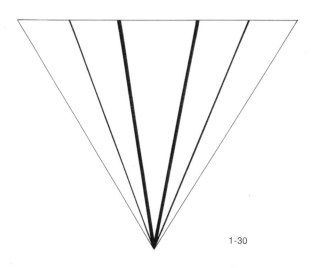

1-30

1-27 — 1-30 Zoom effect. Note the lack of changes in perspective.

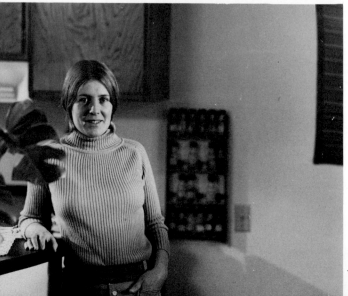

1-28

1-29

This is further illustrated in figures 1-27 to 1-34 by a comparison between the effects of zooming and dollying. When dollying, the spacial relationship between the subjects in the frame — that is, the perspective — changes because the distances change. When zooming, the focal length is changing, yet the effect is like a gradual enlargement of one part of the frame without any change in perspective. For this reason a zoom effect has a flat look.

To make a zoom movement appear more three-

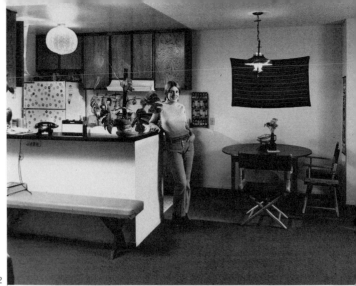

1-32

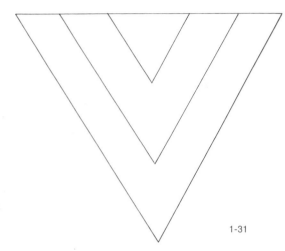

1-31

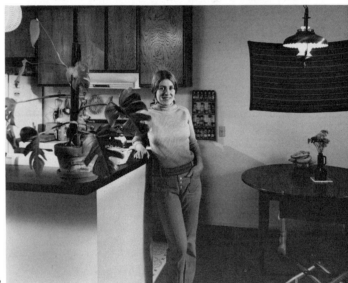

1-33

1-31—1-34 Dollying effect. Note visible changes in perspective. Because a wide-angle lens was used, the closeup was taken from a short distance, resulting in facial distortion. (Photos by author)

dimensional it can be combined with a slight camera movement either up, down, in, out, or to one side. A panning movement also helps, in addition to zooming past or through a foreground such as a row of trees or a picket fence that goes out of the picture as you zoom in. Other times a flat effect may be desired. In this case the cameraman should make a point of avoiding foreground objects and keeping the camera rigidly framed while zooming, or he will accidentally diminish the flat effect.

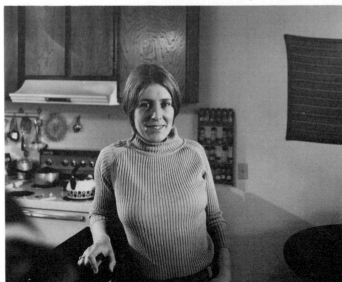

1-34

Practical Lens Use

No lens will yield high-quality results unless it is given proper care and attention.

In all cameras, lens performance depends to a great extent on the viewing system. If prisms in this system are loose or the eyepiece is not adjusted to the operator's sight, even the most excellent lenses cannot be expected to give satisfactory results. The best way to adjust the eyepiece is to remove the lens, point the camera toward a uniformly bright area (sky, wall, etc.), and after loosening the eyepiece locking ring (if there is one), rotate the eyepiece adjustment until the grain of the ground glass or the engraved lines in the viewing system appear sharpest to the operator's eye. Then tighten the locking ring to keep this setting from drifting. In cameras with nonremovable lenses, adjust the eyepiece while aiming at a distant object, focused at infinity and with the f-stop wide open. The eyepiece is designed so that cameramen who wear glasses can usually adjust it for their eyesight and shoot without glasses.

When using a reflexive viewing system, the eyepiece must be covered while the camera is running. Usually the cameraman is covering it with his eye while shooting, but if he should take his eye away during the shot, or if the camera is mounted for a shot without an operator (such as on the bumper of a racing car), the eyepiece must be covered or light will enter it while the camera is running, travel through the system, and fog the film, ruining the shot. This is very important. Many cameras have some provision for closing off the eyepiece. The Arri-S has a small door that swings shut across the eyepiece. The Bolex Rex has an internal door that blacks out the viewing system when the operator turns a knob on the side of the viewer near the front of the camera. Many operators when looking away only for a moment will slip their thumb in between eye and finder and then look away. A light ghostlike apparition and an overexposed effect on the film are possible signs of light entering the viewfinder.

A matte box is mounted in front of the lens to shade it from unwanted direct light. It is usually equipped with a filter holder. Instead, some wide-angle lenses and zooms use a lens shade that attaches directly to the front of the lens.

Follow-Focus

Most cameramen (or their assistants) have a hand on the focus adjustment all the time, ready to compensate for any subject movement. If the camera-to-subject distance changes during the shot, the operator, looking through the viewing system, will have to readjust the focus. This is called "following" or "pulling" focus. In more complex situations where the camera operator cannot pull focus himself, an assistant, called a focus puller, will do it for him, following the markings made on the floor during rehearsal. A combination of fast-moving actors and a dolly or hand-held camera can require a considerable amount of agility at times.

Lens Maintenance

You can clean a dirty lens, but there's not much you can do with a scratched one. So it is wise to clean lenses carefully.

A stream of clean air, such as from an air syringe, is by far the safest way of cleaning a lens. Remember that canned compressed air (from a photo shop) must be used in an upright position or it may spray a gluey substance onto the lens.

A very soft brush, such as one made of camel's hair, is second on the list. It must be used *only* for lens cleaning. Avoid touching its bristles, as fingers are naturally greasy. Your soft lens brush should not be used on the camera, gate, or magazines, because any brush sheds, and the fine, flexible hairs of a lens brush will "travel" in the camera and be wound into moving parts. A brush for camera cleaning should have stiffer bristles that are less apt to be wound into the machinery.

When using a lens brush or air, always hold the lens facing downward so that the dust does not resettle on the lens. This helps when cleaning cameras and magazines too.

Fingerprints and other stains will have to be removed with a photographic lens tissue. (*Never* use a silicone-coated tissue such as those sold by optometrists for cleaning eyeglasses, because it may permanently discolor the lens coating.) Before using the lens tissue, moisten either the lens with your breath or the tissue with a special lens-cleaning solution. Use lens-cleaning solution sparingly; too much may partly dissolve the cement holding the lens elements. Special solutions are available from camera shops, or you can use rubbing alcohol from a drugstore. Rubbing alcohol is not as good as special solution, because it contains menthol and other ingredients that will be left on the lens by the evaporating alcohol. One excellent way to use the lens tissue is to roll it like a cigarette, break it in half, and use the fuzzy end like a brush.

Lenses should be kept clean at all times, even when stored, because fingerprints and other stains left on the lens for long periods may become imbedded in the blue coating of the lens.

Lens Mounting

One of the most sensitive parts of a lens is its mounting. For proper optical alignment with the film, the lens must be precisely locked onto the camera. Much care must be taken to make sure this mounting is not wrenched out of alignment. Repairing such damage is expensive and time-consuming and may never restore perfect mounting.

Because zoom lenses and some wide-angle lenses are of retro-focal design — a complicated optical configuration — they are vulnerable to even the slightest mounting inaccuracy. A retro-focal design is desirable because it permits a larger physical lens size for more expedient handling, while retaining a short focal length. For example, a 5.7mm lens is usually about 4 inches long. If it was actually only 5.7 millimeters long, it would be a very inconvenient size. In the case of zoom lenses, the increased size is necessary to accommodate the wide-angle end of the zoom range. (Retro-focal limitations prevent us from using extension tubes or bellows with zooms and some wide-angles.)

If a zoom lens is imprecisely mounted it may not remain in focus when zooming in or out. Incorrectly mounted wide-angle lenses will simply not be in focus.

Most Super-8 and some 16mm cameras are now manufactured with a permanently mounted zoom lens. This restricts the cameraman in his choice of lenses, but does mean the mounting is usually accurate.

Among 16mm cameras with changeable lenses, there are four common lens mounts. The C-mount is the smallest and therefore the least strong and most sensitive. The Arri mount is stronger and positively locks into the camera. The Arri

1-35 Lens mounts. From left to right: Regular Arriflex, Arriflex Bayonet, Eclair, and C-mount.

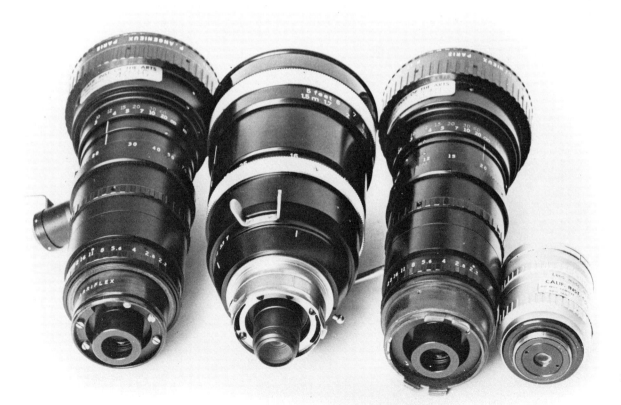

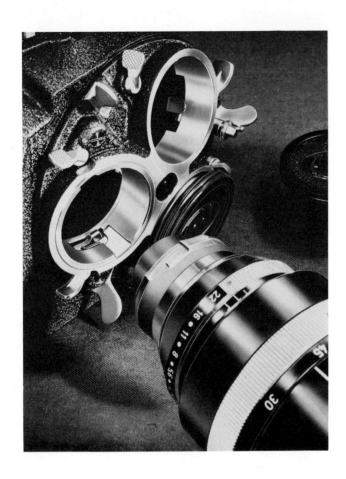

bayonet is a subsequent improvement over the regular Arri mount; a bayonet lens attaches to the camera even more securely and accurately. The regular Arri lenses will fit into either the bayonet or the regular Arri lens sockets, but a bayonet lens requires a bayonet socket and will not fit into a regular Arri mount. A fourth type, an Eclair mount, twists snugly into the camera but without the audible click.

When buying a lens to be used on many cameras, a very good choice is the Arri mount. With an Arri-to-C-mount adapter, an Arri-mount lens can be used with any standard C-mount camera. The standard Eclair NPR camera usually has two mounts, one Eclair and one C, so the Arri lens with C adapter will also usually go onto the Eclair camera. Such a combination is the most versatile. However, when adapters are used the accuracy of the mounting is almost always at least slightly impaired. Therefore, whenever possible, zoom and wide-angle lenses should have the proper mount for the camera to be used.

1-36 The Arriflex S/B camera has one bayonet socket (about to receive bayonet-mount lens) and two regular Arriflex sockets, such as the one at the upper right. (Courtesy of Arnold & Richter)

1-37 Arriflex 16 S/B with extreme telephoto lens, supported by a cradle. (Courtesy of Arnold & Richter)

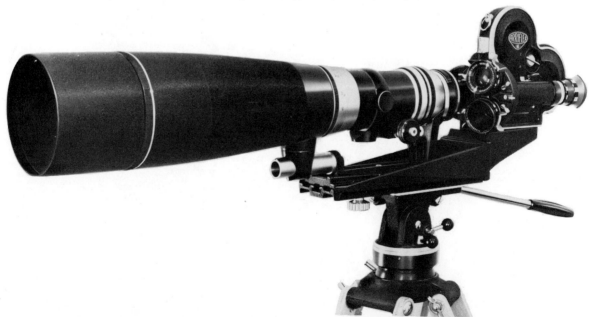

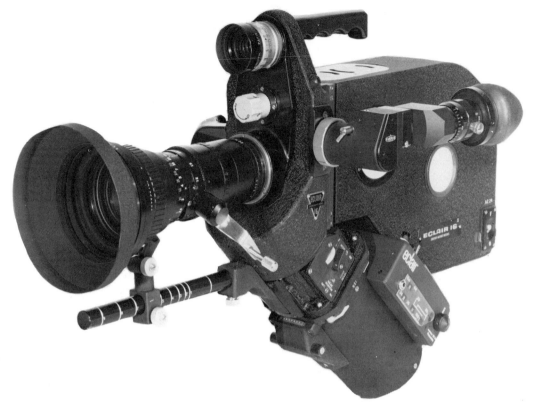

1-38 Eclair NPR with lens support. (Courtesy of Eclair International)

Lens Supports

Long and heavy lenses, such as 250mm or more (especially in C-mount), should rest on a lens support to prevent their length and weight from wrenching the mount out of alignment. A support will also be required for the heavier zooms, such as the Angenieux 12 to 240mm, and also for some of the shorter zoom lenses when they have C-mounts.

The heavier, more sensitive lenses, such as zooms, must be stored in a case to prevent jarring the elements. If the zoom is to be stored mounted on the camera, then the case must firmly support the lens in order to avoid straining the mount.

CAMERA SUPPORTS

On the screen any camera unsteadiness becomes very obvious because the picture is being magnified many hundreds of times. To control camera steadiness, many supporting devices and techniques have been developed. By choosing among them, the cameraman may pick the right equipment for his needs.

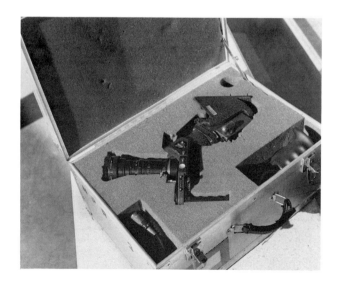

1-39 Eclair NPR with mounted zoom lens in padded case. (Photo by author)

Tripods are the most commonly used supports. They come basically in three sizes: standard legs, baby legs, and "top hat" or "high hat." They also come in different degrees of sturdiness for cameras of different weights.

Leg lengths are adjustable, so the tripod can be leveled when set up on uneven ground. To tighten the leg-length adjustment, always turn the top of the lock to the outside. It can be incorrectly tightened by turning it the other way, but serious bending and disfiguration will damage the tripod. Furthermore, it will not be tight and may collapse, ruining the camera as well.

Some tripods are equipped with a ball-joint leveling device. This is very convenient and can save time by allowing the cameraman to level just the top of the tripod without having to adjust the legs perfectly. This device can be dangerous, however, if it is used carelessly. There is a tendency to level only the ball joint, leaving the tripod legs in a precarious imbalance. For safety, the legs must be almost level before the final adjustment is made with the ball joint.

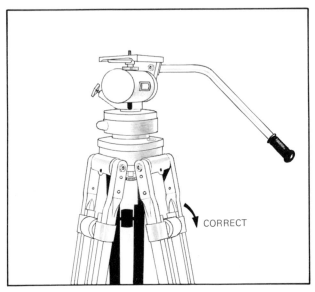

CORRECT

1-41 Correct direction for tightening tripod leg.

1-40 Tripods: standard legs, baby legs, and high-hat. (Manufactured by Birns & Sawyer)

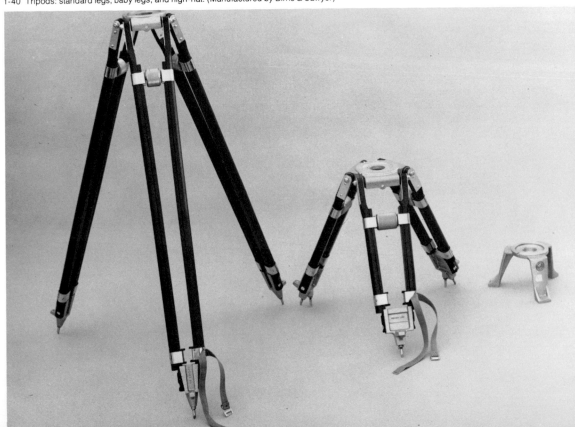

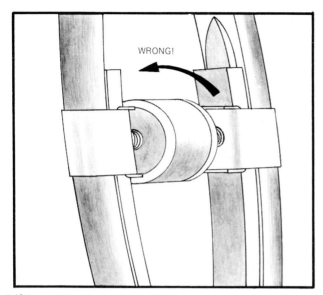

1-42 Incorrect way of tightening tripod leg.

1-43 Ball-joint leveling device. Position is exaggerated for purpose of demonstration.

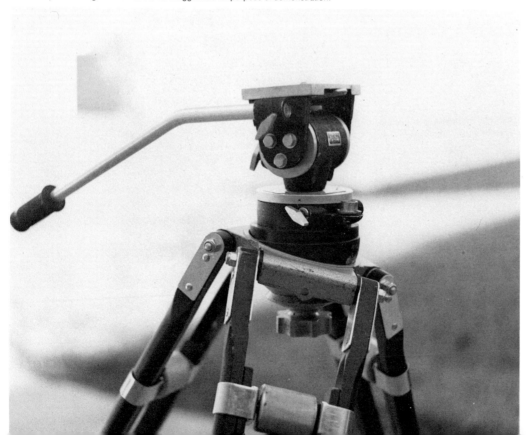

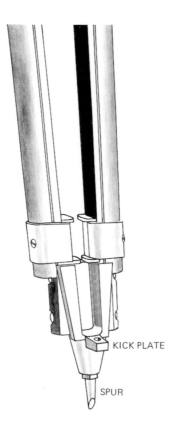

KICK PLATE

SPUR

1-44 Tripod shoe.

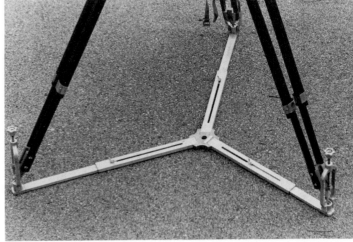

1-45 Spider.

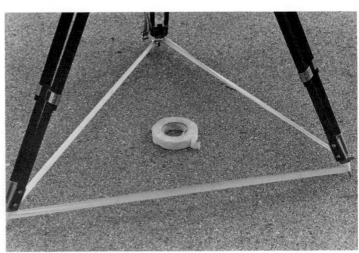

1-46 Tape used as a spider.

The spider (sometimes called the spreader) is an essential part of the tripod equipment. It locks onto the "shoes" to prevent the tripod legs from slipping. In place of a spider, one could use camera tape, a rope, or even a piece of rug or heavy cloth. Sandbags or plastic waterbags are always a useful tool for steadying tripods or stands. Occasionally a length of chain with a turnbuckle can also be used to secure the tripod to a platform.

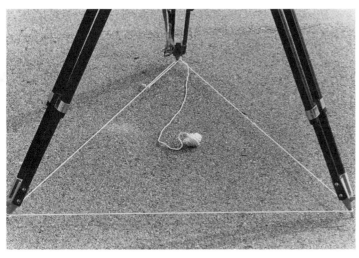

1-47 String used as a spider.

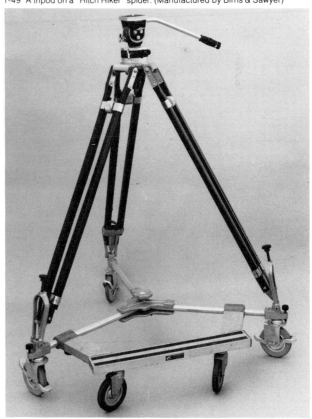

1-49 A tripod on a "Hitch Hiker" spider. (Manufactured by Birns & Sawyer)

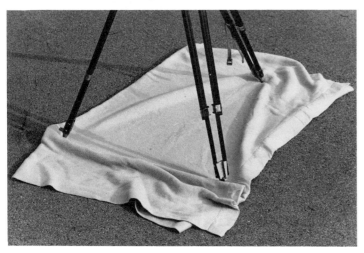

1-48 Blanket used as a spider.

37

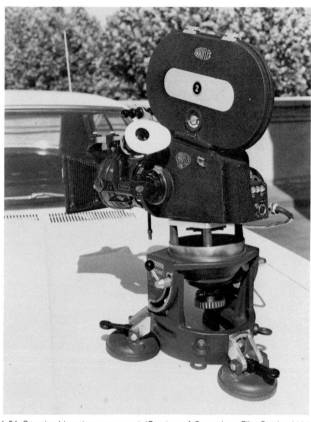

1-51 Samcine Limpet camera mount. (Courtesy of Samuelson Film Service Ltd.)

1-50 Top hat mounted on a "Hitch Hiker" spider. (Manufactured by Birns & Sawyer)

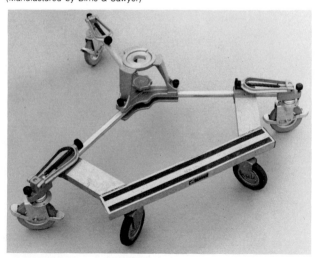

In situations where baby legs are not low enough or the camera is to be mounted on, say, the wing of an airplane, a "top hat" (also known as a "high hat") is practical. Any number of other mounts have been developed for a variety of specialized needs.

For traveling shots, several types of dollies are available. They differ in sophistication and expense. The Elemack and the Colortran are good medium-priced examples. The Jonathan Jib gives the Elemack dolly an interesting boom capability.

The wheelchair has become a favorite location dolly for small-budget productions. Creative cameramen have utilized variations on it, such as the "standolly." Another inexpensive but good dolly is a simple platform with wheels.

1-53 Colortran dolly in low position. (Courtesy of Berkey Colortran, Inc.)

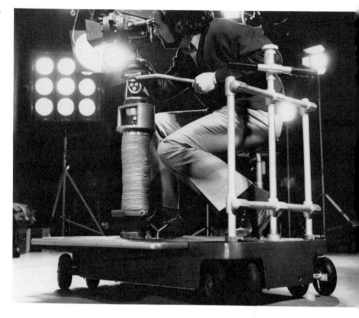

1-52 Colortran dolly in high position. (Courtesy of Berkey Colortran, Inc.)

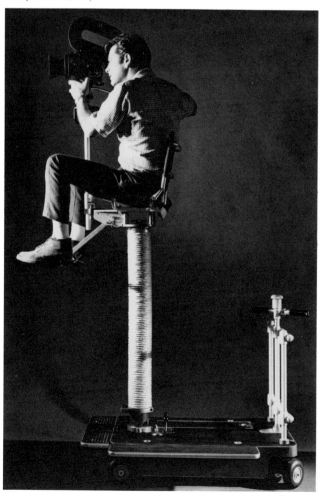

1-54 "Standolly." (Courtesy of Jack Pill and Associates)

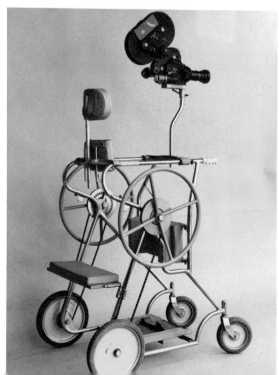

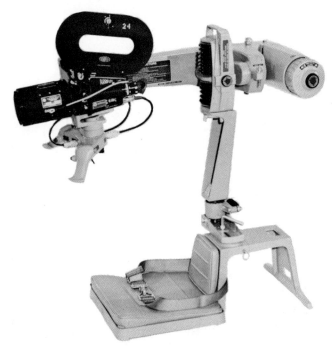

1-55 Tyler 16mm Vibrationless Mini Mount. (Courtesy of Tyler Camera Systems)

can take the manufacturer's suggested weight as a guide, but when selecting a head it is always a good idea to test it with the camera mounted to see how it will behave. Maneuverability and smoothness when panning and tilting are important, but equally vital is the "positive lock." Locking can be tested by tilting the camera forward so that it points below the horizon and locking it in this position. It should remain locked. If the camera is too heavy for the head, it may overpower the lock and continue tilting down until the front of the camera is resting against the tripod leg. The camera may be damaged when hitting the tripod leg, and the weight of the camera when tilted down that far may cause an imbalance that pulls the tripod over, seriously damaging the camera.

Three basic types of tripod heads are available, friction heads, gear heads, and fluid heads. Friction heads, as their name implies, use surface resistance to smooth their movements. Gear heads employ mechanical advantage and are mainly used in 35mm and 65mm. For serious work in Super-8 and 16mm, fluid heads are the best. They use adjustable hydraulic resistance to give their movements a smooth flow.

There are two types of head-to-leg mounts. They are called 16mm and 35mm mounts only because one is larger and is designed to support heavier 35mm cameras. An adapter plate is available that will allow you to put a head with a 16mm mount onto a set of legs with a 35mm mount.

After setting up the tripod the camera is mounted on the head, by a screw that extends from the head and goes into the bottom of the camera. On some heads, such as the O'Connor 50, part of a plate with the screw comes off the head and is separately screwed onto the camera. Then the camera, with this mounting plate attached, is locked onto the head. This arrangement, however, is unusual. There are two sizes of screws: American, and the slightly larger German. Some cameras have two threaded holes so that they can accept either. In addition, a small and inexpensive adapter is available that will enlarge an American screw to German size. This adapter should be a standard accessory carried by all cameramen.

To make sure all the mounts are compatible, *always* set up the camera on the assembled tripod before leaving the equipment room or rental house. This simple practice will save you many headaches. Don't wait until you're on location to find you have different types of mounts·that cannot be put together and no place to get an adapter. This applies not just to tripods, but to *all* equipment.

A traveling shot can often be made smoother by running the dolly on a track made of plywood sheets laid on the floor, by running the camera at a higher speed (only when the change in speed is not betrayed by some moving object, such as a person walking), or by using a wider-angle lens.

Occasionally an automobile is used as a dolly. In this case, bumps can be smoothed out by reducing the air pressure in the tires. When filming at a right angle to the direction of vehicle movement, the auto speed appears almost twice as fast as in reality. Therefore running the camera at a higher speed will both smooth out the movement and compensate for the illusion of increased speed.

When shooting from a helicopter or a moving car, anti-vibration mounts can be used to stabilize the camera. In especially unsteady situations an amazing gyro-stabilized lens system called Dynalens is available.

TRIPOD HEADS

Cameras are mounted onto the tripod legs through the use of tripod heads, which also provide for smooth panning and tilting movements. (Turning horizontally is panning, while turning vertically is tilting.)

The tripod head must be chosen with the camera in mind. Different heads are designed to support different weights. You

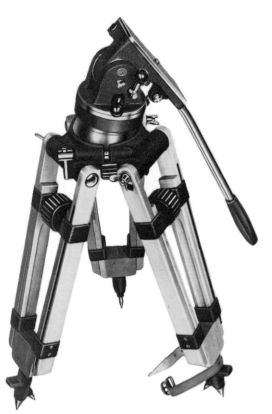

1-56 A friction head. (Courtesy of Arnold & Richter)

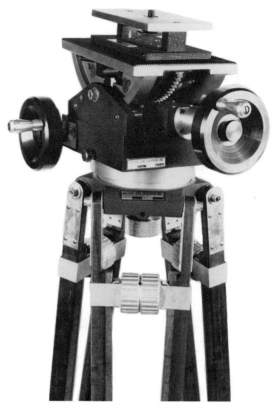

1-57 NCE Cradle gear head. (Courtesy of National Cine Equipment, Inc.)

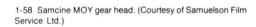

1-58 Samcine MOY gear head. (Courtesy of Samuelson Film Service Ltd.)

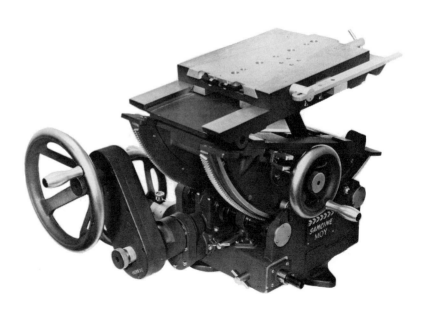

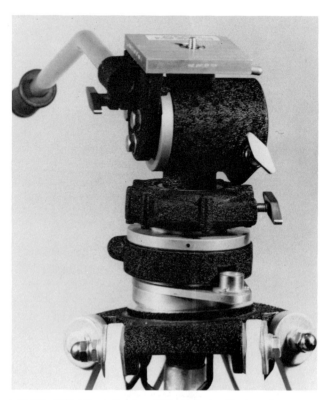

1-59 Miller "F" fluid head. (Courtesy of Miller Professional Equipment)

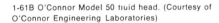

1-60 Miller "Professional" fluid head. (Courtesy of Miller Professional Equipment)

1-61A O'Connor Fluid Head Model 20 was designed specifically for the Eclair ACL and the Arriflex SR-16. (Courtesy of O'Connor Engineering Laboratories)

1-61B O'Connor Model 50 fluid head. (Courtesy of O'Connor Engineering Laboratories)

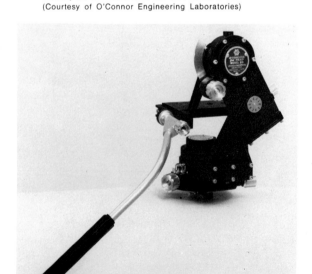

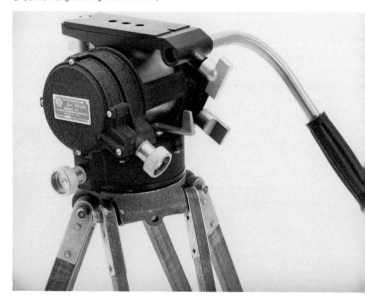

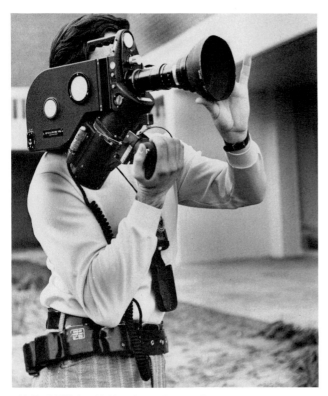

1-62 Eclair NPR, hand-held, resting on shoulder. (Photo by author)

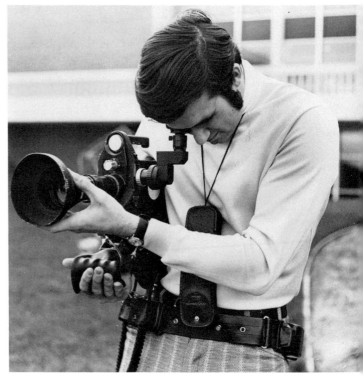

1-63 Eclair held at waist, machinegun fashion. (Photo by author)

HAND-HELD WORK

When hand-holding the camera, our principal concern is controlling the camera for the exact degree of steadiness we desire for the effect, whether it be smooth or jostled and vibrating. Gyroscopic stabilizers are available. They are very effective, but only for relatively simple movements, because the gyroscopic pull sometimes tends to fight the cameraman, preventing him from turning the way he wants. Most cameramen who specialize in hand-held work do not use them.

Hand-held shots can be made steadier by using most of the tricks discussed earlier, such as running the camera at a higher speed or using a wide-angle lens. Jumbled, helter-skelter subject action is often associated with a hand-held shot, such as walking through a panicked crowd. Such activity will often camouflage jerky camera movements.

Steadiness is not our only consideration in hand-holding. Sharpness is also a problem. The 24-fps. camera speed produces a 1/48-second exposure period, which is long enough to cause a relatively fast subject or camera movement to register as slightly blurred on film. Normally this is not noticeable because each single frame is not visible long enough on the screen. However, a jerkily hand-held camera will contribute to even more pronounced image blur. Thus resolution suffers when the camera is hand-held awkwardly.

Steady hand-held work depends to a great extent on the maneuverability of the camera. Ideally the cameraman's body and the camera should be as one. Many cameras and devices have been designed to achieve this unity. Comfortable distribution of the weight of the camera is a big factor. For example, the Eclair NPR puts most of the weight on the cameraman's shoulder, leaving his entire other side free.

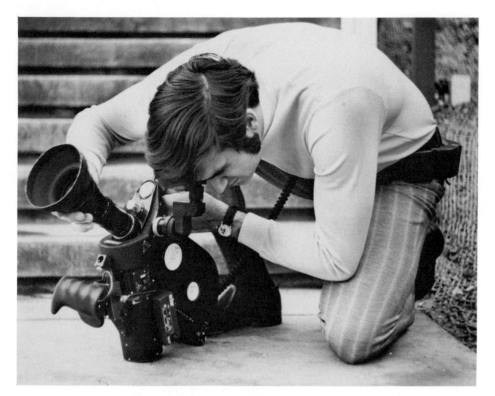

1-64 Eclair used in ground-level shot.
(Photo by author)

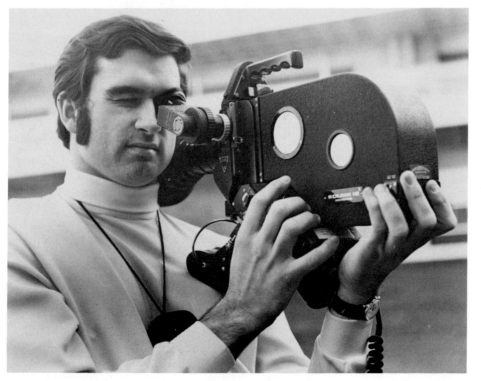

1-65 As seen in these photographs, the rotating eyepiece adds great versatility to a hand-held camera. Here the operator films backward, over his shoulder, obtaining a candid shot without being noticed by his subject. (Photo by author)

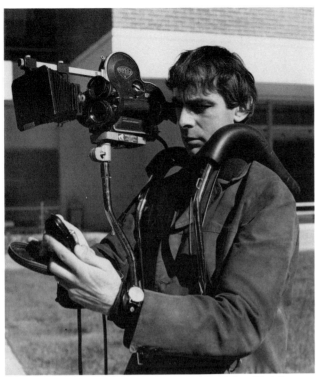

1-66 One type of body pod that leaves the operator's hands free. (Photo by Bob Rogers)

1-67 A Bolex with a pistol grip. (Photo by author)

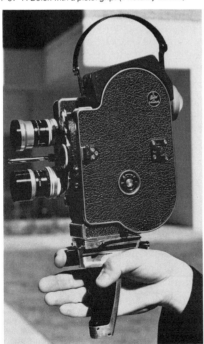

A body pod has been designed to transfer the camera weight directly to the body, releasing one or both hands for the focusing and zooming operations.

There are many designs of body pods, pistol grips, and the like, and the choice is very personal. It depends on the cameraman, the camera, and the shot.

Many of the best cinematographers, like Haskell Wexler, design their own body mounts. One of Wexler's personal inventions, which he calls a "skyhook," transfers the weight of the camera to a back-pack structure. Wexler designed it to stabilize shots taken from the deck of a boat at sea.

Usually a cameraman who investigates commercially available support devices and equipment can pick and choose among them to achieve the right combination for the exact effect he wants.

1-68 The "skyhook." (Courtesy of Haskel Wexler)

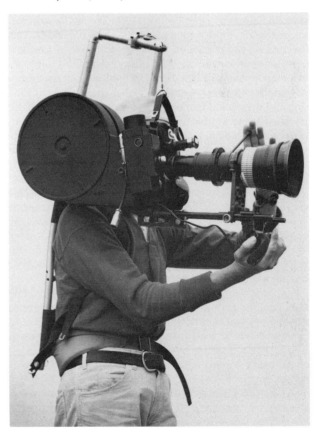

TIME MANIPULATIONS IN CINEMATOGRAPHY

Up until now we have discussed ways of controlling the image recorded by the camera, covering the manipulation of focus, perspective, camera positions, and movements. There remains the time dimension. It has infinite possibilities, and therefore allows for great ingenuity in its use.

Near the beginning of this chapter we introduced time-lapse and slow-motion photography and described how it could expand or collapse time.

Many general-purpose cameras have speeds up to 64 fps available from a wild motor. This is adequate for some slow-motion purposes, but if higher speeds are necessary, there are two general types of cameras to be considered: intermittent-movement and rotating-prism types. Intermittent cameras are the kind we have already described; they arrest each frame for the period of exposure. For this reason they are limited to a top speed of about 1,000 fps but usually less. The rotating-prism camera features a continuous film flow. The film never stops, and the prism rotates to project the image on the passing film. Because the film does not have to stop and start for each exposure, higher speeds are possible, ranging up to 9,000 fps for regular 16mm and up to 18,000 fps when using 8mm single-width or 6mm double-width on 16mm film with 8mm perforations. Special scientific cameras have been designed for much higher speeds, but they are seldom of any practical use to the average film maker.

At high speeds many problems arise. As the exposure time becomes minimal, a great deal of light is required. There is also a "reciprocity failure"; at higher speeds the exposure-time–f-stop relationship gradually changes so that computing the exposure may be difficult. Exposure tests are necessary. To further complicate matters, at very high speeds the reciprocity failure may be different for each layer of color in the emulsion, thus distorting the color.

Film stock for extremely high-speed photography must have "long pitch" perforations. This means the distance between the sprocket holes is slightly greater.

In addition to slowing or speeding a movement, film can be used to remove portions of it. One term cinematographers use for the creative elimination of in-between intervals of movement is "pixilation." Pixilation is much like animation in that it is often taken one or more frames at a time, but unlike animation, its subject is frequently a moving object like cars or people. Where time-lapse cinematography seeks only to speed up action, pixilation removes specific parts of the movement, modifying the apparent nature of the action. For example, an overused pixilation effect is achieved by taking a single frame every time an actor jumps up into the air. Because he is never seen except at the height of his jump, he appears to be suspended above the ground.

Another pixilation technique involves running the camera several frames at a time. Between each interval the actor walks to a different area in the field of view. The result is that he appears for a moment in each position.

Either of these pixilated effects can be achieved by shooting single frames, shooting several frames at brief intervals, or using an optical printer to print only the selected frames from normally shot footage. The creative variations on pixilation are endless and open to experiment.

Most cameras can run backward, providing the opportunity to invert time. Reverse action can be used to make a difficult maneuver possible or to achieve an effect. In one film, a director had the camera run in reverse while filming an actor walking backward in a crowd of normally walking pedestrians. When the film was projected forward, the actor became the only person who was walking forward in the crowd of pedestrians walking backward.

Impossible actions are made possible, such as a man effortlessly jumping straight up onto a roof. The actor starts on the roof, walks to the edge, jumps down, and walks away, all backward. The action is filmed with the camera running in reverse so that when correctly projected, the actor walks to the building, jumps straight up onto the roof, and walks across it.

Another very important use of reverse action is in making complicated maneuvers easier. The most common example is a rapid pan to a very precise framing. If shot forward, we might spend a great deal of footage before we hit just the perfect framing the director wants at the end of the shot. However, filming in reverse, we could start on that precise framing and pan away to the first, less critical angle, achieving the shot while saving time and footage.

Not all cameras feature an ability to run backward. But, reverse action can still be achieved. In 16mm or 35mm the action can be filmed and later reversed in an optical printer. Or reverse motion can be achieved by filming with any camera held upside down! If the image is recorded upside down, we can turn the film over in the projector and show it tail-first. It will be right side up, but the action will be reversed. In the case of single-perforated film stocks, the picture will also be turned around left to right. Double-perforated stocks could be turned over, correcting the left-to-right position, but this would put the emulsion on the opposite side, causing focal problems in printing. When using the upside-down reverse-action method, the best ways to deal with the left-to-right exchange are to avoid lettering or anything else that would give it away or to shoot through a mirror. There is also the possibility of having any lettering printed backward or even exchanging the sides in an optical printer.

The possibilities suggested by time manipulation are endless, and we have touched on only a few. The film maker is limited only by his own imagination. (For further information on special-effects cinematography, see the Bibliography.)

FRONT PROJECTION

Until recently, the process of adding a separately shot background behind a studio foreground has been an expensive luxury practical only to the major film studios. Now with the rapid development of front projection, low-budget productions can afford the use of exotic backgrounds and otherwise expensive sets. This was made possible by the development of a "high-gain" (highly reflectant) screen material, by 3M, called Scotch Light #7610. This screen consists of millions of flint-glass bead-lenses, enabling it to reflect over 200 times more light than is reflected by a person's white shirt. Furthermore, virtually all the light is reflected directly back to the source.

A very thin, optically perfect glass is placed at 45° to combine the optical axes of the camera and the projector. When the camera and projector are perfectly aligned, and equipped with compatible lenses, the image from the projector is reflected by the optical glass onto the screen. The screen returns almost all the light back through the glass into the camera. The 45° glass will reflect away from the camera a certain percentage of light coming from the screen and subject, making exposure compensation necessary. Because of the high-gain reflection, the projection can be of low intensity and will therefore not show on the actor. Because the camera and projector are aligned on the same optical axis, the actor's body will cover his own shadow.

Compared to back projection the lighting is much easier. Because the Scotch Light screen reflects lights back into their own source in a very narrow angle, there is no need to worry too much about side lights washing out your projected background. Even a conventional 45° key light presents no

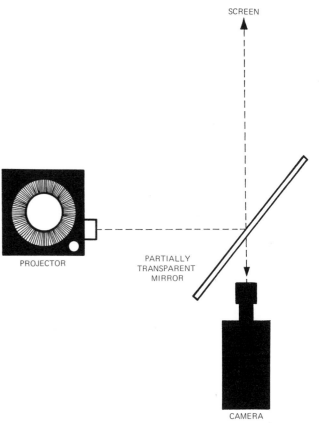

1-69 Front-projection principle.

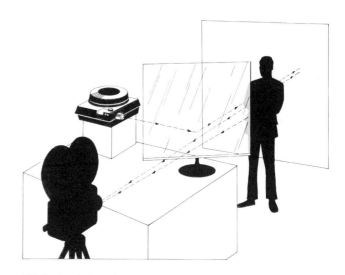

1-70 Front-projection setup.

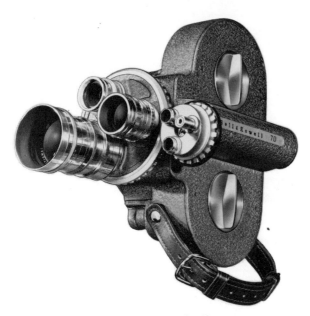

1-71 Bell & Howell DR 70 spring-wound, non-reflex 16mm camera. (Courtesy of Bell & Howell)

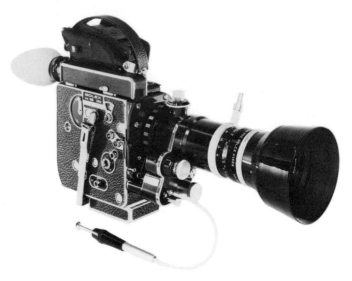

1-72 Bolex H-16 SBM 16mm spring-wound camera, with reflexive viewing system, optional electric motor, and 400-foot magazine. (Courtesy of Bolex/Paillard)

problem, because any of its light that happens to hit the screen will not be reflected into the projector/camera. If anywhere, it will be sent back to the key light.

Because of the narrow angle of reflection, the screen does not need to be taut. It can even be slightly moving and yet return a constantly steady image. Furthermore, seams in the material don't show. This allows us the further luxury of using many planes of depth. Each flat can be cut to the precise shape of the object to be projected on it, and then it is covered with the Scotch Light. The actor can now walk behind it for a truly three-dimensional effect.

A system of this type can be assembled at a relatively low cost and without professional help. The advantages are enormous.

CHOOSING A CAMERA

Having spent the first part of this chapter covering some of the basic camera features and capabilities, we now will try to bring it all to focus. Selecting a camera is similar to choosing a car. You should consider many aspects before committing your money. There is much to be said for renting rather than buying equipment, since needs vary from one filming assignment to another. Secondly, there are rapid changes in camera design, and there is a constant flow of new models, which would be available at rental houses. The decision to rent or buy a camera also depends on how extensively one plans to use it.

Still, many amateurs and professionals prefer to own their own cameras. In this way, if they take good care of their equipment, they can be confident about its dependability. Sometimes they will own their own "stand-by" camera (usually a simple but rugged piece of equipment, such as a Bolex Reflex or a Bell & Howell 70 series), and rent their main camera, such as an Arri, Eclair, Mitchell, etc.

Every few months, camera manufacturers bring forth new designs and improvements in older models. Therefore this book cannot hope to provide an up-to-date consumer's report on every current camera. You will have to investigate the features offered by the designs of leading manufacturers at the time you buy. In addition to providing promotional literature, equipment rental houses can often be very useful in helping you to familiarize yourself with the features and capabilities of different pieces of equipment. Their technicians and repairmen can be of enormous value in pointing out weak points in design or advising precautionary techniques that can save you time, trouble, and money.

When selecting a camera to rent or buy, the primary consideration is the job at hand. No camera is perfect for all tasks.

Cameras can be classified by their sophistication. They fall into four general groups. The simplest cameras are nonreflex and usually spring-wound. Used cameras in this group are often very inexpensive. The favorites on this level include the early Bolex designs (such as the Bolex H-16 S) or the Bell & Howell DR70 series.

48

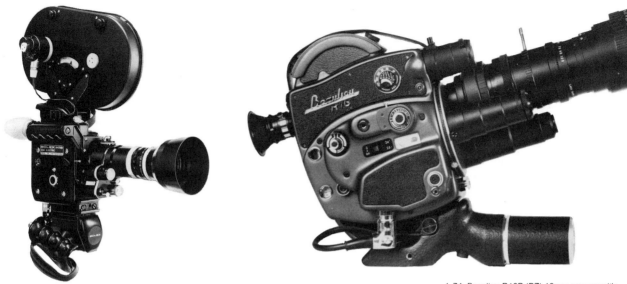

1-73 Bolex H-16 EBM electric 16mm camera with 400-foot magazine and a battery built into the handgrip. (Courtesy of Bolex/Paillard)

1-74 Beaulieu R16B (PZ) 16mm camera with Angenieux 12-120mm auto lens with built-in power zoom. (Courtesy of Hervic Corp./Cinema Beaulieu)

The second group contains cameras with reflexive viewing systems. Electric motors are usually standard equipment. Most of the cameras in this group are equipped with sync-tone "oscillators" or crystal-sync units for sound shooting; however, they are often not quiet enough for succesful sound recording at close quarters. Cameras on this second level take 100-foot or 200-foot internal loads, but some will accept magazines up to 400 feet. The best-known examples of this group are the Bolex H-16 SBM, Bolex H-16 EBM (electric), Beaulieu R16B, Canon Scoopic 16, and Canon Sound Scoopic 200.

1-75 Canon Scoopic 16 camera for 100-foot daylight spool loads with built-in, interchangeable battery. (Courtesy of Scoopic Division, Canon U.S.A., Inc.)

The Beaulieu R16B and Canon Sound Scoopic 200 have automatic diaphragm setting. So do the Bolex cameras when equipped with a proper type of zoom lens. The Canon Scoopic 16 has a built-in light meter next to the lens, and one must be sure not to block it with a hand or a large lens shade.

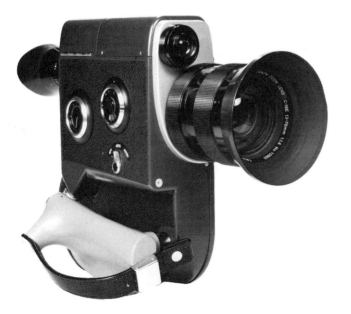

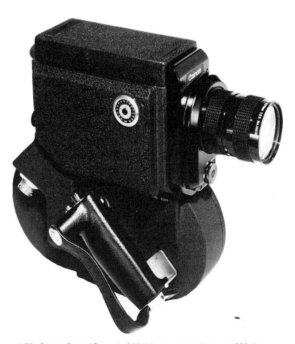

1-76 Canon Sound Scoopic 200, 16mm camera for up to 200-foot daylight spool loads with a single-system sound-recording capability. (Courtesy of Scoopic Division, Canon U.S.A., Inc.)

49

The third group introduces the added sophisticiation of a registration pin, providing an extremely steady picture. Cameras in this group are rather expensive, due to their professional quality. Of these the Arriflex 16 S/B and 16 M/B are most popular because of their rugged durability and extremely high precision. The Eclair CM3 is notable because it can shoot either 16mm or 35mm film by changing magazines and adjusting the aperture plate. Also worth special attention is the 16mm Actionmaster/500 a good general purpose camera which is also good for high speed work. It runs at 24 fps and at 500 fps and five other speeds inbetween. It has double pull down claws and registration pins.

1-77 Arriflex 16 S/B 16mm camera; accepts 400-foot magazine. (Courtesy of Arnold & Richter)

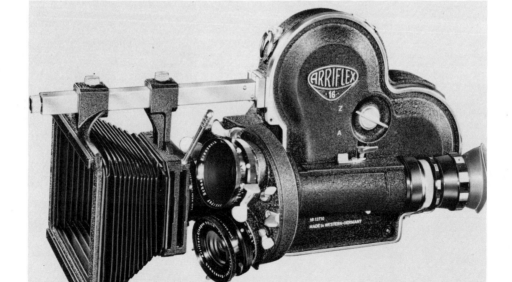

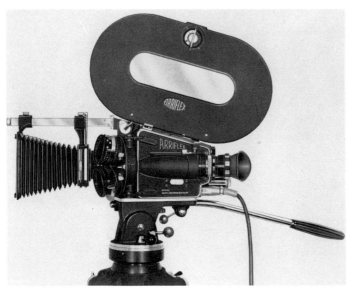

1-78 Arriflex 16 M/B designed for magazines ranging from 200-foot to 1200-foot. (Courtesy of Arnold & Richter)

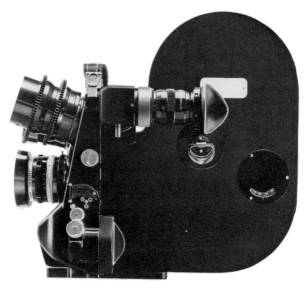

1-79 Eclair CM3 camera adaptable to either 16mm or 35mm operation, with 400-foot magazine. (Courtesy of Eclair International)

1-80 Actionmaster/500 accepts 200-foot, 400-foot and 1200-foot magazines. (Courtesy of Photo-Sonics, Inc. Burbank, Calif.; distributed by Instrumentation Marketing Corp.)

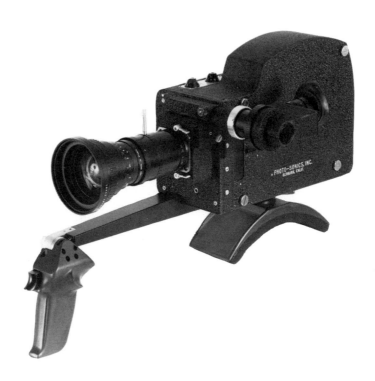

The fourth level includes the highly sophisticated very quietly running cameras. For several years the most widely used members in this group were the Arriflex BL, the Eclair NPR, the rugged Auricons and Auricon conversions. A newer generation of cameras in this group includes the Eclair ACL, the Arriflex 16SR, the Beaulieux News 16, the CP-16/A, the Wilcam W-2+4 and the Aaton 7-16mm/reflex camera.

1-81 A   Arriflex BL noiseless 16mm camera. Accepts 400-foot and 1200-foot magazines. (Courtesy of Arnold & Richter)

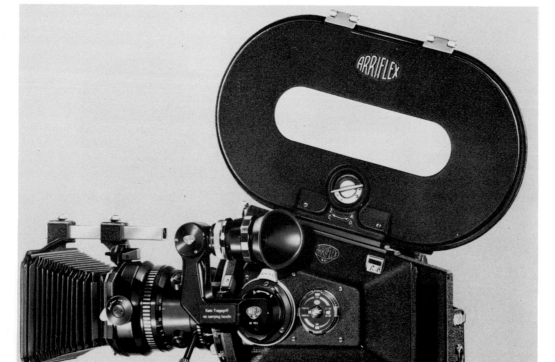

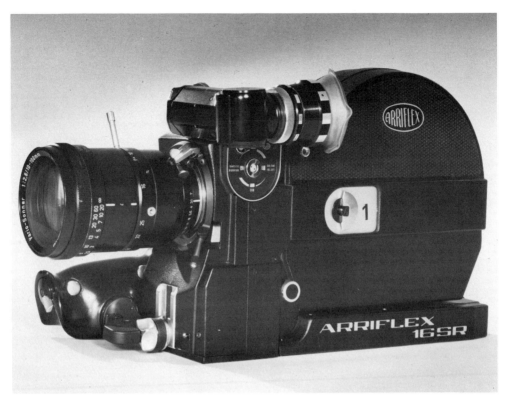

1-81-B The Arriflex 16 SR accepts 200-foot and 400-foot magazines and features an internal battery, automatic exposure and a rotating eye-piece. (Courtesy of Arnold & Richter)

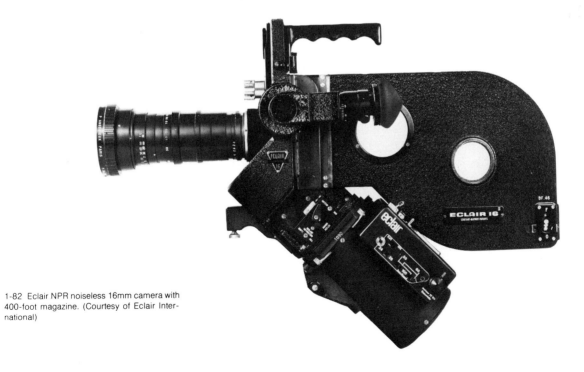

1-82 Eclair NPR noiseless 16mm camera with 400-foot magazine. (Courtesy of Eclair International)

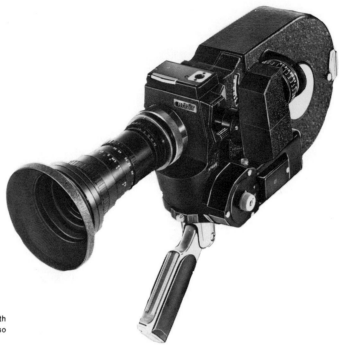

1-83 Eclair ACL noiseless 16mm camera with 200-feet magazine. 400-feet magazine also available. (Courtesy of Eclair International)

1-84 Successful Auricon conversion: "Frezzi-DC-Cordless" TM, noiseless 16mm camera with single or double sound system and internal battery. (Courtesy of General Research Laboratories, division of Frezzolini Electronics Inc.)

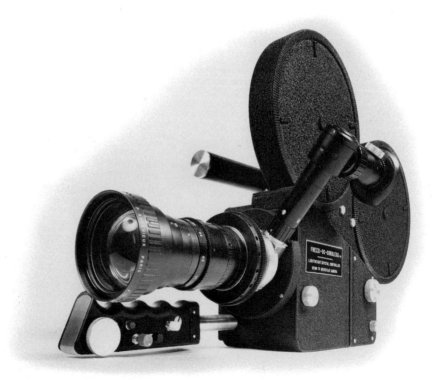

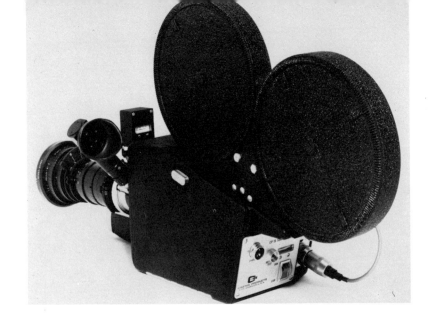

1-85 CP-16/A noiseless single/double system sound camera with internal battery, 400-foot or 1200-foot magazines. (Courtesy of Cinema Products Corporation)

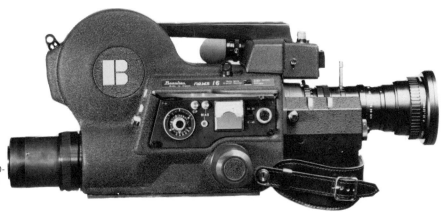

1-86 Beaulieu News 16 noiseless single/double-system sound camera with internal battery and 200-foot capacity. (Courtesy of Hervic Corp./Cinema Beaulieu)

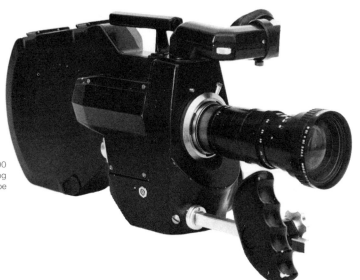

1-87 AATON 7, 16mm/ Super 16 camera with 400 foot magazine. Optional video viewfinder producing video signal directly transmitted to a video tape recorder. (Courtesy Aaton S. A.)

CAMERA TROUBLES AND TESTS

Even the most sophisticated cameras will occasionally fail to operate properly. Usually this is caused by a rather simple malfunction. Amateur cameramen frequently jump to conclusions, suspecting the worst, when the problem is actually some simple thing like a low battery or a bad connection. Therefore, do not panic until you've checked the obvious things first.

Most camera troubles fall roughly into five categories:

I. The camera will not run. This could be caused by:
 1. Dead or low battery
 2. Broken on/off switch
 3. Broken power cable or loose plug connections
 4. Dirty connection between the camera body and the magazine take-up motor (applies to Arri and Beaulieu)
 5. Buckle switch not reset (some cameras have this safety device, which automatically stops the camera if a jam occurs)
 6. Burnt-out or otherwise damaged motor
 7. Extremely cold weather (the camera should be winterized by changing the lubrication from oil to graphite in a camera shop before shooting in very low temperatures)

II. The projected picture is unsteady. Caused by:
 1. Film loops too small or too large
 2. Film stock that has shrunk because of improper storage
 3. Faulty synchronization of the shutter and pull-down claw (causes a vertical blur)
 4. Pressure plate too tight or too loose

III The film is scratched. Caused by:
 1. Dirt or emulsion buildup somewhere along the film path
 2. Rollers in the camera or the magazine are stuck
 3. Film gate scratched or damaged
 4. Film loops too large or too small
 5. Film not properly threaded

IV. The film is fogged. Caused by:
 1. Light leak from an improperly closed camera or magazine door
 2. Reflexive viewfinder open to light — often because cameraman took his head away from the eyepiece
 3. Behind-the-lens filter slot that has been left open (especially on Bolex or wide-angle lenses)
 4. Improper loading or unloading that may have exposed the film to light
 5. An empty lens cavity left open in the turret

V. The picture is out of focus. This is usually the camera operator's fault, but can also be caused by:
 1. Lens not flush in the turret
 2. Lens out of alignment
 3. Viewfinder out of adjustment
 4. Film gate left open when the camera was loaded

Most of these troubles can be avoided by a thorough check. Before the day of shooting, *all* the equipment should be assembled and examined to make sure it is compatible and in working order. Shooting a camera test is a vital step in preparation. It must be done and screened before the shooting begins so that there is ample time to deal with any problems. The main objectives of the test will be to check lens performance and picture steadiness. If two or more cameras are used, it is imperative that the frame lines be compared to make sure that footage from the two cameras can be intercut without the frame line shifting on the screen.

Lens sharpness is best checked by shooting a test chart or even a newspaper, with the lens aperture wide open (lowest f-stop). In the case of a zoom lens, the entire focal range (zoom range) must be tested.

At the same time, test the reflex viewing system and lens calibration by turning the test chart to a 45° angle. Focus visually (or by measured distance) for a marked spot. If the viewing system or the calibrations on the lens barrel are out of alignment the footage will be focused either closer or farther away than the marked spot.

1-88 Lens tested with chart at 45°

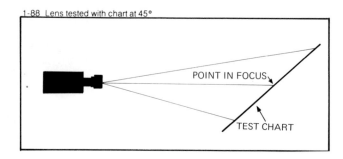

POINT IN FOCUS

TEST CHART

A steadiness test is valuable to check registration stability. It involves exposing the same footage twice, filming a test chart. If the two exposures appear to "breathe" (vibrate) relative to each other, the camera does not have good registration. A quick registration check is achieved by "framing up" the picture while it is projected, so that the frame line is visible in the middle of the screen. Poor registration will cause the frame line to vibrate slightly.

Further tests of such things as emulsion characteristics, lighting, and make-up are also often valuable. For that matter, anything that is in doubt should be tested whenever possible. It is often cheaper to spend a little money on test footage than it is to pay for having a day's or a week's work redone.

CAMERA OPERATION AND CARE

Even the most comprehensive tests cannot eliminate human errors. Most mistakes are due to careless oversights. The camera operator has to keep track of so many small details that he is eventually bound to forget something. When he does, it will be a simple and obvious error.

The beginner is especially prone to such mistakes. Professional cameramen develop a systemized routine of checking everything immediately before shooting. I have my own list of things to check before filming:

1. Level tripod
2. Clean gate
3. Close gate
4. Sprockets engaged
5. Footage counter reset after loading
6. Forward/reverse properly set on both camera *and* magazine motors
7. Motor speed set
8. Magazine take-up taut
9. Viewfinder eyepiece focused for eye
10. Matte box not visible in frame
11. Filter slot covered or closed
12. Filter in place
13. *Check frame for composition, mike boom, set limits, etc.*
14. *Check focus*
15. *Check f-stop*

The last three are the most important, as they are constantly being changed during the shooting day and are therefore the most likely to be wrong when you start to shoot.

The Ditty Bag

The ditty bag contains all the small items a cameraman feels he should have in his immediate reach while filming. The items may vary depending on personal choices but most ditty bags are similar in content. Mine contains:

An *American Cinematographer Manual* (known as the cinematographer's bible)
Air syringe and/or can of compressed air
Orange sticks
A pair of fine tweezers and a dental mirror (for careful removing of film chips and hairs from inaccessible places; these are the *only* metal instruments used for cleaning)
A small flashlight
A *camera brush* made of fairly stiff hair (*not* camel's hair)
A *lens brush* made of extra-soft hair (such as camel's hair)
Lens tissue
Cotton swabs (for cleaning lenses only!)
Lens-cleaning fluid
A compact magnifying glass (cleaning aid)
Assorted screwdrivers
Needle-nose pliers
A crescent wrench
Black camera tape
White camera tape
Gaffer's tape
Grease pencils, marker pens, ball points, and pencils
Camera report cards (can be simple index cards)
Chalk (kept separate because of dust)
Scissors
Spare cores
Spare daylight-load spools
A 50-foot cloth measuring tape
An assortment of spare parts and adapters, such as a German/American tripod screw adapter, a spare core center piece, etc., depending on the type of equipment being used
Stop watch
Contrast-viewing glasses for black-and-white and color

Apart from the ditty bag, these items might also be necessary on location or in the studio:
Spare light meter
Spare light-meter battery
Spare changing bag
Spare film cans with black paper bags

Spare power and sync cables
Extension cables for mikes
Extension cables for lights
All sorts of adapters for electrical supplies; most important, the
    common two-wire to two-wire-and-ground adapter
Spare bulbs and fuses
Spare batteries, such as for tape recorder
Spare camera battery with charger
Spare slate and chalk
Spare magazine take-up belts
Spare lens caps
Spare rubber eyecup
Spare supply of filters
Spare tape-recorder take-up reel
Soldering iron

This list could go on forever. The point is that you should scale your equipment to your production, remembering that you *want* to be overprepared. Camera operation depends on many small details. If one malfunctions, all your footage may be ruined.

Lists of this sort are always of enormous value and should be made up before the day of shooting to make sure that nothing is forgotten.

Here again, as throughout this chapter, we are reminded of the great concentration and attention to detail required from the camera operator in order to maintain control in his work. Only after thoroughly mastering the techniques and mechanics of his craft can a cinematographer develop the consistency necessary to achieve an individual stylistic approach, which is the goal of the cinematographer's art.

CHAPTER 2
FILMS AND SENSITOMETRY

The cinematographer's choice of film stock is a major factor in determining how the image will be recorded, and therefore contributes greatly to the cinematic style. The cinematographer must not only appreciate differences between stocks, but be familiar with every property of the film so that he will know how to manipulate it to achieve the appearance and qualities he wants. Therefore, in our discussion of film stocks we will be concerned with every characteristic relevant to the control of image quality, starting with the most basic.

FILM STRUCTURE

The two fundamental components of film are the base and emulsion. The base (also known as the "safety film support") is usually made of cellulose tri-acetate. The emulsion consists of a thin layer of gelatin in which light-sensitive silver-halide crystals are suspended. This emulsion is attached to the base with a transparent adhesive called the subbing layer.

The base is not completely transparent; it often contains a certain amount of gray dye that serves as an "anti-halation element." Without this, bright points in the frame (such as car headlights) would penetrate through the emulsion, reflect from the back of the base, and create a halo around their images.

These reflections are instead absorbed by the gray dye. This is mainly used in negative films. A different anti-halation technique is employed in some film stocks like Ektachrome Commercial and Kodachrome II. Here the gray dye is replaced by a black coating on the back of the base to stop reflections. This anti-halation backing is removed during the processing. Still a third system places an anti-halation layer between the emulsion and the base, as in black-and-white reversal films.

2-1 Film structure.

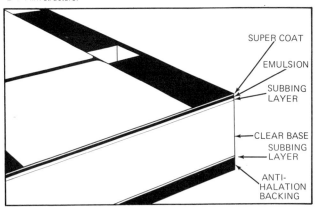

SUPER COAT

EMULSION

SUBBING LAYER

CLEAR BASE

SUBBING LAYER

ANTI-HALATION BACKING

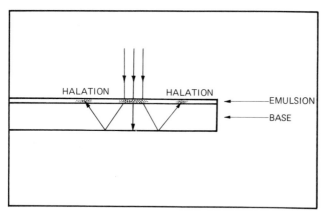

2-2 Halation effect, caused by internal reflections in the film.

PRACTICAL SENSITOMETRY

The science of measuring an emulsion's reaction (sensitivity) to light is called sensitometry. The basic principles of practical sensitometry do not require an extensive knowledge of mathematics or physics. They only require common sense.

As a first step toward a study of sensitometry we should explain roughly how a film is able to record an image. Any scene contains a conglomeration of points reflecting various amounts of light toward the camera. As this light strikes the silver-halide crystals in the emulsion, it causes changes that remain invisible until the film is developed. These hidden changes make up the "latent image." When the film is developed, the areas in which silver-halide crystals received the most light produce more metallic silver than areas that received less exposure. Consider a photograph of a man in a white shirt and black pants. The film is black-and-white negative. The white shirt reflected a lot of light, causing great changes of silver halide into metallic silver. Meanwhile, the black pants reflected only a small amount of light, causing minimal changes in the emulsion. The face had a light reflectance in between the previously mentioned extremes, and so caused a medium change in the emulsion. The developed negative will represent the white shirt as a very dense area with a lot of metallic silver, therefore appearing black. The pants will be the opposite — less metallic silver,

hence more transparent. This is why we call it a *negative*. White objects appear black on film, while black objects appear bright (clear).

Reversal film, on the other hand, results in a positive image on the camera original. It is developed much like negative, and at one point is in negative form. However, the processing does not stop here. The metallic silver of the negative image is removed in a bleach bath and the remaining (unexposed) silver halides are exposed to a weak light in the processing machine. The film is then developed again. This time the image is positive. Black is black and white is clear.

THE CHARACTERISTIC CURVE

Many beginners have been misled into believing that for any scene there is only one proper light level and one correct exposure. This notion is reinforced by automatic exposure systems, which magically divine the correct setting for the entire scene. This unfortunate· idea is misleading and will hamper the film maker's understanding of exposure.

Every scene contains an infinite number of reflected brightnesses. White objects reflect much light and dark objects reflect little light. The film will faithfully record only a part of the range the human eye is capable of adapting itself to. Take, for example, a scene in which the range runs from a bright sky to a black telephone in a shadow. From one vantage point our eye can probably see these extremes because it readjusts itself when looking at each one. As we glance up from the telephone our eye closes its iris and refocuses for the brighter sky. It is difficult, however, to see both clearly at the exact same time. The film has the same problem. If two such extremes are in the field of view at once, it is impossible for the film to record both faithfully. The range of light levels in many scenes is greater than the range the film can correctly record.

Therefore in filming a·scene we must decide what objects are the most important and calculate an exposure that will place the brightness levels of those objects within the range that the film will faithfully reproduce.

To define the optimal range of each film, we will determine how increasing amounts of light cause deeper reactions in the emulsion. We chart the levels of exposure against the resulting densities in the processed film, arriving at a graph known as the "characteristic curve." It is not a practical on-the-set aid, yet its thorough comprehension is indispensable in helping us

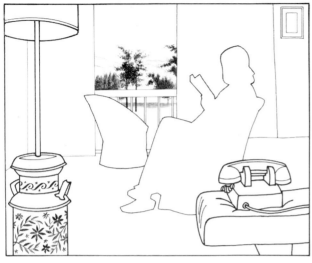

2-3 Graphic representation of extremes in the scene brightness range that were not distinguished in the photo. See Figure 2-6.

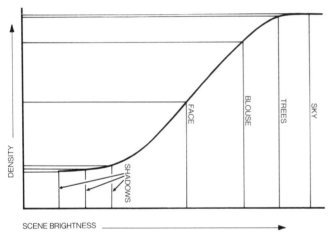

2-4 Scene brightnesses located on a characteristic curve.

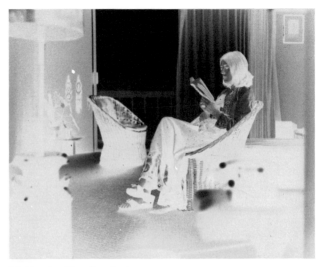

2-5 Negative. (Photo by author)

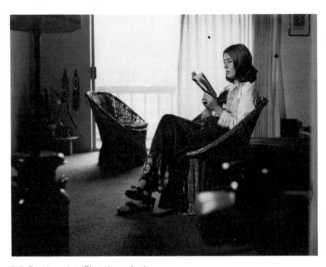

2-6 Positive print. (Photo by author)

understand how the film emulsion interprets the subject's brightness range.

The curve is established by placing a short strip of an unexposed film into an instrument called a sensitometer, where it is exposed to increasing levels of light. The film is then processed, and the density resulting from each light level is measured with a device known as a densitometer. By plotting the results on a graph we arrive at the characteristic curve, describing the relationship between light levels and densities for this particular emulsion.

Let us consider an everyday exposure problem and relate it to the characteristic curve. In the example of figure 2-3, I was confronted by a huge range of brightnesses in the scene. I

decided that for this scene it was most important for the person in it to be represented faithfully, so I used an exposure that would bring the face within the optimal range of the curve. The blouse was brighter and the skirt was darker, but they too fell within the range and were recorded proportionately lighter and darker. However, designs on the lamp stand and the telephone in the shadow were so far underexposed that all details were lost. This is because at the low end of the curve (called the "toe"), where the lamp stand and telephone were, the shadows were "squashed." Note in figure 2-4 how a large difference in scene brightness was represented as a minute different in densities on the film, and thus detail was lost. The same is true of the other extreme, where the trees outside were

61

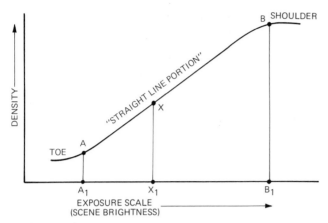

2-7 Characteristic curve.

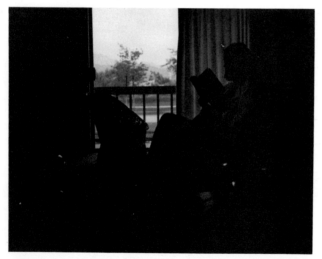

2-8 Exposure calculated for trees outside. Compare with Figure 2-6. (Photo by author)

lost because at the high end of the curve (called the "shoulder") the great difference between the trees and the sky was represented on film as only a small difference in density, and therefore the two are not distinguishable from each other.

Ideally the curve might be a straight 45° line, not squashing anything, but, in fact, no such film exists. The nearest to this ideal is the straight-line portion of the curve (between A and B in figure 2-7). Actually this portion between the toe and shoulder is rarely perfectly straight. However, any scene that stays under the limits of the straight portion (e.g., between A-1 and B-1 in figure 2-7), will be faithfully reproduced in *correctly related* densities. That is, an increase in the brightness will cause the image to be proportionately brighter, without squashing.

Some scenes, such as a foggy landscape, may be so narrow in brightness range (low contrast) that they could fit into the straight-line portion of the curve twice over. In practical terms this means that such a scene could be exposed anywhere within the straight-line portion and still yield a negative with correctly related densities. It is very common for a photographer using black-and-white negative film to give such a scene a minimal exposure, positioning the brightness range on the lower portion of the curve yet still within the straight-line portion. In this way he obtains a fairly thin (not dense, more clear) negative that gives more finely detailed reproduction. The lab technician will later compensate for this minimal exposure by printing it lighter. This technique is only used for black-and-white negative film. When shooting in color negative or any reversal emulsion, the important brightness range should usually be placed near the middle of the straight-line portion to obtain the best rendition.

In negative, the horizontal length of the emulsion's straight-line portion (A-1 to B-1 in figure 2-7) and the size of the scene brightness range (for example A-1 to X-1) together determine latitude. In this example the latitude is from X-1 to B-1. In negative, latitude is any range outside the scene's brightness range, yet still within the straight-line portion. In the original example in figure 2-4, there was no latitude because the scene brightness range was greater than the straight-line portion.

It should be noted that we have been talking about negative film only. Latitude for reversal films is thought of differently. Reversal films are much less tolerant of overexposure and underexposure. There is not a wide range of acceptable exposures. When using reversal film, we place the most important brightness range (objects) in the center of the straight-line portion and think of latitude as the adjacent tolerance range (acceptable over- and underexposure). In other words, latitude is a measure of how far clearly separated details extend into the bright and dark areas (i.e., how large the optimal range is).

Therefore when calculating exposure we are not exclusively interested in one reflected light level. Our real consideration is a range of brightness levels present in the subject, from which we choose one. We calculate an exposure for it that will place it and the other adjacent levels on the curve where they will be represented in correctly related densities. For example, in the situation of figure 2-6, if we had decided that the view outside the window was the most important element to see clearly, we could have calculated an exposure that would have brought the trees near the center of the straight-line portion, as in figure 2-8.

There are two complications we have previously ignored in the interest of keeping things simple. First of all, color employs not one but three emulsions—one for each of the primary colors, blue, green, and red, each of which has its own characteristic curve. Ideally they should be parallel and very close together, but this is not always the case (figure 2-9).

The second previously unmentioned complication is that because reversal films yield a positive image, their curves slant opposite to negatives. That is, in negative a low light level yields a low density (clear area on the film), while a high light level causes a dense area on the film. In reversal, however, this is opposite. A white object is recorded as bright (clear) and a dark object is recorded as dark (dense), so the curve slants in the opposite direction, from upper left down to the lower right.

EXPOSURE VALUES

It was earlier stated that the exposure value (f-stop) was selected so that the important light levels would be placed within the optimal range of the characteristic curve. To understand how this is done, it must be noted that the "scene brightness" side of the graph represents the light *actually reaching the film* — that is, the amount of light allowed to pass by the f-stop. The horizontal and vertical (density) scales increase logarithmically, as do f-stops. (Logarithms are common in film making; many film makers understand and use them without realizing it.) If a scale is logarithmic, it simply means that each succeeding step *doubles* the value of the previous one. Logarithms could also triple or quadruple between steps, but in film making we are almost always talking about "logs" that double the value with each increasing step. Take the example of f-stops. As you remember from Chapter 1, each wider f-stop setting doubles the amount of light passing through the lens. Therefore f-stops are designed in a logarithmic progression.

Light is measured in logarithms because it naturally increases that way. Suppose we start with one light bulb on and then turn on a second. Of course the illumination appears to increase. To make the light appear to increase again *by the same amount,* we must turn on *two* more bulbs. To increase it the next time will require four more bulbs if the increase is to appear as great as each of the previous steps.

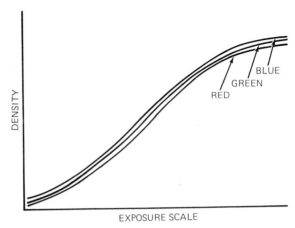
2-9 Characteristic curve for a hypothetical color negative.

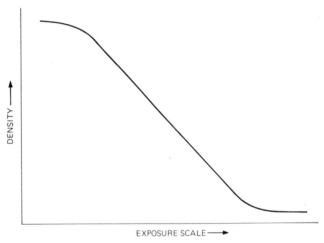
2-10 Curve for a reversal film.

Step number:	1	2	3	4	5	6	7
Number of bulbs:	1	2	4	8	16	32	64

This is a logarithmic scale. The light doubles with each succeeding step. Yet the light *appears* to increase by the same percentage between each step, making a logarithmic scale the most convenient system for discussing light.

Because f-stops and the scene-brightness scale of the characteristic curve are both calibrated in logarithms, the two can be related. It happens that each stop equals 0.3 on the horizontal scale. That is, between 0.00 and 0.6 there are two stops. Between 0.00 and 2.4 there are eight stops. We could determine where the various scene brightnesses would fall on the horizontal scale. For example, a given object, such as a face, might be exposed so as to fall on the middle of the scene-brightness scale. An object one stop brighter in the scene would fall one .3 division to the right of the face on the scene-brightness scale. An object reflecting two stops less light will fall .6 to the left on the horizontal scale, and so on. Remember that the scene-brightness scale of the characteristic curve refers to the amount of light actually reaching the film. Therefore, if we now reduce the exposure one f-stop, all the scene brightnesses will shift .3 to the left on the horizontal scale. Similarly, if we increase the exposure by one f-stop, all the brightnesses would shift .3 to the right.

Consider the example in figure 2-4. We decided that the face was the most important object in the scene and therefore calculated an exposure that brought the face within the straight-line portion of the characteristic curve. We could instead have used an f-stop that would have brought the trees within the straight-line portion, but the face would be lost in the shadows (see figure 2-8). Therefore, by selecting the proper f-stop, we are able to "position" the brightnesses of our subject within the straight-line portion of the characteristic

curve. Thus to calculate the exposure we need to know the brightness of the subject and the sensitivity of the film.

The overall degree of sensitivity of a film is expressed by the position of the characteristic curve in relation to the horizontal scale (scene brightness). Our goal is to find some way of arriving at an f-stop that will place the range of important scene brightnesses within the straight-line portion. Therefore, for practical purposes the sensitivity of each film is rated by an ASA (American Standards Association, now called the American National Standards Institute) exposure index, sometimes also referred to as EI number.

Faster films are more sensitive and have higher ASA numbers. They are designed for filming under low light level. Because they require less light, the straight-line portion of their characteristic curve will appear slightly to the left (see figure 2-11). Slower emulsions are less sensitive and have lower ASA numbers. They are designed for shooting scenes with brighter illumination levels.

The ASA value doubles as the sensitivity of the film doubles. For example, an exposure index (ASA) of 200 represents an emulsion twice as fast as one of ASA 100. ASA 200 describes a film four times as fast as ASA 50.

Notice how f-stops relate to ASA values. For example, we have a set amount of light (say 800 foot-candles), which will remain at that level. Then for the following ASA values we would use the following f-stops:

ASA 25	ASA 50	ASA 100	ASA 200	ASA 400
f/4	f/5.6	f/8	f/11	f/16

2-11 A fast and a slow emulsion. This fast emulsion starts reacting to light one stop (0.3 increment) before the slow emulsion. Notice that of these two hypothetical emulsions, the fast emulsion has a slightly longer useful portion. Notice also that the faster emulsion has a higher fog level (i.e., higher minimum density inherent to the emulsion).

Every time the exposure index (ASA) doubles, it means the film is twice as sensitive, therefore requiring *half* as much light. As each succeeding f-stop cuts the light by half, we can see how f-stops relate to ASA; every time the ASA doubles it signifies that one stop less light is required.

Therefore, we sometimes describe a film as so many stops faster or slower than another film. For example, a film of ASA 200 is eight times faster than a film of ASA 25 (25 x 8 = 200), but we may also say this by stating that the film of ASA 200 is three stops faster than the film of ASA 25 (25 doubled three times equals 200). This tells us that a film of ASA 25 requires three stops more light than one of ASA 200. This relationship is vital. Although it may seem puzzling at first, it will seem quite simple once you have mastered it.

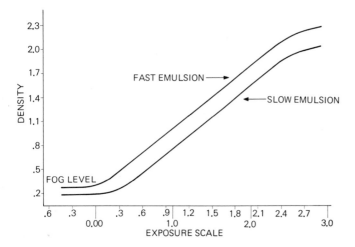

DAYLIGHT VERSUS TUNGSTEN EXPOSURE INDEX

The exact color of light differs depending on the source. The slight difference between the color of sunlight and the color of tungsten illumination is hardly noticeable to the eye. The film, however, is quite sensitive to variations in the color of the light, and therefore black-and-white films are given two ASA values, one for daylight and one for tungsten. Color film will magnify color variations, yielding unacceptable results, unless we use the proper filter to modify the incoming light, tailoring it to the color requirements of the emulsion. This will be discussed at much greater length in Chapter 3.

FORCED PROCESSING

The ASA number is only the manufacturer's *recommended* sensitivity. The sensitivity can be changed by increasing or decreasing the period of development. Increasing the developing time will have the effect of increasing the ASA. This is called "pushing" or "forced processing." Most emulsions can be pushed two stops (multiplying the sensitivity by four), but pushing will result in quality losses, such as higher grain, less sharpness, and changes in color and contrast (higher contrast in negative film and lower contrast in reversal film). The amount of quality loss depends on the amount of pushing and the type of emulsion being used. Because of this most labs protect their quality reputations by refusing to push more than two or sometimes three stops.

The effect of pushing shows up in a family of characteristic curves. Here in figure 2-12, for example, light level A would normally yield a density of X, but by pushing the film one stop it results in a density of Y. Note that these curves are not parallel.

The more the negative film is pushed, the steeper the characteristic curves become. This means that we can expect an increase in contrast with increased pushing of negative.

Pushing reversal causes a slight decrease in top densities. The blacks in the scene are recorded as gray, resulting in lower contrast.

Excessive pushing will also desaturate color, giving the film a muddy look.

For a practical example of how to use a film with the intention of pushing it, suppose you are using a film of ASA 50. You want to shoot a scene where there is not enough light.

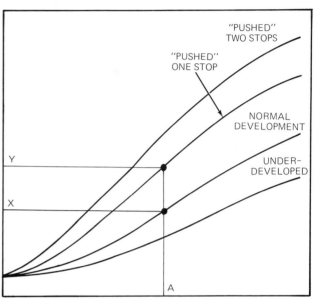

2-12 A "family" of characteristic curves.

2-13 Camera stock versus a print stock.

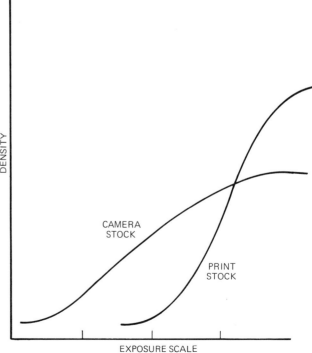

If you had a film of ASA 100 you would be all right. So you decide to use the ASA 50 film and push it one stop in the development. One stop pushing doubles the exposure index to 100. Set the light meter to ASA 100 and expose the entire scene accordingly. When you send this roll of film to the lab, clearly indicate that it has been exposed at ASA 100 and request one stop pushing. This information should be written on the film carton, on the can, and on the lab report.

Pushing is occasionally described as "developing to a higher gamma." Gamma is a measure of the slope of the straight-line portion of the characteristic curve, which, as you can see in figure 2-12, becomes steeper with more pushing. A higher gamma indicates a steeper curve. Therefore, a higher gamma means more contrast. The gamma standard for the majority of camera negatives is 0.65. (This is not vital to our discussion, but for those interested in knowing where this figure comes from, it is the tangent of the acute angle between the straight-line portion and the horizontal axis of the grid.) Print stocks are slower and of much higher gamma.

DEFINITION

Up until now we have been mainly discussing sensitometry — that is, ways of measuring a film's sensitivity. Yet when we compare film stocks we are equally interested in another aspect, the film's definition. It is a key factor in determining the texture of the images as they appear on screen. The photographic definition of a film depends on three contributing factors: the grain, the sharpness, and the resolving power.

Graininess is one of our primary concerns. When the grains of metallic silver forming the image are visible, they create a texture like boiling sand when projected. The degree to which these grains are visible will depend upon their size and their concentration (density). As explained earlier, the grains of silver halide are struck by light and then processed to yield an image formed by grains of metallic silver. It seems that the larger a silver-halide crystal is, the more easily it is affected by light. Faster emulsions achieve their increased sensitivity partly by using generally larger crystals. Therefore faster emulsions show more grain than slower emulsions. Secondly, the denser the developed original film, the more grain. In negative film this means that overexposure will increase grain, because overexposure of negative will yield a denser original image. Reversal is just the opposite. In reversal, underexposure will result in a more dense original and hence more grain.

To reduce grain, some experienced cameramen may slightly *under*expose *negative* film. Reversal film could be slightly *over*exposed to reduce grain, but because reversal has less latitude than negative, this effect is not recommended.

As one could well imagine, pushing will also increase grain. This is because additional speed has been obtained by increasing the densities through prolonging the development time. The extended development time tends to make the grains clump together. The opposite is also true; by underdeveloping one reduces the speed of the emulsion and thereby decreases the grain. However, underdeveloping will reduce the contrast and distort the color as well. Some films (usually the slower emulsions, which have finer grain to begin with) will take pushing better than other stocks.

In discovering the grain characteristics of a given film stock, tests and practical experience are more reliable than the manufacturer's promotional literature.

Sharpness is another key factor influencing photographic definition. It represents the precision with which the emulsion records sharp edges in the scene. An "acutance" test measures sharpness by using a densitometer to determine how quickly the density drops across a sharp shadow line, such as in a picture of a knife edge. A reversal film will yield a sharper image than a negative of the same ASA rating.

Resolving power is the third factor contributing to the overall picture definition. It is the film's ability to record fine detail. Resolving power is measured by photographing a chart composed of fine sets of parallel lines, separated by spacings of the same width. The lines and spacings become gradually thinner from set to set. After processing the film is examined under a microscope to determine the maximum number of lines per millimeter that the film is capable of distinguishing. For example, Plus-X Negative Type 7231 can resolve 33 lines per millimeter if the contrast ratio between the lines and the background is 1.6 to 1, or 112 lines per millimeter if the ratio is 1000 to 1. As we see in this example, the resolving power is dependent on the subject's contrast. In addition, it will be influenced by other factors. A fairly slow, fine-grain emulsion, properly exposed and processed normally, will usually deliver high resolution. However, over- or underexposure, over- or underdevelopment, or the use of a faster film would reduce the resolving power. It should further be noted that lens quality also contributes to the overall resolution of the image.

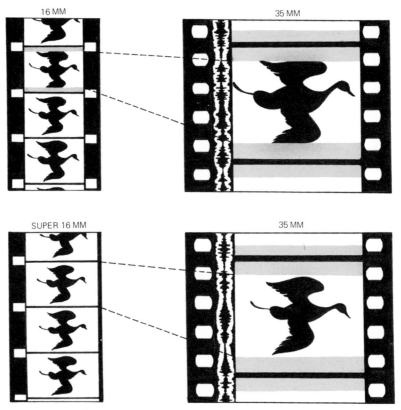

2-14 Advantage of Super-16 original when blowing up to 35mm for release.

FILM GAUGES

A key factor in apparent definition is the size of the film format. For example, a frame of 35mm film is approximately 4 times larger in area than a frame of 16mm film. If projected onto equal-size screens, the 16mm film must be enlarged much more than the 35mm film. As a result, the grain appears larger and the details less distinct in 16mm than in 35mm. This difference is not caused by different emulsions, as most 35mm emulsions are available in 16mm. The difference is merely the result of the reduced image size in 16mm. Similarly, even though the same emulsion may be used, 16mm pictures appear much clearer and less grainy than 8mm. Super-8 has a slightly larger image area and so is superior to regular 8mm. In fact, the Super-8 film format has not only virtually replaced the regular-8 stocks, but is now encroaching on some 16mm television applications. Many stations are discovering that the quality of Super-8 is adequate for television use, because of the relatively small size of television screens. The absence of fine detail shows less on the small screen. TV reporting with Super-8 is cheaper, easier, and in many ways faster and more mobile.

As the quality of film stock continues to improve, the smaller formats become capable of recording better and better images. Twenty-five years ago, 16mm film was considered strictly amateur, while now it is a fully professional stock.

16mm film is, in some cases, replacing 35mm in the filming of many television shows and even feature films. In the case of features, the finished 16mm original is blown up to 35mm for theatrical release. This unfortunately introduces a noticeable loss in quality. Some labs have been quite successful doing such enlargements as a specialty, but the reduced definition is still apparent.

The Super-16 format was especially developed to minimize this loss. It is used for films that are shot in 16mm and blown up to 35mm for release. When normal 16mm is blown up to wide-screen 35mm, the great magnification results in more graininess and poorer image quality. The problem is further aggravated by the fact that the top and bottom of the 16mm frame are lost in changing the image to the wide-screen ratio (see figure 2-14). Super-16 extends the image into what was formerly the sound-track area. This provides for not only a larger image, but one that is already in wide-screen ratio. Thus the Super-16 format requires less magnification when blowing up to 35mm wide-screen, and hence there is a much smaller loss in quality.

In adapting a 16mm camera to the Super-16 format, the lens must be recentered and the aperture modified. Not all camera designs are easily converted.

FILM STOCKS

At first glance, the list of available motion-picture stock could be overwhelming to a beginner. But after becoming familiar with different films, one will be able to relate each film to the specific tasks or situations for which it would be used. There is a great choice of film stocks available in 16mm. Super-8 has less variety but is catching up slowly.

After deciding between black-and-white and color, the next choice is negative versus reversal. (In Super-8 all films are reversal.) There are several reasons for the popularity of reversal stocks in 16mm. In addition to having finer grain, reversal film is easier for lab technicians and editors to handle. Scratches and dust specks on reversal print black, but from negative they print white and are much more visible. Furthermore, in the printing stages the timing and optical work (such as fades) are much easier in reversal. Negative, on the other hand, has the advantage of less contrast for better tonal gradations and a greater tolerance for under- and overexposure. This gives negative greater latitude.

In this book we will limit ourselves to one manufacturer's line of film stocks.

Eastman Black-and-White Negative Stocks

PLUS-X NEGATIVE BLACK-AND-WHITE
TYPE 7231 (16MM)
ASA: day 80; tungsten 64
Plus-X Negative is medium-speed and has fine grain. It is useful for both indoor and outdoor photography. It is generally used on exteriors and in the studio where light levels are high. It has good deep blacks.

DOUBLE-X NEGATIVE BLACK-AND-WHITE
TYPE 7222 (16MM)
ASA: day 250; tungsten 200
Double-X became a great cameraman's favorite because it is three times faster than Plus-X and has relatively low grain and great latitude. It permits great economy in studio lighting and saves a lot of lighting problems on location. It responds well to forced development and thus can easily be pushed a stop, giving us a forced speed of ASA 500 in daylight and 400 with tungsten lights. Double-X is a good choice for the cameraman who wants to simplify his work by using one emulsion for all circumstances. Its resolution is almost as good as Plus-X, but Double-X has about 50 percent more grain.

4-X NEGATIVE BLACK-AND-WHITE
TYPE 7224 (16MM)
ASA: day 500; tungsten 400
4-X has a high ASA and is designed for extremely low light levels such as are encountered in documentary conditions. Unfortunately, 4-X has high grain and reduced resolution. Given my choice, I would rather push Double-X one stop in development than use 4-X at its normal speed.

Eastman Kodak Black-and-White Reversal Stocks

PLUS-X REVERSAL BLACK-AND-WHITE
TYPE 7276 (16MM)
ASA: day 50; tungsten 40
Plus-X Reversal is a fine-grain, medium-speed film with good contrast and beautiful tone gradation (many distinguishable shades). You would use it for daylight exterior shooting and in the studio situation where adequate lighting is provided (250 foot-candles for f/2.8).

TRI-X REVERSAL BLACK-AND-WHITE
TYPE 7278 (16MM)
ASA: day 200; tungsten 160

Where there is not enough light to shoot Plus-X Reversal, Tri-X is suitable. It has more grain than Plus-X, but good tonal reproduction and good halation control (halos around bright objects are kept to a minimum). Tri-X can be pushed at the expense of even higher grain.

4-X REVERSAL BLACK-AND-WHITE
TYPE 7277 (16MM)
ASA: day 400; tungsten 320

4-X is designed for extremely low light levels, or for situations in which a very grainy picture is desired for an effect. The anti-halation characteristics are good. The speed can be pushed by forced development at the cost of even more grain and poorer definition.

Eastman Color Negative

Eastman offers only one color negative film in 16mm. Although standard in 35mm, color negative is prohibitively expensive in 16mm, because of the high cost of making corrected prints.

COLOR NEGATIVE
TYPE 7247 (16MM)
ASA: day 64 (with Kodak Wratten #85 filter); tungsten 100

Color negative is more tolerant of exposure errors, has greater latitude, and is more easily color-corrected than reversal. Nevertheless, it is not favored by the majority of film makers in the United States, who prefer 16mm reversal because it is easier to handle in editing and less expensive in final printing.

Eastman Kodak Color Reversals

EKTACHROME COMMERCIAL
TYPE 7252 (16MM) — ECO
ASA: day 16 (with Kodak Wratten #85 filter); tungsten 25

Also called ECO, this is the most often used 16mm color film. It is designed for shooting outdoors (with a #85 filter) and in the studio where adequate light is available. It has a fairly slow ASA but it can easily be pushed one stop with only a minimal loss in quality. Its very fine grain does not drastically increase when pushed. ECO is not intended for direct projection. It has a low-contrast characteristic, and the proper contrast will show only in the print. The original emulsion is soft and would easily be scratched in the projector or moviola.

Unlike other color reversals, the latitude of ECO will allow up to one stop overexposure without a fatal degrading of color. However, at one stop underexposure, the color tends to become muddy.

EKTACHROME MS
TYPE 7256 (16MM)
ASA; day 64; tungsten 16 (with Kodak Wratten #80 A filter)

MS has a very fine grain and can be directly projected. It is balanced for daylight but could be used under tungsten lights with a filter. It is mostly used for scientific analysis.

EKTACHROME EF DAYLIGHT
TYPE 7241 (16MM)
ASA: day 160; tungsten 40 (with Kodak Wratten #80A filter)

EF Daylight is a high-speed film intended for low-level daylight illumination. Its high ASA makes it ideal for slow-motion sports photography. Its exposure latitude allows for one stop underexposure without drastic color loss. It has noticeably more grain than ECO. According to the manufacturer it can be pushed up to three stops with "some loss in quality," but there are not many labs that would risk their quality reputation by pushing it more than one or two stops.

EKTACHROME EF TUNGSTEN
TYPE 7242 (16MM)
ASA: day 80 (with Kodak Wratten #85 filter); tungsten 125

EF Tungsten is designed for shooting indoors where there is not enough light for ECO. EF Tungsten is the second-most-used color reversal stock. Generally, a cameraman will use ECO outdoors or indoors when there is enough light, because ECO renders better resolution. But when light levels are too low for ECO, EF Tungsten is the common choice. It has more grain and contrast than ECO.

EF Tungsten has become the film most often used for filming TV news coverage, because it readily adapts to almost any situation. It can be exposed indoors with only one or two portable lights or sometimes with just available light. With the use of a #85 filter it easily adapts to daylight illumination. Unlike ECO, EF Tungsten shows its proper contrast in the original, so this same material can be broadcast without the need of a print to correct the color. However, the emulsion of EF Tungsten, like ECO, is soft and will be scratched by projectors and moviolas. Therefore if prints are to be made, the original should not be projected. In the case of news coverage, the film will be projected only once for broadcast, risking a few scratches picked up in one or two runs.

Prints made from EF films (both 7241 and 7242) tend to be rather contrasty and thus intercut poorly with ECO. To cut down the contrast in the original (yielding a more natural print), some labs offer a service known as "post-flashing" or "post-fogging." Before developing, the original film is rewound in front of a very weak light source. This introduces a small amount of overall exposure, which reduces the contrast. After this the film is developed in a normal manner. Post-fogging EF gives softer, more naturally subtle color renditions than unfogged, and looks better when cut with ECO. EF that has not been post-fogged looks noticeably more contrasty when cut together with ECO. If you require post-fogging, indicate it on every can of film to be post-fogged, and write it on your lab order form in red letters (so it will be noticed). Indicate post-fogging *first* on the form above all other instructions.

There are two more often-overlooked color reversal films that should be mentioned:

KODACHROME II
ASA: day 25; tungsten 6 (with Kodak Wratten #80A filter)

KODACHROME II-A
Balanced for 3400° K
ASA: day 25 (with Kodak Wratten #85 filter); 3400°K photoflood 40; 3200°K tungsten 32 (with Kodak Wratten #82-A filter)

Both Kodachrome II and Kodachrome II-A are manufactured mainly for amateur use where prints will not be made from the original. The colors are rich while blacks are deep. Unfortunately, this means Kodachrome is quite contrasty. Prints made from it increase this contrast even more. Another disadvantage is the lack of edge numbers, which help the editor.

Nevertheless, Kodachrome emulsions are the best stocks available for shooting color titles such as high-contrast graphics with rich colors, making Kodachrome an excellent animation stock. The deep rich blacks also make it especially good for shooting so-called "burn-in" titles (white letters, superimposed). Even in black-and-white films burn-in titles may be shot on Kodachrome.

SHOOTING TESTS

The best way of familiarizing yourself with the characteristics of a given emulsion is by shooting tests. To maintain consistency, tests should be shot using film from the same emulsion batch to be used in the production, exposed using the same light meter and (if possible) the same camera, and processed at the same lab. The exact shape and location of the characteristic curve will often slightly vary between labs.

The most useful information can be obtained by photographing three objects: a gray scale chart, a color chart, and a human face. This combination should be shot using a variety of successive exposures, such as starting with five stops overexposed, going down one stop at a time to the "correct" exposure, and then closing the lens iris through five stops of underexposure. We may even test half-stops of under- and overexposure. Each stop tested must be clearly indicated in the shot along with the type of film and the emulsion batch. When processed and evaluated, this series of varying exposures will give us:

1. The most correct ASA rating. For example, accumulating variables might make the film look best when one half-stop overexposed in relation to the suggested ASA exposure index.
2. Emulsion latitude and contrast. The number of steps distinctly visible on the color and black-and-white charts will demonstrate the latitude and contrast characteristics. For example, a film might allow one stop overexposure with less quality loss than one stop underexposure.
3. Color rendition. On black-and-white film the color chart will appear as a gray scale. By studying the relative appearance of the color bars we can determine how color is reproduced by the given black-and-white stock. For color stocks we study the faithfulness of the color reproduction and see how color changes as the exposure varies. The face is an important item here, as it provides us with a skin-tone reproduction.

Any other variables should be tested. For example, when considering using a film pushed one or two stops a test will help us to predetermine the degree of quality loss. Similarly, if some old, outdated stock is to be used, it would be a good idea to test some of it first to make sure it hasn't deteriorated. As was said before, anything that is in doubt should be tested.

FILM STORAGE AND HANDLING

To prevent undesired changes in the film stock, such as changes in color, sensitivity, and fog level, and to prevent shrinkage, all films should be properly stored and handled. Color film is especially sensitive to high temperature and extremes in humidity and therefore should be stored in a refrigerator. Black-and-white film may be stored in a refrigerator or a reasonably cool and dry place. All films should be kept in a can, sealed airtight (preferably with the original tape).

When being stored for periods of one to six months, the best storage temperature is about 55°F for all films except color negative, which does best when kept at 50°F. For longer periods the temperatures should be lower.

When film is taken out of the refrigerator, it must be allowed to warm up before it is opened or moisture may condense on its cold surface. It should take about 30 minutes to warm up to room temperature. If the humidity is very high (like 90 percent) it could take as long as an hour. A carton of several cans may take as much as nine hours to warm up.

When shooting on location the film is usually preloaded into camera magazines, which should be kept in dustproof and moisture-tight metal magazine cases. These cases must be left in a cool place. When your car is parked in the sun its trunk becomes like an oven, so never keep your film there, even for a short period.

Before filming in really hot or humid areas, familiarize yourself with the appropriate Kodak pamphlets *and* the section in the *American Cinematographer Manual* dealing with film handling in these conditions. The same should be done before filming in extremely cold areas.

When bulk film and magnetic tape has to travel on commercial airlines, advise the airline officials that it is perishable in extreme heat and that it should not be X-rayed or submitted to strong magnetic fields. Also write these instructions and the contents on the outside of the case in large red letters.

Film deteriorates fastest between exposure and development, and so it should be processed as soon as possible after being shot.

FILM ORDERING INFORMATION

Schools and independent film makers can buy their raw stock directly from Kodak at a very substantial discount from the prices of most retail camera stores. The Eastman Kodak Company Educational Marketing Division in Rochester, New York, can give you the address of the local distribution center.

When ordering film, make sure to specify the type of perforations and "wind" that are correct for your camera. Almost all cameras require film wound *emulsion side in.* Single-sprocket cameras use either B-wind film or double-sprocket film. Some cameras will accept double-perf film only. Very few cameras will accept A-wind film. It is mainly for printers.

"Pitch" refers to the distance between sprocket holes. High-speed cameras and print stocks require long pitch.

Emulsion is made up in batches, which yield thousands of feet of film. When ordering raw stock for a given production, it is advisable to secure all the footage with the same batch number. Two different emulsion batches may have slightly different characteristics.

Film is cheaper when bought in bulk. It is common for amateurs to buy film in rolls of 400 feet or more and then break it down into 100-foot spools. This is often more trouble than it is worth. It should be pointed out, however, that when winding unexposed stock from reel to reel in a darkroom, there is a chance that spots and patterns will be caused by static electricity on the film. This can be prevented by grounding the rewind arms and winding the film slowly at an even speed.

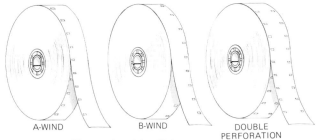

A-WIND   B-WIND   DOUBLE PERFORATION

2-15 Film winds. Film wound emulsion side in.

CHAPTER 3
FILTERS AND LIGHT

A cinematographer's primary concern is the manipulation of color, contrast, and texture. These qualities can be controlled either by changing the way in which the light falls upon the subject (as we will discuss in the next chapter), or by introducing a filter between the subject and the camera. To understand how light can be manipulated by filters, we will start by exploring just a little bit of light theory. Then we can discuss specific filters and their functions. (*Note:* There are several filter manufacturers, and some have different designation systems. For the sake of simplicity I will use Kodak Wratten filter numbers, unless I specify otherwise.)

THE ELECTROMAGNETIC SPECTRUM

The electromagnetic spectrum extends from cosmic rays to telephone impulses and beyond. Within this enormous range of wavelengths there is a narrow range of visible energy, called light. The rest is darkness to our eye. At each end of this visible spectrum there are invisible wavelengths — ultraviolet and infrared — that are not visible to the human eye but can be recorded on film.

The most common human experience of the entire visible spectrum is the rainbow. All the colors of the rainbow are generated by the sun. *Together they appear white.* But when dispersed by the moisture in the air or refracted by a prism, the wavelengths are spread, thus creating a rainbow effect.

FILTER THEORY

The color of an object comes from the light falling on it. When white light (which contains all the visible wavelengths) falls on an object, some hues are absorbed. The other colors are reflected, giving the object an apparent color. For example, when white light strikes a "blue" object, the surface of the object reflects the blue light and absorbs all the other visible wavelengths, mainly red and green.

The color of the object will change when the light falling on it is not white. For example, when a "blue" object is illuminated by light *not* containing blue wavelengths, the object will appear black.

This brings us to the basic principle of filters. Filters modify light by absorbing certain colors and allowing others to pass.

When using filters we think of the spectrum as three primary colors: blue, green, and red. Any other color is a mixture of

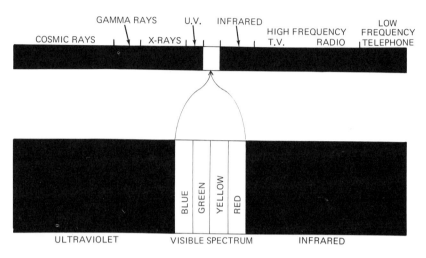

3-1 The electromagnetic spectrum.

COSMIC RAYS · GAMMA RAYS · X-RAYS · U.V. · INFRARED · HIGH FREQUENCY T.V. · RADIO · LOW FREQUENCY TELEPHONE

BLUE GREEN YELLOW RED

ULTRAVIOLET · VISIBLE SPECTRUM · INFRARED

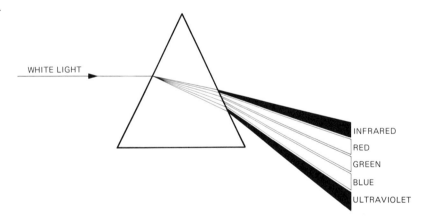

3-2 White light refracted by a prism.

WHITE LIGHT

INFRARED
RED
GREEN
BLUE
ULTRAVIOLET

3-3 The color of an object depends on: *A,* the color absorbed by the object; *B,* the color of the light falling on the object.

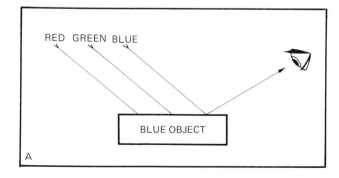

RED GREEN BLUE

BLUE OBJECT

A

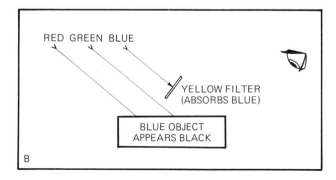

RED GREEN BLUE

YELLOW FILTER (ABSORBS BLUE)

BLUE OBJECT APPEARS BLACK

B

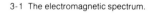

73

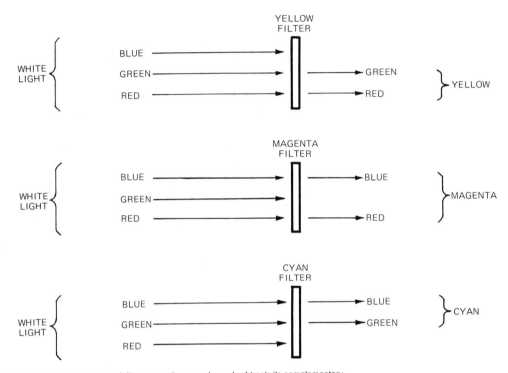

3-4 Subtractive filter principle. A filter passes its own color and subtracts its complementary.

these three. We manipulate the primary colors by using their so-called complementaries: yellow, magenta, and cyan.

Yellow is called "minus blue," because a yellow filter stops blue and passes green and red, which together make yellow light.

Magenta is called "minus green," because a magenta filter stops green light and passes blue and red, which together make magenta light.

Cyan is called "minus red," because a cyan filter stops red light and passes blue and green, which together make cyan light.

These are the basic principles of filter formulas. In practice we do not always deal with pure primary and complementary colors, and so a wide variety of filters have been designed, each for a specific and limited job. There are three main areas of filter use: black-and-white, color, and all-purpose. But before going further we must first consider filter factors.

FILTER FACTORS

All filters absorb a certain amount of light and therefore will decrease the amount of light reaching the film. With certain filters (such as ultraviolet) the loss is so minimal that it can be disregarded. However, the majority of filters require an exposure compensation, depending on their rate of absorption. This compensation is expressed as a filter factor. The filter factor represents the *number of times we need to double the exposure.*

Factor	Compensation	Factor	Compensation
2	1 stop	6	2½ stops
3	1½ stops	7	2¾ stops
4	2 stops	8	3 stops
5	2¼ stops	9	3⅛ stops

For example, if the exposure for a picture is f/11 with no filter and we then decide to use a filter with a factor of 2, the exposure will have to be increased one stop to f/8.

When using more than one filter we *multiply* their factors, not add them. An alternate method is adding the required f-stop compensations for the filters. For example, suppose we were combining two filters with factors of 2 and 3 respectively. If we multiply factors, 2 x 3 = 6, and a factor of 6 requires 2½ stops compensation. If we add compensations, factor 2 requires 1 stop compensation, factor 3 requires 1½ stops compensation, and 1 stop + 1½ stops = 2½ stops compensation, the same result as by adding factors.

Exposure compensation tables are provided in the filter manufacturer's literature, and in the *American Cinematographer Manual*.

USING FILTERS FOR BLACK-AND-WHITE FILM

Black-and-white film reproduces color in shades of gray. The human eye is not equally sensitive to all colors, seeing some colors, such as green, as brighter than other colors, such as blue. Similarly, black-and-white films also have their own peculiarities. For example, they see blue as brighter than green and will record blue objects in a lighter shade of gray than green objects, the opposite of the human eye.

In black-and-white photography, filters are used to manipulate the emulsion's response to colors. You may *correct* the emulsion's response to match that of the human eye, or augment *contrast* between two colors that would otherwise appear as the same shade of gray.

Because black-and-white emulsions are "oversensitive" to blue light, the most common problem is the overbright sky. In such cases the sky appears as dead white. To correct this, we use a yellow filter, which absorbs blue light, thus slightly darkening the sky. Because the shadows are illuminated by blue light from the sky, they will also be darkened, thus increasing the overall scene contrast.

The orange filter goes farther in darkening the sky and shadows. If we want to make cloud formations very visible, an orange filter can be used to accentuate the clouds by overdarkening the sky. A red filter will render the sky black and greatly accent clouds and contrast for a night effect. Of course these effects are based on the elimination of blue light. If the sky is overcast (that is, white and not blue), such filters will not successfully darken the sky. (It should be noted that at altitudes above 3,000 feet the blue sky is much darker and often no filter is necessary to correct it. Even a light-yellow filter may make it quite dark.)

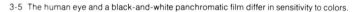

3-5 The human eye and a black-and-white panchromatic film differ in sensitivity to colors.

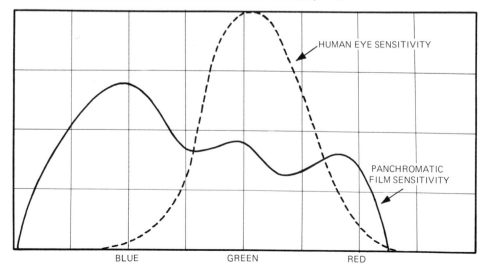

HUMAN EYE SENSITIVITY

PANCHROMATIC FILM SENSITIVITY

BLUE   GREEN   RED

Another very important use of the orange filter is for penetrating haze. Normally, haze is created by tiny water and dust particles suspended in the atmosphere. It scatters the shorter wavelengths of light, most notably blue. Because it absorbs blue, the orange filter can be used to diminish the effect of haze. However, haze cutting must be done with moderation, as haze gives a picture three-dimensional aerial perspective. If *all* haze were eliminated (such as with a red filter), the picture would appear flat.

When the subject is farther away from the camera, there is more atmosphere (hence potential haze) between the camera and the subject. For this reason, lenses longer than 250mm will frequently require an orange filter for outdoor use. This is because the subject is usually a considerable distance away when such a lens is used.

To *increase* haze, as when one wants to exaggerate atmospheric depth, a pale-blue filter will help.

For portraits, filters are often used to improve or modify skin tones. In close-ups the orange filter will darken blue eyes and eliminate all or most of the freckles and skin blemishes. A #15G filter is commonly used for this purpose. A green filter, on the other hand, would darken the skin for a suntan effect while emphasizing freckles and blemishes.

Filters can be used to improve the rendition of foliage. In nature our eyes can distinguish many shades of green. Without filters, black-and-white film emulsions tend to darken greens and eliminate tonal gradations. A green or a green-yellow filter will help to differentiate the green tones, but will not lighten foliage as much as we might expect. Actually foliage reflects much red light and infrared radiation, and therefore an orange or red filter will brighten greens. If infrared film is used with an infrared filter the foliage will appear as white. (See Chapter 9 for more on infrared cinematography.)

FILTERS FOR COLOR USE

In black-and-white photography, colored filters can be used to augment contrast or in some other way alter the way in which the emulsion translates colors into shades of gray. However, when filming in color the film will record the color of the filter. Therefore in color work the principal task of filters is to keep the colors faithful.

As we mentioned before, white light contains all the colors of the spectrum. But the *exact* color of the light depends on the *temperature* of its source. For example, if we heat up a piece of metal it will glow red. If we heat it up even more it will

glow white. The sun is burning "white-hot" and therefore glows white. The tungsten filament in a light bulb, however, is burning at a lower temperature and therefore only emits a reddish-yellow light.

Our eye adapts so easily between these color temperatures that we see them both as white unless they are placed side by side. If such a comparison were made, the outdoor light would appear to contain just a bit more blue light and the artificial light would show more reddish. Color film will not adapt so easily between these different sources. Therefore, an emulsion must be designed for a specific color temperature.

To define the exact color temperature of a given light source, scientists compare it to a "black body." This laboratory instrument is dead black when cold. As it is heated, it starts glowing, changing color as the temperature rises. The temperature is measured in degrees Kelvin. Each color radiated by the black body can be described by its color temperature in degrees Kelvin. We think of red as a warm color and blue as a cold color, but the Kelvin degree ratings show them as just the opposite. Some color-temperature ratings of common light sources are:

Source	Color temperature
Candleflame	1500° K
60-watt household bulb	2800° K
Film-studio lights	3200° K
Photoflood lights	3400° K
Sunset in Los Angeles	3000° to 4500° K
Noon sunlight	5400° K
Blue sky light	approximately 10,000° K
Clear blue northern sky	up to 30,000° K

Color emulsions are balanced for one of three color temperatures: 3200° K, 3400° K, or "daylight." By this we mean that 3200° K light will appear white on color film balanced for 3200° K. Normal daylight will appear white on film balanced for daylight.

If the light source and the emulsion balance do not match, the color reproduction will be biased. For example, if a "tungsten" emulsion (3200° K) is shot outdoors in noon daylight (6000° K), the entire scene will appear bluish. The opposite is also true. A daylight-balanced film shot indoors under tungsten illumination without the proper correction filter will yield an orange picture.

In such situations we must use a *color-conversion filter* to

KODAK Light Balancing Filters

Filter Color	Filter Number	Exposure Increase in Stops*	To obtain 3200 K from:	To obtain 3400 K from:
Bluish	82C + 82C	1⅓	2490 K	2610 K
	82C + 82B	1⅓	2570 K	2700 K
	82C + 82A	1	2650 K	2780 K
	82C + 82	1	2720 K	2870 K
	82C	⅔	2800 K	2950 K
	82B	⅔	2900 K	3060 K
	82A	⅓	3000 K	3180 K
	82	⅓	3100 K	3290 K
No Filter Necessary			3200 K	3400 K
Yellowish	81	⅓	3300 K	3510 K
	81A	⅓	3400 K	3630 K
	81B	⅓	3500 K	3740 K
	81C	⅓	3600 K	3850 K
	81D	⅔	3700 K	3970 K
	81EF	⅔	3850 K	4140 K

*These values are approximate. For critical work, they should be checked by practical test, especially if more than one filter is used.

3-6 Kodak light-balancing filters. (Courtesy of Eastman Kodak)

correct the color balance of the light entering the lens. The most common conversion by far occurs when indoor (3200° K) film is being shot outdoors. This requires an orange Wratten #85 filter, which "warms up" the daylight, lowering the color temperature of the incoming light to 3200° K in order to agree with the film.

Although rarely done, the opposite conversion — daylight emulsion used under 3200° K lights — can be accomplished by using a Wratten #80A blue filter.

Kodachrome II-A is one of the only 16mm Kodak emulsions rated for 3400° K that is the color temperature of the photoflood lights used by amateur film makers. Kodachrome II-A is adapted to 3200° K light by using a #82A filter. Another related conversion is the use of photoflood lights (3400° K) with 3200° K film. In this case one uses a Wratten #81A yellowish filter.

Color-conversion filters are for broad modifications of color. A second category includes *light-balancing filters*, which are used for minor variations in color temperature. For

example, daylight emulsions are balanced for noon daylight. However, the color temperature of daylight changes from reddish at sunrise to bluish at noon and back to reddish at sunset. From about two hours after sunrise until about two hours before sunset these changes are minor and can easily be corrected in the lab. But in the early morning and late afternoon the color is changing much more rapidly. During these hours of quickly changing color temperature, if we are filming a scene that must later be edited together, we should use light-balancing filters to keep the color temperatures fairly close together so that the color will not drastically change between shots. Fine color corrections can be done later in the lab.

Often it is not desirable to "correct" the color temperature. For example, if we are filming a reddish sunset, it is better to leave it uncorrected than to change it into white daylight using a light-balancing filter.

The key question to ask is whether the nonwhite light is "motivated." If two actors are standing near an open fire it is

Kodak COLOR COMPENSATING FILTERS

Peak Density and Exposure Increase in Stops

CYAN (Absorbs red)		MAGENTA (Absorbs green)		YELLOW (Absorbs blue)	
CC025C	—	CC025M	—	CC025Y	—
CC05C	+ 1/3	CC05M	+ 1/3	CC05Y	—
CC10C	+ 1/3	CC10M	+ 1/3	CC10Y	+ 1/3
CC20C	+ 1/3	CC20M	0 1/3	CC20Y	+ 1/3
CC30C	+ 2/3	CC30M	+ 2/3	CC30Y	+ 1/3
CC40C	+ 2/3	CC40M	+ 2/3	CC40Y	+ 1/3
CC50C	+ 1	CC50M	+ 2/3	CC50Y	+ 2/3

Red (Absorbs blue and green)		Green (Absorbs blue and red)		Blue (Absorbs red and green)	
CC025R	—	—	—	—	—
CC05R	+ 1/3	CC05G	+ 1/3	CC05B	+ 1/3
CC10R	+ 1/3	CC10G	+ 1/3	CC10B	+ 1/3
CC20R	+ 1/3	CC20G	+ 1/3	CC20B	+ 2/3
CC30R	+ 2/3	CC30G	+ 2/3	CC30B	+ 2/3
CC40R	+ 2/3	CC40G	+ 2/3	CC40B	+ 1
CC50R	+ 1	CC50G	+ 1	CC50B	+ 1 1/3

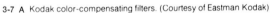
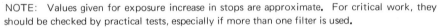
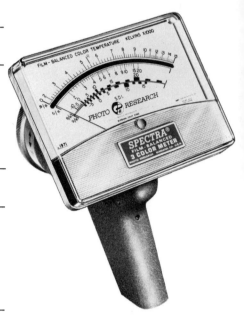

NOTE: Values given for exposure increase in stops are approximate. For critical work, they should be checked by practical tests, especially if more than one filter is used.

3-7 A Kodak color-compensating filters. (Courtesy of Eastman Kodak)

3-7B Spectra Film Balanced 3-Color meter. (Courtesy of Photo Research)

entirely reasonable that their faces be illuminated by reddish light. In fact, at times we may use color filters to distort the color, making it appear more logical. For example, if an actor is outside at night, supposedly illuminated only by moonlight, a light-blue filter might be required for psychological realism. We will discuss this further in the next two chapters.

To determine the proper light-balancing filter for converting a given light to the correct color temperature we use a color-temperature meter. The color-temperature meter will determine the exact color temperature of the light falling on the subject. Until recently color temperature meters have been made with two selenium (light-sensitive) cells, one covered with a red filter and the other with a blue filter. If the measured light contains more red than blue, the cell with the red filter will generate a stronger current than the cell covered by the blue. The red will have a stronger effect on the indicator needle when these two currents are averaged, so the needle will indicate the color balance of the light source. Some color-temperature meters also indicate the filter required to achieve the proper color balance.

A relatively inexpensive yet quite accurate color-temperature meter is the Gossen Sixticolor.

Recently, the Spectra 3-Color Meter introduced an entirely new design, using red, blue *and* green filters which precisely match the spectral sensitivity of the color film exposed through typical camera lenses.

Unlike reflectant meters, there is no danger in pointing a color-temperature meter directly into the sun. In fact, the meter *should* be pointed directly into the light source being measured.

It should be emphasized that this meter has nothing to do with calculating exposure. It measures the *color* of the light.

For many film makers the color-temperature meter is more of a luxury item than an indispensable tool. In most situations the minor light balancing can be done by the lab. Usually the only time a film maker uses a color-temperature meter is when employing light-balancing filters to approximate the correct color balance while filming under a changing light source or when filming under some irregular sources (household bulbs) that need to be partially corrected.

A third category of filters are the *color-compensating*, or CC, filters. They are used extensively in the lab for the minor color corrections mentioned earlier. They come in six basic colors, three primary and three complementary. They are available in various densities. Occasionally they may be used while shooting — for example, if the color rendition is critical. When film from two emulsion batches must be intercut, they should be tested to determine the difference between their renditions. If the two are close, there is no problem, but if the difference is substantial, color-compensating filters may be used to bring them closer together.

STARTING FILTERS AND EXPOSURE INCREASES FOR
TEST SERIES WITH FLUORESCENT ILLUMINATION

EASTMAN COLOR FILMS	Type of Fluorescent Lamp[†]					
	Daylight	White	Warm White	Warm White Deluxe	Cool White	Cool White Deluxe
FILM BALANCED FOR DAYLIGHT	40M + 30Y + 1 stop	20C + 30M + 1 stop	40C + 40M + 1 ⅓ stop	60C + 30M + 1 ⅔ stop	30M + ⅔ stop	30C + 20M + 1 stop
FILM BALANCED FOR 3200°K TUNGSTEN	85B‡ + 30M + 10Y + 1 stop	40M + 40Y + 1 stop	30M + 20Y + 1 stop	10Y + ⅓ stop	50M + 60Y + 1 ⅓ stop	10M + 30Y + ⅔ stop

†When it is difficult or impossible to gain access to fluorescent lamps in order to identify the type, ask the maintenance man.

‡KODAK WRATTEN Filter No. 85B.

3-8 Starting filters and exposure increases for test series with fluorescent illumination. (Data courtesy of Eastman Kodak)

FLUORESCENT LIGHT

Fluorescent light is an odd light source that rates a discussion of its own. Its peculiar characteristics make it somewhat of a headache when filming in color.

As we mentioned at the beginning of this chapter, white light contains all the colors of the rainbow. Tungsten light also contains all the colors, but in a different proportion — more red and less blue. Fluorescent light, on the other hand, does *not* contain the entire spectrum. The electrified gas inside a fluorescent tube emits only a few distinct wavelengths, not all the wavelengths of the visible spectrum. There are many different types of fluorescent lights, all of which have this "broken-spectrum" characteristic. They fall basically into two categories: the "daylight" type and the "warm white" variety.

Because of the broken-spectrum characteristic, fluorescent light is unsuitable for faithful color reproduction. Left unfiltered, it will reproduce on tungsten emulsion as greenish-blue when the tube is of the daylight type and brownish when the tube is of the warm-white type. Nevertheless, there are frequent situations in which we are forced to use it. Unfortunately, the older designs of color-temperature meters are not very effective when dealing with a discontinued spectrum. This difficulty is overcome by the Spectra 3-Color Meter which indicates the exact filter combination to be used with any irregular light source, including the various types of fluorescent light. Without such a meter the only way to find a suitable combination of color-compensation filters is by trial-and-error tests shot at the location.

Some manufacturers, like Tiffen and Optivision Company, make filters that approximately correct the basic types of fluorescent lamps, like daylight or warm-white. There are also Kodak recommendations as to the starting combinations when shooting tests under fluorescent sources.

Although it is the general practice to use tungsten-balanced emulsions with fluorescent light, it is worthwhile to experiment with daylight emulsions when shooting under daylight-fluorescent sources. For example, I understand that some cameramen at the Mission Control Center in Houston use EF Daylight (ASA 160) in the main control room, where there is very low-level fluorescent illumination and a great number of bluish monitors. It is pushed one stop in the processing and then a timed, color-corrected print is made on Eastman 7388 print stock. This yields a final result with the *equivalent* of almost 1000 ASA, and the color seems acceptable for broadcast use. (This was reported in Charles Loring, "Meanwhile, Back at Mission Control," *American Cinematographer*, October 1969.)

When shooting in wide areas, such as airport terminals, factories, or offices, filters are about the only thing we can use

Kodak Wratten Neutral Density Filters No. 96

Neutral Density	Percent Transmission	Filter Factor	Increase in Exposure (Stops)
0.1	80	1¼	⅓
0.2	63	1½	⅔
0.3	50	2	1
0.4	40	2½	1⅓
0:5	32	3	1⅔
0.6	25	4	2
0.7	20	5	2⅓
0.8	16	6	2⅔
0.9	13	8	3
1.0	10	10	3⅓
2.0	1	100	6⅔
3.0	0.1	1,000	10
4.0	0.01	10,000	13⅓

3-9 Kodak Wratten neutral density filters #96. (Courtesy of Eastman Kodak)

to improve the color in long shots. But when filming closeups we can bring in tungsten light and get the skin tones correct even if the colors in the background are still not right. Actually, audiences today will accept many such technical inaccuracies because, with the rise in amateur photography, they have become used to this type of misrepresentation and it does not distract them as much as it would have, say, thirty years ago.

MIXED DAYLIGHT AND TUNGSTEN SOURCES

A similar problem arises when daylight is visible in an artificially lit scene. Most often this is daylight seen through a window. The conflicting color temperatures can be ignored, but the result will be that the indoor colors look proper with the outside appearing blue. There are two other solutions. The most popular is a #85 window gel, available in large rolls that can be stretched across the window. This will convert the daylight to match the 3200° K balance of the indoor emulsion and lights. Alternatively we could convert the emulsion to daylight by using a #85 filter and convert the tungsten lights to daylight color temperature by using "dichroic filters" or blue gels. Dichroic filters are a special type of glass designed to reflect excessive red and pass the blue end of the spectrum,

and they are often used for converting tungsten light to daylight color temperature.

ALL-PURPOSE FILTERS

Some filters are suitable for use with either black-and-white or color films. These include ultraviolet, neutral density, diffusion, and polarizing filters.

Ultraviolet filters are much like the other filters we have been discussing, in that they eliminate a certain group of wavelengths — those in the ultraviolet area. Only a small part of the ultraviolet radiation coming from the sun actually reaches the earth's surface. Most of it is absorbed by ozone layers, haze, and air pollution. UV radiation is stronger in high mountains where the atmosphere is thinner and more clear. It also seems higher in the summer months.

Light meters do not read ultraviolet rays, yet the film is sensitive to them. If not controlled, UV radiation will overexpose your picture (particularly the sky). Therefore, in outdoor photography, especially in the mountains, a UV filter should be employed. It does not affect the visible spectrum and requires no exposure compensation. Many photographers leave a UV filter on the lens all the time. This also protects the lens from dirt and scratches. When green, yellow, orange, or red filters are used, the UV filter is unnecessary because all these filters absorb UV radiation. When used for color photography, UV filters should be of the colorless variety.

Neutral density filters are designed to cut down overall brightness and reduce all colors equally. They are often used when the light intensity is too high for the given emulsion (for example, when shooting on a fast emulsion outdoors in bright sunlight). Neutral density filters are also used to avoid having to stop the lens down too far. There are two reasons for doing this. Lens optics are better at f/11 than at f/16 or f/22. Furthermore, stopping down increases the depth of field, which may not be desirable, if, for example, we want to separate the subject from the background.

Neutral density filters are calibrated by their density. Many other filters are manufactured in combination with a neutral density filter. For example, an 85N3 is a single filter combining a #85 color-conversion filter with a .30 neutral density filter.

Like all filters, neutral densities are available as "graduated" filters that will darken the upper part of the frame (such as the sky) but gradually become transparent toward the bottom of the frame. No exposure compensation is usually used with this type of neutral density filter. The graduated neutral density is most often used to darken the sky when using color film. Unfortunately, panning and other camera movements may betray the presence of this filter, so the camera should usually remain stationary when it is being used.

So far all the filters discussed absorb colors. *Diffusion filters,* on the other hand, scatter light and thus reduce resolution. Such devices were quite often used in Hollywood films to soften the faces of aging actresses. 16mm is not as sharp as the 35mm format and therefore diffusion in 16mm is not necessary for quite the same reasons. It is rather used for strong desaturation of color and for special effects.

Professional diffusion filters are made of two pieces of glass laminated together. Finely ground patterns on one of the inside surfaces delicately diffract the light, diffusing the picture without causing halos or star effects.

The effectiveness of such a filter depends on the contrast, the exposure, and the subject's size in the frame. For example, if the details are portrayed in high contrast they will be more prominent and harder to diffuse. The amount of diffusion will also be reduced by underexposure. Conversely, diffusion is increased by either overexposure or lower contrast (either in the lighting or by the type of emulsion). Furthermore, in a closeup, the detail to be diffused is larger and therefore

more visible, requiring more diffusion than in a long shot. To evaluate the degree of the effect, look at the scene through the diffusion filter held together with a contrast-viewing glass. The viewing glass (to be discussed in the next chapter) is designed to show the scene contrast exactly as it will appear on film.

There are many types of diffusion filters. Harrison & Harrison diffusion filters require no compensation factor. The range runs from 1 to 5, and each step doubles the previous one in diffusion. Mitchell Camera Corporation diffusion filters are rated A, B, C, D, and E, from light to heavy effect. "Star filters" are exaggerated diffusion filters with grid grooves spaced 1 to 3 millimeters apart. They create sparkling star effects on each "hot spot" or bright glitter of light in the scene. Star filters should be used only on static shots, as panning will often cause a sort of stroboscopic effect that may not be desirable.

In addition to such specially designed filters, many materials have been used for diffusing "scrims," such as black net, wire mesh, muslin, nylon stockings, etc. If the lens is considerably stopped down, scrim materials will tend to cause small flares on hot spots. Another homemade diffusion filter is made by smearing vaseline or glycerin onto a piece of optical glass. It should be remembered that scrims and other homemade diffusion devices may require exposure compensation, which can be calculated by holding such a device in front of a light meter.

Like diffusion filters, Harrison *fog-effect filters* scatter light. However, they are designed for the special task of creating fog by scattering light from the bright picture areas into the shadows, thus creating a grayish appearance and low contrast. No exposure compensation is required, because the light is merely scattered, brightening the shadows. Fog filters are available in a range of effects. Numbers 2, 4, 6, and 8 are the most widely used. (Remember these numbers are *not* factors.)

Different in structure are Harrison *double-fog filters.* They create the effect of fog without reducing definition. At their lowest density range (i.e., numbers ⅛, ¼, ½, or 1) the fog will be minimal. This provides an excellent way of cutting down the inherent contrast and saturation in reversal emulsions such as Ektachrome Commercial.

However, there are filters especially designed for this reduction of contrast and color saturation. These are the Harrison *low-contrast screens,* which do not diffuse the image or flare the highlights. They are available in a range of 1 to 5.

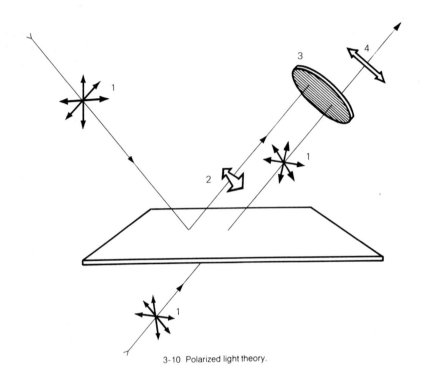

3-10 Polarized light theory.

They have the effect of expanding the midtones so that there are many distinct shades of gray. The loss of blacks and lightening of other shades sometimes creates a slightly overexposed appearance. A minor exposure reduction, ½ to 1½ stops, is *sometimes* advisable in order to keep the brightness levels within the optimal exposure range. This will prevent a "flare" effect.

Unlike fog and diffusion filters, which scatter light rays, the *polarizing filter* "straightens" the light into parallel planes in which the light vibrates in the same direction.

1. Light vibrates in all directions along its axis (path). See figure 3-10.
2. When light reflects from surfaces like glass or water it becomes polarized (i.e., vibrates in only one direction).
3. A polarizing filter correctly positioned can stop polarized light.
4. This filter will *pass* previously unpolarized light, *polarizing it in the process.*
5. This light will be the image that reaches the film.

A polarizing filter can be used to minimize the reflections in glass (such as in shop windows) and is most effective when the angle between the optical axis and the glass surface is about 34°. If the surface is being photographed "straight on" (about 90°) the filter will have little or no effect. This filter must be used in moderation, however. Complete elimination of all glare and reflections dulls the picture, giving it a flat look. If overdone, it could even make the surface disappear. For example, if you are photographing a beautiful clear pond and use a polarizing filter to make the bottom more visible, the pond might appear not to have any water in it.

Unlike glass or water, metal surfaces do not polarize light, and so to eliminate glare from metal surfaces, polarizing filters must be put on both the camera lens and on the light sources.

When setting a polarizing filter it is rotated to obtain the desired degree of effect. It will have either a dot or a handle that when pointed toward the source of light (such as the sun) gives maximum glare elimination. This effect is most pronounced when the sun is at 90° to the lens-subject axis.

In color photography, polarizing filters (of the colorless

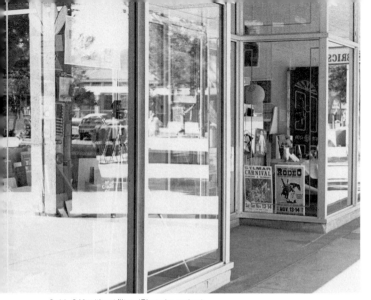

3-11 34° *without* filter. (Photo by author)

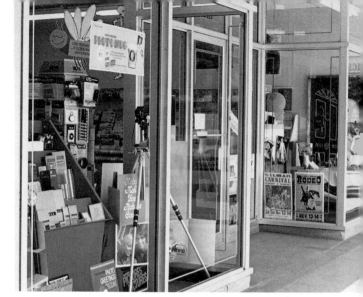

3-12 34° *with* filter. (Photo by author)

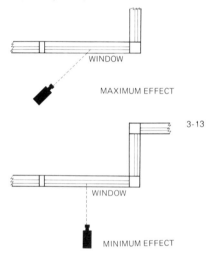

WINDOW

MAXIMUM EFFECT

3-13

WINDOW

MINIMUM EFFECT

3-14 90° *without* filter. (Photo by author)

3-15 90° *with* filter. (Photo by author)

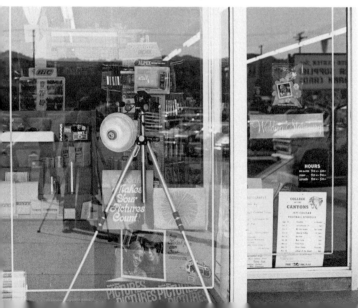

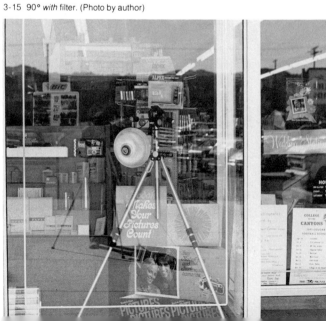

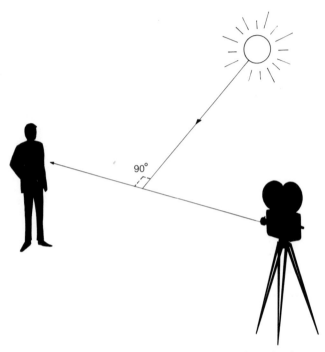

3-16 A polarizing filter most effectively eliminates glare when the sun (or other light source) is 90° to the lens-subject axis.

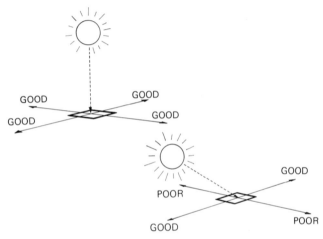

3-17 A polarizing filter most successfully darkens a blue sky when the lens-subject axis is 90° to the sun.

variety) have several important functions. Blue sky can be effectively darkened if the sun is 90° from the optical axis. If we are shooting either toward the sun or 180° away from it ("down sun"), the effect is minimal. The white clouds against a blue sky will be accentuated when the sky is darkened. However, if the sky is white, as it often is down near the horizon or on overcast days, the polarizer will have little or no darkening effect.

In color photography a polarizing filter is also used for haze penetration.

Because a polarizer will eliminate glare from the surface of objects that normally would have a certain amount of it, such as leaves, flowers, certain textiles, etc., the color saturation will often increase.

A *fader device* for amateur cameras can be made from two polarizing filters. The two filters are placed on the lens and counter-rotated for a gradual elimination of light. This is not a

professional practice, and serious film makers have such effects done in the lab.

The filter factors for polarizing filters are not constant. The basic factor is about 3 (i.e., 1½ stops), regardless of the filter's position. An additional factor of up to 2 (i.e., one more stop) may be needed, depending on the rotation and light angle. The total factor can be measured by placing the filter in front of the light meter at the same angle of rotation as it will be on the lens. When taken from the camera position, such a reading is fairly accurate. A "spot meter" (to be discussed in the next chapter) is ideal for this purpose, as it allows you to take the reading while looking through the meter to see the degree of glare reduction.

Beginners frequently make the mistake of overcompensating for a polarizing filter. Therefore one should use caution to avoid overexposing the picture, losing color saturation and washing out detail.

PHYSICAL CHARACTERISTICS OF FILTERS AND GELS

There are five common ways of constructing a filter:

1. Gels are optically the best because they are thin. Unfortunately they are soft and easily scratched. Once damaged, they cannot be repaired and must be replaced. Fortunately, gels are the least expensive type of filter. To prevent damage, they should be handled by their edges. Fingerprints on the surface cannot be removed. A soft camel's-hair brush or an air syringe might be used to remove dust, but not much else can be done. Gels are also sensitive to moisture or prolonged direct sunlight. As a result they should be stored flat in a dry place. Gels can be used not only on the lens, but on lights as well (a cheaper kind). In this case, scratches are not as critical as when the gel is used on the camera. A scratched gel used on the front of the lens may easily cause reduced definition. When a damaged filter is used *behind* the lens, it might even be close enough for the scratches to show on the film. Actually, any filter that is not optically perfect will reduce definition. If more than one filter is used at a time, the definition loss is even greater. In the case of gels, when two are used together, sandwiched with surfaces touching, this will often cause "Newton's rings," irregular refraction patterns. This is why manufacturers bother to make filters that combine functions, such as the #85N3 (combining the effects of a #85 filter with a .30 neutral density), so that both objectives might be achieved with a minimum loss of definition. Gel filters are available in many sizes, ranging from large sheets ("window gels") for covering windows to sizes commonly used on lenses: 2-inch, 3-inch, 4-inch, or 5-inch squares.

2. Kodak Ektalux filters are made of semirigid, thermosetting resin, and feature a quality equal to optical glass. They are lightweight and resistant to moisture, heat, and scratching. Unlike gels they can be cleaned with lens cleaner or breath moisture and used indefinitely when given proper care.

3. Another type of glass filter consists of a colored gel cemented between two sheets of optical glass. Although usually not quite as optically perfect as gels alone, this type is more durable and therefore easier to handle. They can be cleaned but should be given the same careful treatment as a good lens. They should be stored in a case and kept dry, because the gel inside is sensitive to moisture. Should it become moist it will swell and the filter will be ruined.

4. An excellent type of glass filter is made by laminating two pieces of optical glass together, with organic dyes mixed in the cement.

5. The cheapest and least satisfactory filters are made by adding the dye directly to the glass during the manufacturing. In this process it is difficult to control the exact color rendition given by these filters.

When shooting footage that is to be edited together, it is a good idea to stick to one brand and design of filters. Different brands may have slightly different colors.

As lenses vary in size, so do the filters. One must be sure to get the proper size and type of filter so that it will fit onto the equipment being used.

Above all, the quality of the filter is most important. It is ridiculous to spend several thousand dollars on an excellent lens and camera and then save money by getting a poor filter or by using a gel that is slightly damaged and should be replaced.

CHAPTER 4
LIGHTING

Lighting is the most important element in cinematography. It is the task to which a cinematographer gives his primary attention. He studies the characteristics of his film stock so that he may predict what effect it will have in translating his scene onto the screen. He then manipulates the lights accordingly. Filters are an aid in modifying that translation. But it is lighting that shapes the reality in front of the lens, giving it depth or flatness, excitement or boredom, reality or artificiality. Cinematography attempts to create and sustain a mood, captured on the screen. In this respect lighting is at the heart of cinematography.

CHARACTERISTICS OF LIGHT

As discussed earlier, a certain overall *quantity* of light is necessary to register the picture on film. However, the way in which the scene will be portrayed on screen depends on the *quality* and *distribution* of the light. There are three distinct aspects to be considered: whether the source is "hard" or "soft," the angle of the "throw" (the path the light follows), and the color of the light.

A source can be described as hard or soft, depending on the type of shadows it creates. Light that travels directly from the filament of the bulb to the subject with only a lens in between will usually cause sharply defined deep shadows. If the light is bounced off some diffusing reflecting surface, or diffused by some translucent substance suspended between the light and the subject, the shadows will be weaker and less sharp. The diffusing surface acts as a multitude of small sources, all washing out one another's shadows.

The hardness or softness of light depends on the size and distance of the *effective* source. For example, if the effective source is a large surface from which the light is bounced, it creates a softer illumination than would be obtained if the light came directly from the filament of the bulb. The most extreme example of a soft light is a blue or overcast sky. As for distance, the sun — by no means a small source — creates sharp shadows because it is so far away that its rays are almost parallel when they reach the earth. On the moon, where there is no atmosphere to scatter and diffuse the sunlight, this hard quality is most pronounced. The sky is black, shadows are dramatically dark, and contrasts are extreme. On earth the atmosphere scatters the sunlight. Our sky acts as an enormous soft source that fills in the shadows left by the sun. If the sun is completely diffused by the atmosphere, as on an overcast day, the gray sky would be the only source and the soft light would create a shadowless effect.

The second aspect of light quality is the angle of the throw. The direction from which the light comes will suggest the mood of the scene, the time of day, and the type of location. It will also model the objects in the scene, bringing out their shape and texture, or perhaps intentionally not revealing shape and texture.

The third aspect of a light source is its color. Often the creative use of color is not aimed at realism, or the situation justifies a color light source other than the proper color temperature. In such cases, gelatin filters might be used on the light *sources.*

Studying the light around us in every type of location, time, weather, and season is the best way of learning about these light characteristics. The second best way is to watch films with lighting in mind (preferably without sound).

STYLES IN LIGHTING

In the traditions of motion-picture lighting, it is possible to distinguish various stylizations, just as in the work of the great masters of painting. The three most pronounced styles used by cinematographers are high-key (such as in the paintings of Turner, Whistler, and some of Degas), low-key (such as in the paintings of Rembrandt and Caravaggio), and graduated-tonality (such as in the paintings of Ingres).

A *high-key* scene is one that appears generally bright. It is best achieved in cooperation with the art director, as the sets and costumes should be in light tones. The lighting for a high-key effect will often employ much soft, diffused illumination with relatively few shadows. It is important to include at least a few dark areas to indicate that the highlights are not simply overexposed.

If, on the other hand, only a few areas of the frame are well lit and there are many deep shadows, the effect is *low-key.* There is a popular fallacy that to achieve a low-key effect one has merely to underexpose. In fact, it is the *ratio* of dark shadow area to adequately lit areas that creates a low-key effect. Here again the art director can help, this time by providing darker sets and costumes.

Graduated tonality is intended to produce a tonal effect of graduated grays. It is often achieved by soft light evenly illuminating the scene, creating weak shadows, with the tonal

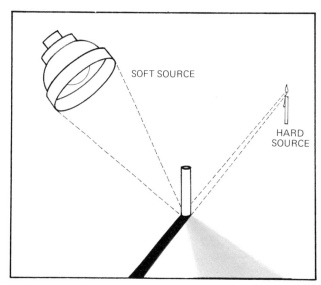

4-1 Hard versus soft light.

4-2 A soft light. Light from the bulb reflects from the large inner back surface, creating soft illumination.

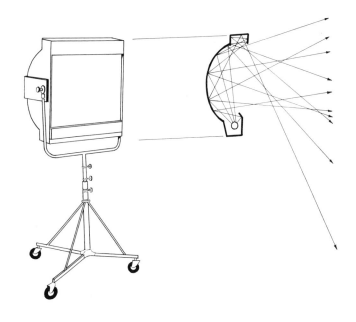

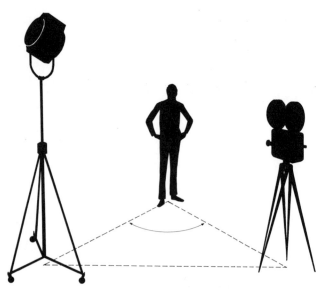

4-3 Key light "outside the actor's look." The actor's sight line runs between the camera and the light.

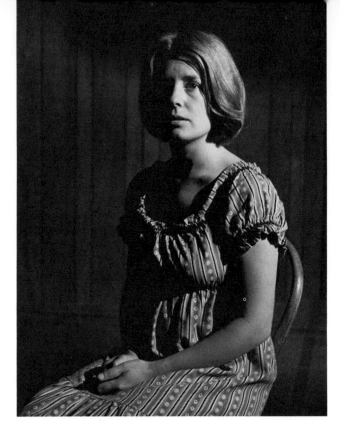

4-4 Key light only.

gradations often painted onto the sets or created in the actor's costumes and makeup. Sometimes artificial shadows are painted on.

These three stylizations by no means cover all the approaches to lighting the film.

Long before shooting, the director and the cinematographer should discuss the style or approach to be taken in the film. This will depend to a great extent on the mood and character of the story, or perhaps of each scene. For example, a drama is most often done in a low key while a comedy is usually more effective in a high key. All sorts of films *could* be done in gradated tonality. There are no set rules about what style should be used with what type of film. It is all up to the director and cinematographer.

LIGHT FUNCTIONS

In creating and maintaining a style, the haphazard approach is bad. We have to know exactly what each lamp is doing for us and why we are putting it in a given spot. To simplify things a terminology was developed, naming the functions of the lights.

The *key light* is the main source of light for a given character while at a certain place in the scene. (If the character moves about he may have several key lights, one for each of his locations.) There are no set rules on the placement of the key light. A traditional starting place is 45° from the camera and 45° off the floor, but the mood or location of the scene usually leads the cinematographer to put it elsewhere. Another rule of thumb suggests that the key should come from "outside the actor's look." That is, if the actor is looking off camera, which is usually the case, the key should come from the other side of his line of sight so that he is looking between the camera and the key light. This means the downstage side of his head will be in shadow, giving his features a pleasant three-dimensionality, but this rule, like the 45° rule, is very frequently ignored. It is very interesting to note that many of the masters of painting most frequently use a "key light" coming from the left side of the canvas. A cinematographer rarely has so much freedom. The final position of the key light will depend on the mood, the actor's features, the set topography, the supposed time of day, etc. The key's position will determine the shadow pattern on the face.

A *fill light* is used to fill in the shadows created by the key light. It should not create additional shadows and therefore usually comes from fairly near the camera. In Hollywood studios, fill light was sometimes introduced by a frame of

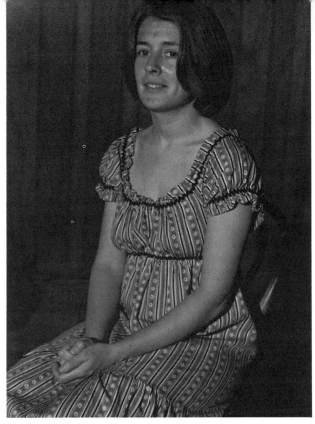

4-5 Fill light only.

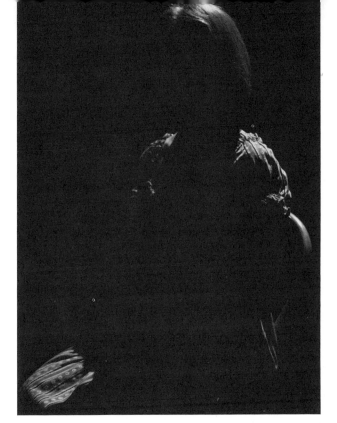

4-6 Back light only.

4-7 Kicker light and back light only.

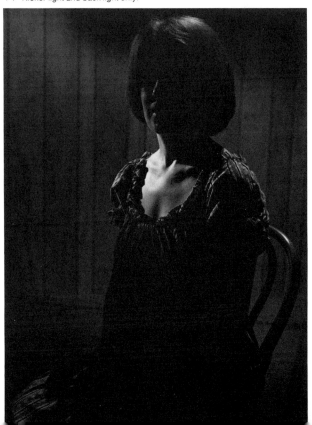

bulbs around the lens. This practically eliminated the possibility of creating shadows visible through the lens. Today, soft-light sources are often used for fill. The shadowless quality of soft light allows for greater freedom in placing the fill, and is especially useful in television studios where all lights are hung from above and the action must be properly lit for several cameras at a time. When trying to achieve dramatic low-key effects the fill light is frequently omitted.

The third principal light is the *back light,* which is designed to separate the actors from the background. This adds three-dimensionality to the picture. This light is often omitted by cameramen who believe in realism and do not want an unmotivated source of light illuminating the picture. The back light is positioned above and behind the actor. It illuminates the top of his shoulders and head.

Similar in function but different in placement is the *kicker light.* It works from a three-quarter-back position on the opposite side of the key light. It is often placed lower to the floor than the back light. The use of back lights and kickers depends entirely on the situation. Sometimes one, both, or neither will be used. They are introduced at the discretion of the director of photography.

The lighting may also require effects lights — for example,

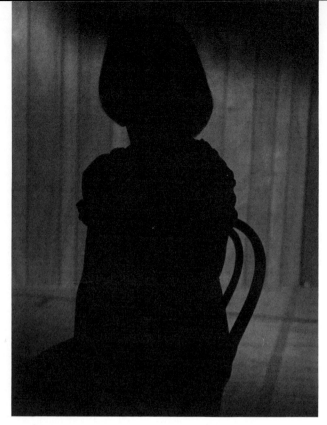

4-8 Set light only.

4-9 Portrait illuminated by key, fill, back, kicker, and set lights. (Photos by author)

4-10 Placement of lights for figures 4-4 through 4-9.

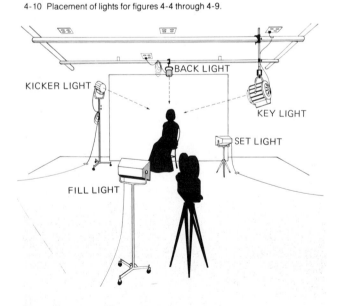

a clothes light to bring up the texture of a costume. Another effect light, the *eye light,* is usually a small hard-light source either positioned near or mounted right onto the camera. It acts as a weak fill light that mainly fills in the actor's eye sockets. Its reflection provides a lively sparkle in the actor's eye. It is recommended when photographing an actor with dull or deeply set eyes. Some cinematographers mount the eye light on the camera, just above the lens, and use it in every shot because they like its effect.

Set lights illuminate the walls and furniture. There may also be *practical lamps* (lamps that are part of the scene), *backdrop lights* illuminating painted or photographed backdrops seen through a window or doorway, and other special light sources such as fireplaces, passing car headlights, etc.

LIGHT MEASUREMENT

In lighting a scene, the relative intensities of the lamps are almost as important as their placement. For example, the key

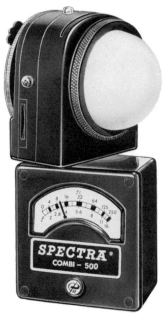

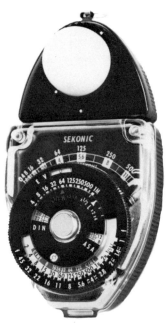

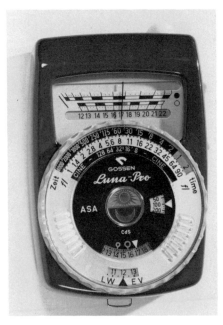

4-11 Spectra Combi-500 incident light meter. Can also be used as a reflected light meter. (Courtesy of Photo Research)

4-12 Sekonic L28C incident light meter. Can also be adapted for use as a reflected light meter. (Courtesy of Kanematsu-Gosho U.S.A., Inc.)

4-13 Gossen Luna-Pro light meter. Mainly a reflectant meter but also functions as an incident meter. Special attachment available for narrow-angle light measurement. (Courtesy of Kling Photo, Woodside, N.Y.)

light should be more intense than the fill light, but by how much?

There are two distinct types of light measurements: incident and reflected. Incident light meters measure the intensity of the illumination coming from the lamp and express the reading in foot-candles. Reflected light meters measure the light reflected from the subject and yield a reading in candles per square foot, or in foot-lamberts.

The more widely used incident meters, like the Spectra or the Sekonic, have a hemispherical "light collector" in front of the light-sensitive cell. This plastic device is designed to represent the general curvature of a human face. When pointed from the subject directly toward the camera it registers the amount of light falling on the face. In addition to the hemispherical collector, these meters could be used with a flat disk, preferred by some cameramen for measuring individual lights. The incident light meter gives a very objective measurement, unaffected by the skin or background color, and therefore it is constant from scene to scene. An incident light reading is extremely convenient when working to a given illumination level, setting the f-stop and then manipulating the

lights to arrive at the proper foot-candle values. We can quickly check those values while walking about the scene with the sphere of the meter pointed toward the camera.

One thing to remember when using an incident light meter is that the reading will not be influenced by the background. Especially when filming outdoors in the shade, an overbright background may spoil the shot, and therefore an incident light reading must be intelligently interpreted. For example, it may be desirable to modify the reading by a half to three-quarters of a stop to allow for an overbright or overdark background.

For reasons such as these, many cinematographers prefer reflected light meters for outdoor work, while depending on incident light meters when in the studio, although they usually carry one of each.

There are two types of reflected light meters. The common type has a rather wide angle of acceptance and therefore measures *and averages* the brightness levels in a wide area. Although satisfactory for determining the average brightness range, this meter must be used with special alertness. Such things as a very light or very dark background, light sources in its view, or any other extremes in scene brightness will

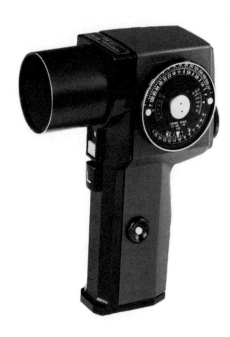

4-14 Honeywell Pentax 1°/21° (spot) exposure meter. (Courtesy of Honeywell, Inc.)

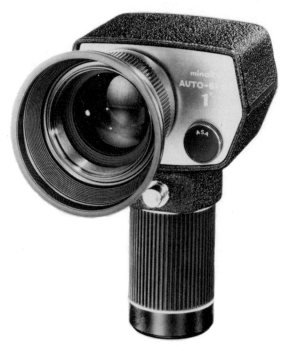

4-15 Minolta Auto-Spot 1° exposure meter. (Courtesy of Minolta Corporation)

influence the reading and possibly lead to exposure errors. For example, a closeup is taken against a setting sun. When measuring the face, some light from the bright sunset could very easily enter the meter and drastically affect the reading. As a result the face would be underexposed. Our picture might show a very dark face silhouetted against a properly exposed sunset. With such perils in mind we must evaluate reflected light readings intelligently. Most automatic exposure systems employ a meter of this type. When using a camera with such a system, one should be constantly aware of its limitations and be ready to recognize problem situations when they come up. Most good automatic exposure systems have a manual override, which should be used when photographing scenes with such extremes.

The second type of reflected light meter is the spot meter. It overcomes the above problems by featuring a very narrow angle of acceptance (such as 1°). It permits scanning the entire scene so that individual brightnesses can be measured and compared. Because of the narrow angle, the measuring

can be done from the camera position by looking through the meter and sighting on the various parts of the scene. This is very handy when shooting with a long lens from a distant position. Looking through the meter, the cameraman can see the exact spot he is measuring. The calibrations on the spot meter are equal to one stop, making it quite easy to measure the brightness ratios between different parts of the scene.

A spot meter should have a lens shade to protect it from unwanted directed light. Also, some spot meters have a certain "time lag" when the meter is first used after being stored, and so the lens cap should be removed a minute or so before taking the first reading.

18% GRAY CARD

It is very important to keep in mind that reflected light meters are calibrated for the so-called "medium-gray" (18% reflectance). A reflected light meter always indicates the exposure required in order to have the measured subject represented

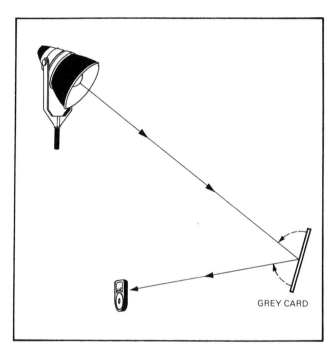

4-16 18% gray card angled halfway between the light and a reflected light meter.

as medium-gray on the film (or its equivalent in terms of color brightness). Therefore a cameraman using a reflected light meter must ask himself if he wants the subject to be represented as medium-gray. Obviously the answer is quite often no.

For example, a Caucasian face has about 35% reflectance. On the other hand, a black face reflects less than 18%. If the reflected light readings are blindly followed, both faces will be represented as similar shades of gray (on black-and-white film). The Caucasian face will appear a bit dark and the black face a bit light. For a more faithful representation, the Caucasian face should be given half a stop to one stop "overexposure" and the black face the same amount of "underexposure." This is actually not over- or underexposing, but intelligently interpreting the readings so that the subjects will be correctly represented.

One way to avoid guesswork is to use an 18% gray card, measuring it instead of the subject. This guarantees that objects that are medium-gray in the scene will be medium-

gray on film. Thus the reading is not biased by the shades (light or dark) of the objects in the scene. When using a reflected light meter with an 18% gray card, the readings will be as objective as those taken with an incident meter. An incident meter, as you remember, reads the light coming from the source. Its spherical light collector approximates a medium-gray readout.

When using a medium-gray card and reflected light meter, the card should be angled halfway between the light angle and the camera to get the most accurate reading.

CONTRAST-VIEWING GLASSES

Viewing glasses are very important and often overlooked lighting aids. When looking through them, the cameraman can see approximately how the contrast ratio will appear on film. It is invaluable in setting the relative values of the key, fill, back, and kicker lights.

There are three types of contrast-viewing glasses: one for panchromatic (black-and-white) film and two for color (tungsten and daylight). Viewing glasses often vary among manufacturers, and one should always try to use the brand to which one is accustomed. The cinematographer should not keep the glass at his eye for long periods, because if the eye is given too much time to adapt to the filter the judgment will be less accurate.

After establishing the key light at a given level, some *experienced* cameramen use the viewing glass and not the light meter, while setting all the other lights. Then the final exposure is checked with a light meter before shooting.

MEASURING CONTROLLABLE LIGHT

Indoors, where all the sources are under control, professional cinematographers use one f-stop for an entire scene. The incident light table for an emulsion gives the number of foot-candles required for a proper exposure at a given f-stop. The cinematographer chooses a combination and uses it throughout a scene. Considerations for choosing a level include the depth of field required, the actor's comfort, and power/light economy. Say a cinematographer chooses f/2.8, which requires 400 foot-candles with Ektachrome Commercial film. He will therefore, in this hypothetical example, use an exposure of f/2.8 for the entire scene and light with a key-plus-fill light level of 400 foot-candles in each shot.

Because of the popularity of this method, the incident light meter has become the basic tool for studio lighting. The immediate readout in foot-candles makes the incident meter the best instrument to use when setting up the lights. Sometimes, in addition, a reflected light meter (especially a spot meter) is helpful in evaluating the brightness range, but of the two, the incident meter is the most important when shooting under controllable light situations such as are found when shooting indoors.

The mood of the lighting is principally established by the ratios of intensity between particular lights. Most significant is the ratio of key to fill light. Measuring the ratio of key to fill is quite often misunderstood and even misrepresented in professional literature. The fill light usually is placed so that it illuminates not only the darker side of the face, but the key-light side as well. Therefore, if the key light alone is 250 foot-candles, and the fill light is 125 foot-candles, the lighting ratio is not 2:1 but 3:1. This is because both the key light and fill light illuminate the key-light side. Their sum is 375 foot-candles. The fill light alone fills in the shadows with its 125 foot-candles, making the ratio 375 to 125, or 3:1. Therefore, when considering the lighting ratio we are usually talking about key-*plus*-fill light versus the fill light alone.

The combined reading of key plus fill is the one used in calculating the exposure. We always expose for the bright side of the face. When taking a light reading of key plus fill, one must be sure to shade the light meter from the back light and kicker, which might otherwise influence the reading.

The contrast viewing glass is very helpful for visually evaluating lighting ratios.

It should be noted in passing that actors in the background may have to be lit to a higher ratio than those in the foreground in order to appear the same. For instance, if the foreground is 2:1, the background might be 3:1 or 4:1. Without this added contrast, the background may appear dull and lack three-dimensionality. This principle applies to outdoor shooting as well. Distant sunlit actors may not require any fill light, while actors in the foreground will generally need a fill light in order to soften the harsh shadows created by the sun.

To determine what lighting ratios look best for the emulsion to be used, a test is advisable. The lighting ratio test is of great importance when familiarizing yourself with the film stock to be used in the production. The aim of this test is to discover how much darker one side of the face can be before the details start disappearing into the shadows. This depends on the latitude and contrast characteristics of the specific emulsion. Black-and-white films will generally withstand higher ratios than color. Because negative films have lower contrast and more latitude, they will often stand higher ratios than reversal stocks.

Manufacturers recommend 3:1 as the maximum acceptable ratio for color film, although tests prove that even an 8:1 ratio will show *some* detail in shadows, but the color will be deteriorated in these underexposed areas. Light-ratio tests should include six setups: 2:1, 4:1, 8:1, 16:1, 32:1, and 64:1. (Notice that because the fill light drops by *half* between each of these steps, we might relate these ratios to f-stops, describing 2:1 as "fill one stop less than key and fill combined," 4:1 as "fill *two* stops less than key and fill combined," 8:1 as "fill *three* stops less than key and fill combined," etc.)

To make the difference between the key and fill sides of the face clear, the key light for these tests should be 90° to one side. The fill light should be near the camera. Also, when shooting tests, make sure the model receives only the light intended and there are no reflections from walls, light from windows, etc.

Generally speaking, color requires more fill light than black-and-white because underexposure causes unfaithful colors. Also, because reversal emulsions are more contrasty by nature, reversal films require generally more fill light than negative.

The levels for the back light and kicker are more subjective. They will depend entirely on the subject and the situation. In the first place, the incident meter is designed to be pointed toward the camera from the subject, which is *away* from these lights. Nevertheless, many technicians will point an incident meter toward the back light and kicker, knowing from experience how to evaluate the reading. The color and texture of the actor's hair and costume are the main factors influencing the amount of light reflected toward the camera. For example, a brunette will require more back light than a blonde in order to be separated from the background. The experienced cinematographer will take this into account and set his lights accordingly. A brunette in a dark costume may require a back light and kicker brighter than the key light, while a blonde could do with a back light one-third the intensity of the key. In color cinematography, one could use color gels over the lights to give a blonde an amber back light or a brunette a blue back light to further increase the depth. In addition, the background, the mood of the scene, etc. may help to determine the proper levels for the back light and kicker. For example, if the actor is standing in front of a properly lit wall,

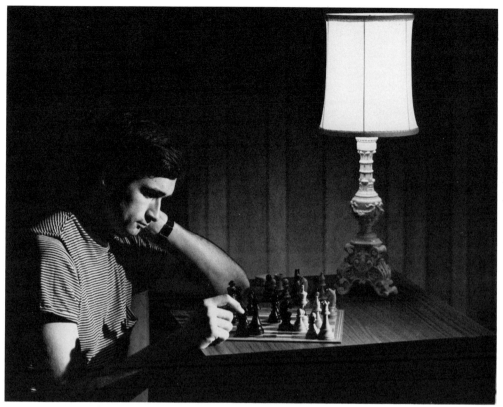

4-17 Practical lamp 2 1/2 stops brighter than the face. (Photo by author)

he may be sufficiently separated from the background so that a back light is not necessary. In most cases, visual judgment (perhaps aided by a spot meter) is the best method of evaluating the effect of these lights.

When appraising the brightness ratio of face to background, the incident meter is not much help, because it does not take the subject's color brightness into consideration. Here a spot meter can be very useful. Depending on the mood of the scene, the face may be lighter or darker than the background, but in most cases it should not be the same. One also uses the spot meter when determining the brightness of so-called practical lamps. Take, for example, a man sitting at a table on which there is a practical lamp. As a rule of thumb, this lamp will look convincing if it is approximately 2½ stops brighter than the face. (The exposure is set for the face.)

When shooting film intended for television, extreme contrasts must be avoided. Television film should be limited to a 32:1 ratio between the brightest point and darkest detail. We will lose details that are more than five stops darker than the brightest point in the screen. This happens when the film is translated into electrical signals. According to international agreement, video signals are confined to a one-volt variation. The brighter the picture, the more voltage it generates. Now, if we have, for example, a face against a very bright background, such as a white wall or sky, the shot may look all right on a theater screen. But when fed through the TV film chain, the bright background will generate much voltage. Therefore, the overall video signal will be lowered in order to stay within the one-volt limit. Lowering the signal darkens the picture, and as a result the face might be reproduced much too dark, possibly appearing as a silhouette. To avoid this, one should try to have 1½ to 1¾ stops difference between the brightest spot in the frame and the face. The total brightness range among details to be seen must not exceed five stops.

In practice, cinematographers shooting filmed television shows just light their scenes normally, as though they were for theater release, yet they avoid extreme contrasts, such as by eliminating very bright backgrounds and by keeping pure-white objects to an absolute minimum. Actually, television engineers recommend that each shot have a small bit of "reference white" to allow them to set their controls. This helps them to achieve the most faithful rendition. Without reference white, the dark picture will be electronically "pushed up" to achieve the standard voltage, resulting in a muddy-gray picture. Therefore, out of self-protection, careful cinematographers try always to have a small pure-white object such as a handkerchief in the frame whenever possible.

When shooting film for video, it is also wise to avoid large uniform areas, because they sometimes show electronic "noise" (like vibrating grain) when translated to television signals. Similarly, stripes and geometric patterns should be avoided when possible, as they occasionally appear to vibrate when their edges happen to coincide with the scanning lines of the video signal.

LIGHTING EQUIPMENT

Today there are enough types of lighting equipment available to fill volumes. We will try to cover the most important types. One should pay particular attention to the practical working characteristics of each light, namely, the *quality* of the light produced by the given instrument and its physical capabilities in the way of mounting, controlling beam size, etc.

We will be using the terms "quartz" and "incandescent," which are frequently misused in practice; they are thought of as denoting different types of bulb. Quartz lamps are actually a type of incandescent bulb, distinguished by elements and structure. Quartz lamps are properly called tungsten-halogen lamps. In conventional incandescent lamps the tungsten filament slowly evaporates and deposits itself on the inside of the bulb wall, darkening it and lowering the color temperature. Quartz lamps are similar, but they contain halogen gas, which combines with the evaporating tungsten and deposits it back onto the hot filament, thus forming a restoration cycle. This cycle requires a high operating temperature, and therefore quartz glass is used because it can withstand the heat. This self-cleaning characteristic allows quartz lamps to maintain their original light output and color temperature throughout their life. Other advantages include longer life, smaller size, and quieter operation. (Conventional incandescent bulbs sometimes hum.) A quartz bulb should *never* be touched with bare fingers, as they would leave a deposit of natural chemicals that weaken the quartz glass. Any fingerprints should be removed immediately with alcohol.

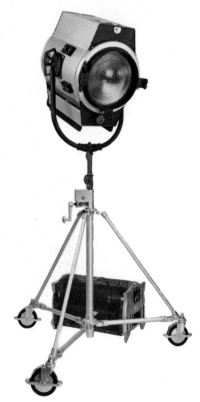

4-18 Arc spotlight. 225-amp Baby Brute Molarc. (Courtesy of Mole-Richardson Co.)

Most lighting instruments fall into three basic categories: arc spotlights, incandescent spotlights, and open reflector lights (which have no lens).

Arc Spotlights

Because of their physically small light source, arcs give sharp shadows. They are powerful enough to illuminate large areas. They are so bright that they can be used as fill lights outdoors in bright sun. All arcs require color gels in front of their lenses when used with daylight or tungsten emulsions. Carbon arcs operate on DC current and on location require special generators because of their huge power consumption. They are rather heavy and require operators. All this makes them somewhat expensive to use.

Spotlights

The second group contains the family of spotlights, including the spherical-reflector Fresnel-lens lights and ellipsoidal-reflector spotlights. Of this group, the Fresnels are the most widely used studio instruments. They are mainly used as key lights, back lights, kickers, and set lights because they can produce the hard light desirable for those functions.

Fresnels are available in many sizes, ranging from 50 watts to 10,000 watts, with either traditional heavy-duty housing or lightweight aluminum construction.

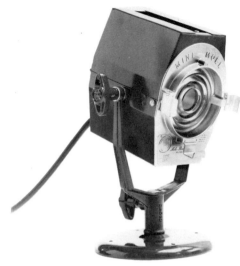

4-19 A Very small Fresnel instruments accepting bulbs from 50 watts to 200 watts are popularly called "inky-dinks." This particular version is a Mini-Mole Solarspot. Inky-dinks are very convenient when shooting on location with fast emulsions.

4-19 B 1000-watt Fresnel light. Molequartz Baby-Baby Solarspot.

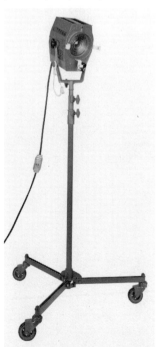

4-19 C 2000-watt Fresnel light. Molequartz Baby Junior Solarspot.

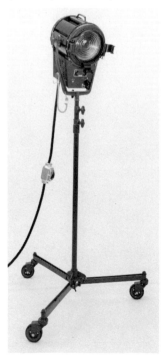

4-19 D 5000-watt Fresnel light. Molequartz Baby Senior Solarspot.

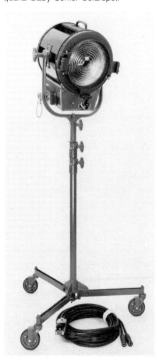

4-19 E 10,000-watt Fresnel light. Molequartz Baby Tener Solarspot. (Series courtesy of Mole-Richardson Co.)

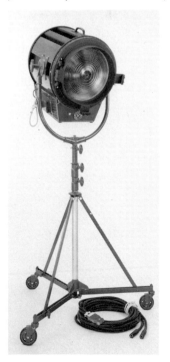

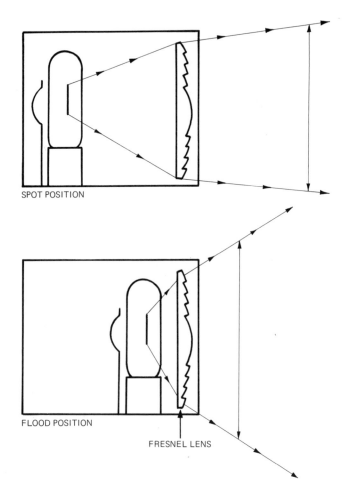

SPOT POSITION

FLOOD POSITION

FRESNEL LENS

broader area. When working in a hurry, the spot/flood adjustment can be used to set the intensity of the light. Flooding spreads the light over a greater area, therefore making it less intense than when spotted into a small area. It is quite common for the cameraman or gaffer to stand in the actor's position reading a meter while an electrician follows his orders to spot or flood the lamp until the desired level is obtained.

When pointing a Fresnel at a subject it is first spotted. This narrows the beam so the electrician can clearly see exactly where the center of the beam falls. He turns the lamp until the beam is hitting the center of the area to be illuminated. The Fresnel is then flooded to the desired degree.

Strangely enough, when the lamp is flooded the shadows are sharper than when it is focused. The reason is that when the lamp is focused (spotted), the entire lens acts as a light source. When flooded, the bulb is in the front of the lamp and almost visible, thus constituting a smaller light source and creating sharper shadows. If the spotted position seems sharper it is only that the greater intensity makes the shadows more prominent. To obtain the sharpest shadow from a Fresnel lamp one can remove the lens altogether.

The other type of spotlight is the ellipsoidal-reflector spotlight. It casts a sharp-edged pattern that can be shaped by irises or shutters or by inserting a cutout pattern. Lights of this design originated in the theater, and so their rating is generally low, ranging from 250 to 2000 watts.

4-20 Fresnel lens lamp with adjustable beam width.

4-21 An ellipsoidal-reflector spotlight.

BULB

ELLIPSOIDAL
REFLECTOR

SHUTTER
OR IRIS

LENS

The Fresnel lens remains stationary while the bulb and spherical mirror can be moved together, either closer or farther from the lens, allowing us to control the beam of light, either "spotting" or "flooding" it. When the bulb and mirror are farthest away from the lens, the light rays are more converged. This is the spot position, and it narrows the beam to a smaller area of coverage. Flooding the lamp moves the bulb and mirror to the front of the housing, near the lens. When in the flood position the lamp throws a wider beam, illuminating a

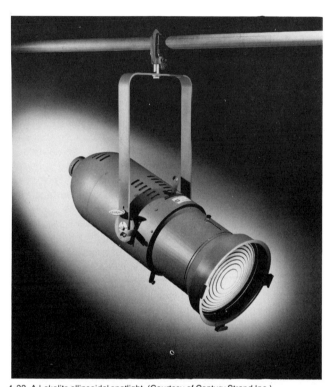

4-22 A Lekolite ellipsoidal spotlight. (Courtesy of Century Strand Inc.)

4-23 An ellipsoidal-reflector follow spot. (Courtesy of Berkey Colortran, Inc.)

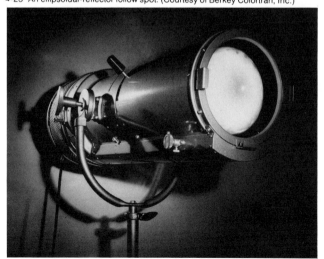

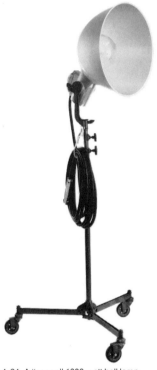

4-24 A "scoop" 1000-watt bell lamp.
(Courtesy of Mole-Richardson Co.)

Open Lights

Open lights are those instruments that do not have lenses. They are generally softer in quality and cast a wider beam than lamps with lenses. Most open lights use quartz lamps.

Open lights come in many variations. The oldest type in cinematography is the *scoop*, which has been used for many years as a source of soft light and is very commonly employed as a fill light. Scoops are frequently equipped with quartz lamps, but for economy reasons, conventional incandescent bulbs are also widely used, especially when these lamps are to be left on for long periods, for example when used as work lights in the studio. Scoops range in size from about 500 watts with a 15-inch diameter to 5000 watts with a 27-inch diameter.

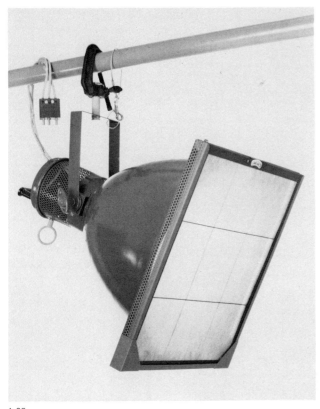

The largest size is sometimes called a "sky pan" or "sky light" and used as the overall fill for the entire set, or to illuminate huge backdrops. The most widely used scoops are the 1000-watt type, often used in clusters of two or four.

Soft lights, as their name implies, are open reflector lights that produce very soft and shadowless light. It is so even that it is often compared to northern-sky illumination. The quartz bulbs are not visible. The light is completely diffused by being bounced off the white surface at the back of the housing. None of the light reaches the subject directly. Some modern designs can be collapsed into suitcase size. Soft lights are available in sizes from 750 to 8000 watts. To maintain a constant color temperature, the white reflecting surface must be kept clean.

Strip lights are a type of open light used for lighting cycloramas and other large backdrops. They are available in units of one to twelve lights. They use quartz bulbs. The highly portable Bardwell & McAlister "Clipstrip" is collapsible. It includes a 10-foot powered bar. Up to ten separate lights can be attached and plugged directly into the bar, eliminating the need for separate cables.

4-25

4-25 A 2000-watt Molequartz scoop. Note the diffuser scrim further softening the light. (Courtesy of Mole-Richardson Co.)

4-26 750-watt Colortran Soft-Light. (Courtesy of Berkey Colortran, Inc.)

4-27 2000-watt Colortran Soft-Lite. (Courtesy of Berkey Colortran, Inc.)

4-26

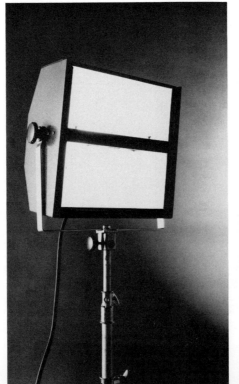

4-27

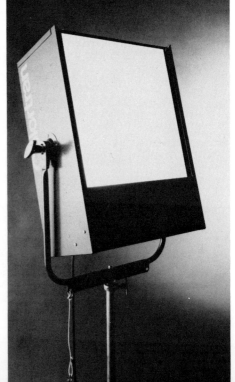

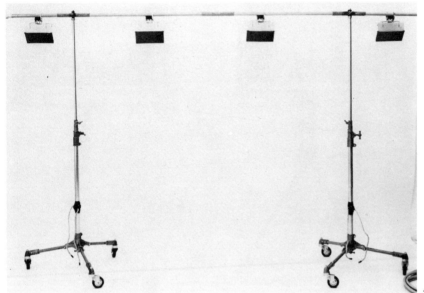

4-28 A, B Bardwell & McAlister "Clipstrip" kit. (Courtesy of F & B Ceco of California, Inc.)

4-28A

4-28B

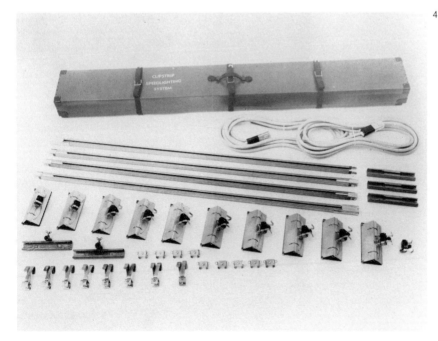

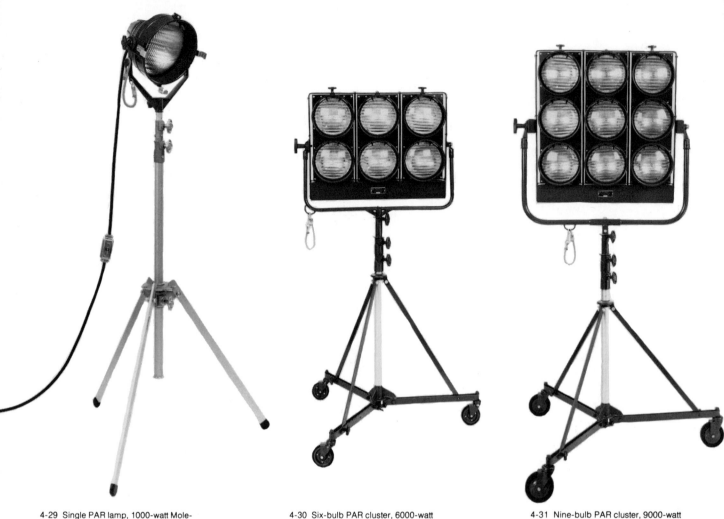

4-29 Single PAR lamp, 1000-watt Mole-quartz Molepar. (Courtesy of Mole-Richardson Co.)

4-30 Six-bulb PAR cluster, 6000-watt Molequartz Molepar. (Courtesy of Mole-Richardson Co.)

4-31 Nine-bulb PAR cluster, 9000-watt Molequartz Molepar. (Courtesy of Mole-Richardson Co.)

Clusters of quartz lights are designed in models containing up to twelve bulbs. These bulbs have an internal reflector and are usually either 650 or 1000 watts. They are officially coded as PAR lamps (Parabolic Aluminized Reflector). Within the PAR grouping there are many subtypes, each described by a three-letter designation that specifies the variable characteristics, such as beam width, voltage, wattage, color temperature, etc. For example, a FAY bulb is one of the more popular types within the PAR group. A FAY bulb is 650 watts and has a color temperature of 5000° K, making it useful as an outdoor fill light. The terms for the instruments themselves and for the bulbs seem somewhat confused in popular usage. The larger 1000-watt PAR instruments are commonly referred to as "Par" lights, while the instruments accepting the smaller 650-watt PAR lamps are often called "Fay" lights. In the Mole-

Richardson line, they are designated as Molepars and Molefays, while the Colortran nomenclature is Maxi-Brutes and Mini-Brutes.

"Par" and "Fay" bulb clusters can be used to do some of the work normally assigned to arcs. Indoors they can be used as powerful light sources, either direct or bounced off some surface. Although they cannot provide a harsh shadow, such as sunlight produces, they are useful as outdoor fill lights when the sun is the key light, or on gloomy days to raise the overall light level. For daylight use blue gels should be employed, or the bulbs could be of the dichroic coated type. However, the daylight color temperature of some lamps may drop with prolonged use, in which case the lamps should be filtered with a blue gel of a color density designated as one-half 26 blue.

102

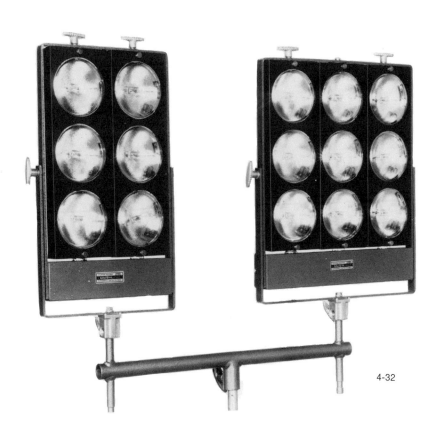

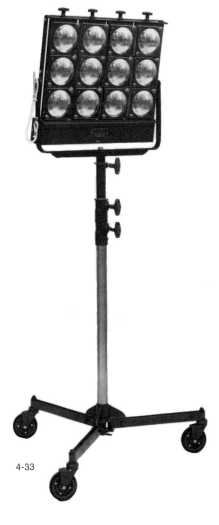

4-32

4-32 Clusters of 650-watt bulbs, Mini-Brute 6 (3900 watts) and Mini-Brute 9 (5850 watts). (Courtesy of Berkey Color-tran, Inc.)

4-33 Twelve-bulb FAY cluster, Molequartz 12-light Molefay. (Courtesy of Mole-Richardson Co.)

4-33

103

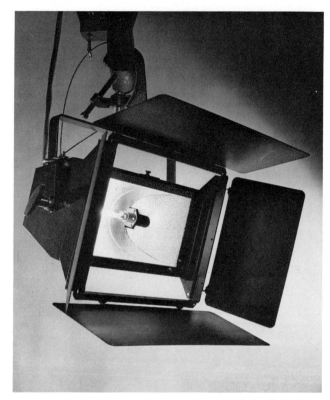

4-35 A 1000-watt "broad," useful as a fill light. (Courtesy of Berkey Colortran, Inc.)

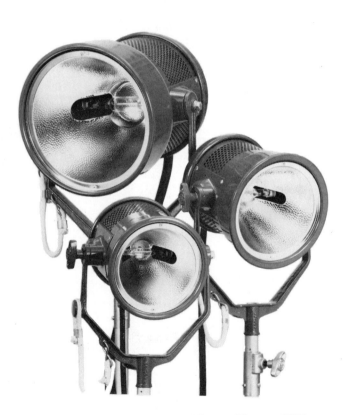

4-34 A family of open reflector quartz lights, 650-watt, 1000-watt, and 2000-watt. (Courtesy of Mole-Richardson Co.)

Other miscellaneous open reflector lights include a wide variety of recently developed quartz lamps that do not fit into clearly cut categories. Some are very light and portable, useful in either studio or location work. Others come as location lighting kits. All open reflector quartz lights lack some of the controllability of Fresnels. This is only a small sacrifice in television lighting, but for film-studio work the cameraman may want to depend more on Fresnels and use the open sources just as fill lights and as overall shadowless illumination. On location, however, the smaller size, lighter weight, and constant high light output of open reflector quartz lights may be more important than the controllability of Fresnels.

Within this group manufacturers recommend certain lamps as having either key-light or fill-light characteristics. There is a wide choice available among constantly changing designs.

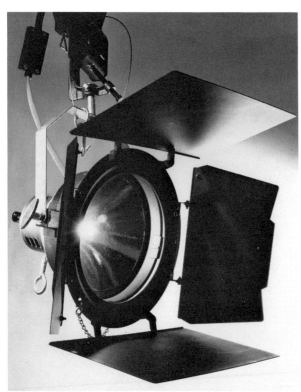

4-36 A "Super-10," focusable and useful as a key light. (Courtesy of Berkey Colortran, Inc.)

4-37 A set light. (Courtesy of Berkey Colortran, Inc.)

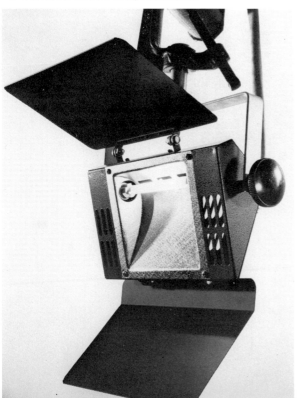

4-38 Location lighting kit. Contains two "key" and three "fill" open reflector quartz lights, each 1000 watts. (Courtesy of Berkey Colortran, Inc.)

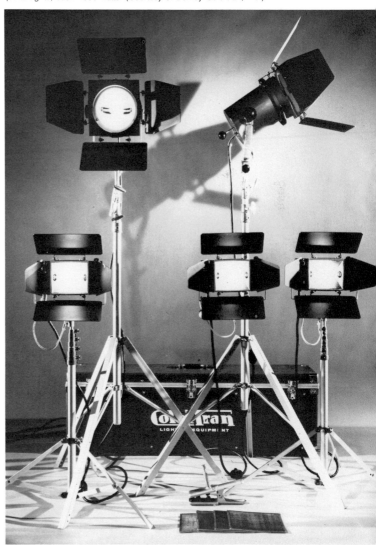

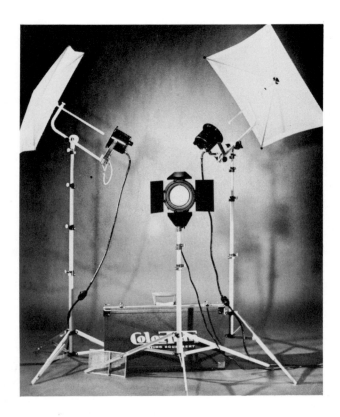

4-39 TV/Portrait kit. One 600-watt Mini-Pro lamp and two similar 650-watt hard-light sources that can be used with two reflective umbrellas for diffused light. (Courtesy of Berkey Colortran, Inc.)

4-40 Mini-Pro kit. Three 600-watt hard-light sources. (Courtesy of Berkey Colortran, Inc.)

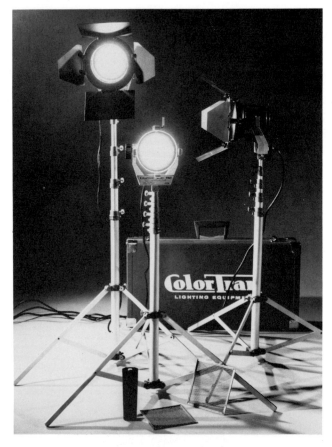

Photoflood incandescent bulbs are used in the inexpensive Lowel-Light units, but more important, they are useful in practical lamps, where a household fixture is in the frame and a conventional-looking bulb with a 3200° K color temperature is required. They are also available for 3400° K and daylight.

Photofloods come in a household shape or with a built-in reflector. In addition, the reflector type is manufactured in both flood and spot designs.

Battery-powered portable lamps such as Sylvania "Sun Guns" have an obvious application for newsreel work or when filming in such places as moving cars where power is not available. Most such battery-powered lights will yield up to 50 minutes with a 150-watt bulb or 22 minutes with a 250-watt bulb. The color temperature drops as the battery weakens.

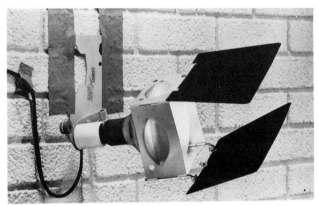

4-41 A Lowel-Light and barndoors affixed to a wall with gaffer tape. (Courtesy of Lowel-Light Photo Engineering)

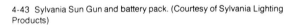

4-43 Sylvania Sun Gun and battery pack. (Courtesy of Sylvania Lighting Products)

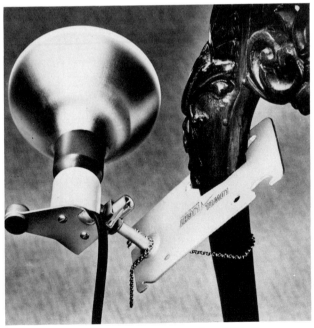

4-42 A Lowel-Light attached to a chair. (Courtesy of Lowel-Light Photo Engineering)

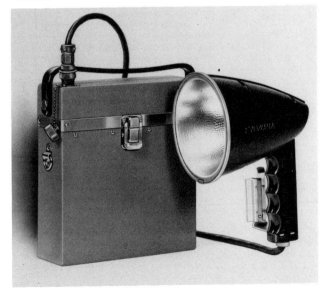

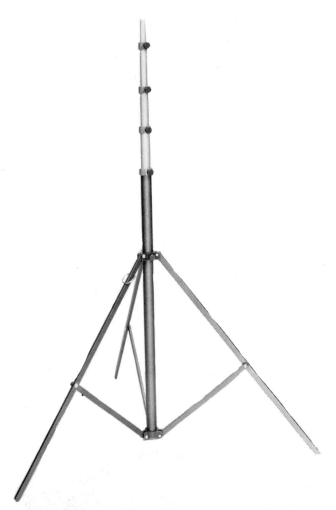

4-44 A lightweight stand. (Courtesy of Mole-Richardson Co.)

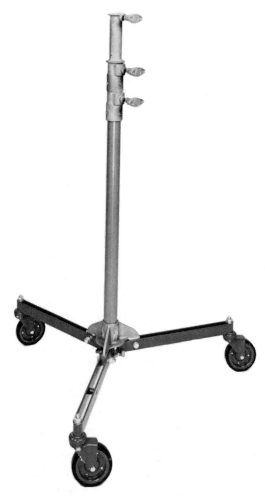

4-45 A light stand on casters (pedestal). (Courtesy of Mole-Richardson Co.)

Mounting Accessories

A studio light usually can be ordered as either a hanging model or a standing model. The hanging model comes with a shorter cable and *without* an on/off switch. It should be ordered with a C-clamp that is the proper size for the grid. The standing model comes with a 25-foot cable and an on/off switch. Standing models must be ordered with a pin that is the proper size for the stand to be used. These models can be interchanged by exchanging the C-clamp for a pin or vice-versa.

Stands vary in size from heavy-duty to lightweight. Some are equipped with casters. They are adjustable for different heights and can be equipped with many types of side extenders, boom arms, etc. Some are power-operated for elevating large heavy lights.

Other available mounting instruments include trombones, wall plates, base plates, etc.

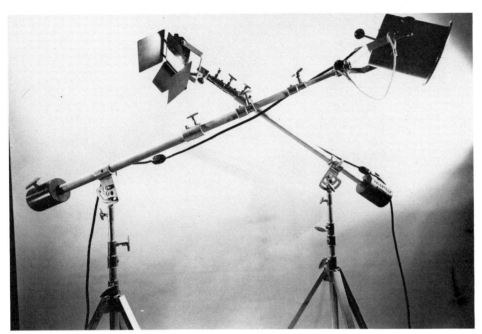

4-46 Boom arms. (Courtesy of Berkey Colortran, Inc.)

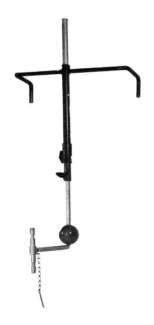

4-47 A trombone. The arms hook over the top of the set wall and the light mounts on the pin at the bottom. (Courtesy of Mole-Richardson Co.)

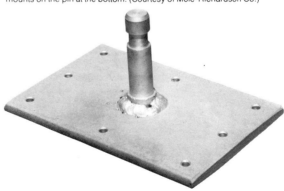

4-48 Wall plate. (Courtesy of Mole-Richardson Co.)

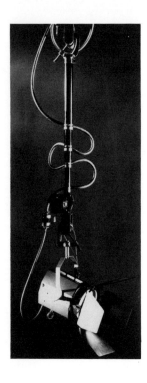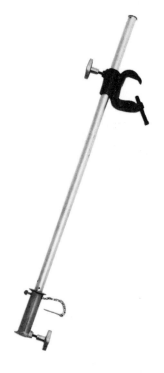

In studios equipped with a grid of fixed height we may have to use lamp hangers of various designs, such as telescoping Anti-G hangers or ordinary adjustable-rod hangers in various heights.

Scaffoldings (also called parallels) are often used for mounting lights, both in the studio and at outdoor locations.

"Polecats" are extremely useful as compact portable grids for indoor locations.

Securing Devices

Every lamp on the grid and every barndoor, snoot, etc., must be secured with a safety chain or cable. The bases of lightweight lamp stands — especially on location — should be steadied with sandbags. Stands can also be taped or lashed to almost any supporting structure, such as a wall, furniture, or a window frame. Light stands are pulled over most frequently by people tripping on badly secured cables left lying loose on the floor. All cables, especially those in areas where people will be walking, should be taped to the floor with gaffer's tape, an extremely strong heat-resistant adhesive tape, sold in film-supply houses. Sometimes a ring is provided at the base of the stand and the cable is put through it, so that if someone trips on the cable the jerk will be less apt to pull the lamp over. For extra stability, one leg of the stand should point in the direction of the light — that is, be directly under the lamp.

Accessories for Controlling Light

An ability to control and manipulate light is necessary for its creative use. There are five objectives in controlling a light beam: changing the intensity, changing the effective size of the source (diffusing), manipulating the pattern, adjusting the color, and, in special circumstances, eliminating heat.

To cut down *light intensity,* scrims can be introduced between the light and the subject. These are usually made of metal mesh and may come in round or square shapes to fit in the holder on the front of the light, or may be of larger size for positioning at some distance in front of the light. There are two common densities for scrims. A "single" scrim cuts the light by half a stop. A "double" reduces the light by one stop. Scrims are available in different shapes, such as half-scrims, which cover only half the light. Often several scrims are used at once.

By placing a *diffusing* material in front of the light source, we are able to change the effective size of the source, making the light softer. Like scrims, diffusers are often made of a mesh material, but a mesh will only diffuse if the gaps between the threads are narrower than the thickness of the threads themselves. The common materials are silk, Dacron, frosted glass, fiber glass, and heat-resisting plastics. Many other substances are also used.

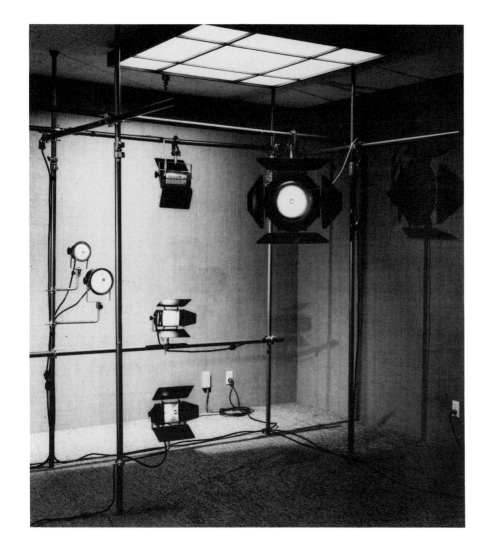

4-51 Colortran Pole Kings. (Courtesy of Berkey Colortran, Inc.)

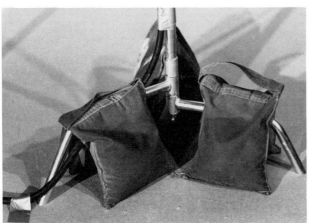

4-52 Sandbags steadying a stand. (Photo by author)

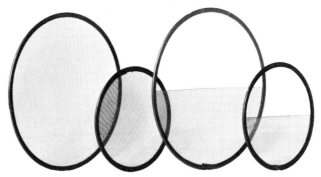

4-53 Scrims. Left to right, a single, a double, a half single scrim, and a half double scrim. The physical size varies according to the size of the light instrument. (Courtesy of Mole-Richardson Co.)

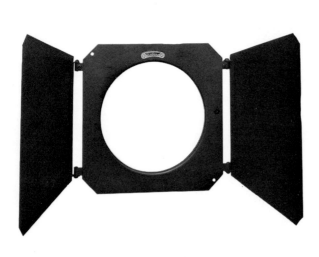

4-54 Two-leaf barndoors. (Courtesy of Mole-Richardson Co.)

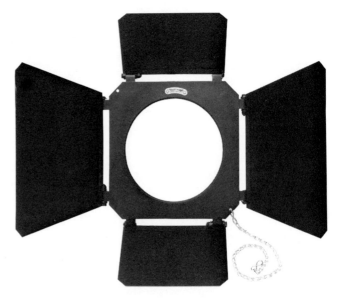

4-55 Four-leaf barndoors are preferable. (Courtesy of Mole-Richardson Co.)

"Barndoors" are the most versatile instruments for controlling the *light pattern*. Almost any light (all Fresnels and most types of open reflector quartz lights) should always be equipped with barndoors, preferably of the rotating four-leaf variety. They can be used to keep lighted areas from overlapping. By restricting the light pattern they can prevent unwanted shadows, such as from the sound boom, keep light off shiny surfaces, and protect the camera lens from direct light. They can also be used to create desirable shadows such as the "fall-off" at the top of an interior wall. Barndoors generally enable the cameraman to create the desired lighting patterns.

"Snoots" are similar in function. These funnellike devices of different diameters are even more restricting, casting circles of light.

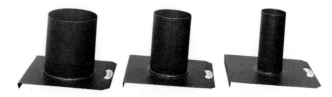

4-56 Snoots. (Courtesy of Mole-Richardson Co.)

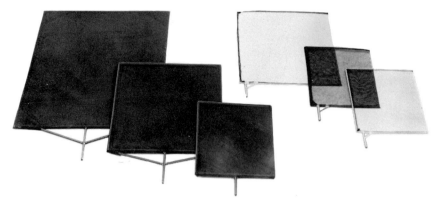

4-57 Flags (black) and scrims (nets). (Bardwell & McAlister, courtesy of F & B Ceco of California, Inc.)

"Flags," "dots," "fingers," and "cookies" differ in size and shape, yet they are all used for introducing shadow patterns. Unlike barndoors or snoots, they are usually on "century stands" or goosenecks that hold them between the light and the subject. One very important use of a flag is shading the camera lens from direct light. The "cucaloris," or "cookie," can be used to create the random shadow pattern usually associated with foliage. Some cookies are made of a frosted plastic material and give a very soft shadow pattern. A cookie will often substantially improve the appearance of woodwork or furniture, giving it a deep, rich look.

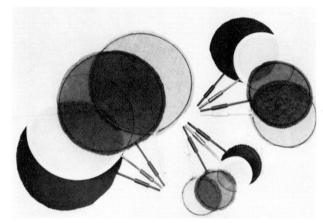

4-58 Assortment of dots and targets. (Bardwell & McAlister, courtesy of F & B Ceco of California, Inc.)

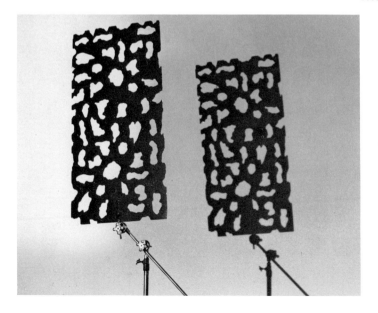

4-59 A cucaloris (cookie). (Photo by author)

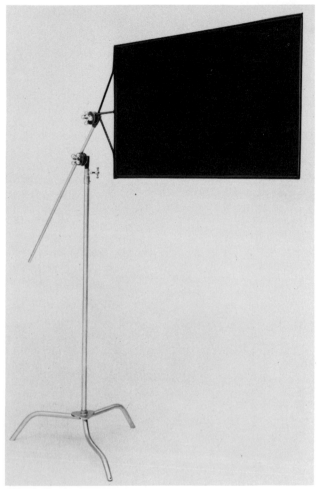

4-60 A flag on a century stand. (Bardwell & McAlister, courtesy of F & B Ceco of California, Inc.)

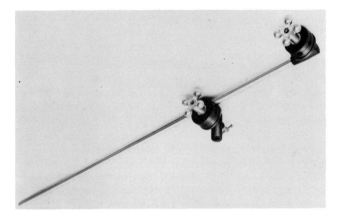

4-61 "Gobo Head" on the arm of a century stand. (Bardwell & McAlister, courtesy of F & B Ceco of California, Inc.)

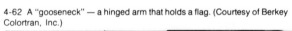

4-62 A "gooseneck" — a hinged arm that holds a flag. (Courtesy of Berkey Colortran, Inc.)

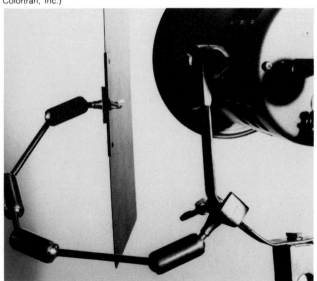

These shadow-making devices serve many functions, not the least of which is the breaking up of evenly illuminated areas. Often, and especially when lighting set walls, an even illumination gives the set a flat, uninteresting look. A few random shadows here and there will break up the monotony, making the background seem more alive and three-dimensional. The shadows do not need an established reason for being there, yet they shouldn't directly violate logic. For example, a couple of flags and fingers may be used to create shadows that might be coming from the crosspieces of a window. We don't see the window in the scene, yet as long as it's logical that a window might be there and cast such a shadow, the audience will accept it without even thinking. The darker the set is and the more random its design and colors, the more one can get away with. The opposite is also true. A lightly colored bare wall will advertise the shadows thrown onto it, so they have to be especially logical to prevent the audience from being distracted. In all such cases, subtlety is advisable. Remember too that by using shadow patterns to make a set more alive, its visual appearance becomes more pleasing. Therefore, be sure that an attractive appearance is not in conflict with the mood the director is trying to create.

In placing any shadow-making device, the shadows will be more distinct if the light is from a hard source such as a Fresnel, and they will also be sharper if the device is farther from the lamp.

For *adjusting the color,* a gelatin filter can be mounted on the front of most lights in a special holder that positions it some distance from the lens. Gels that are not heat-resistant will have to be mounted on a stand and held farther away from the lamp.

Glass *heat-removing* filters can be used to prevent excess heat in special applications, such as in filming an ice-cream commercial or in close-up zoological work. These filters cause a slight loss in color temperature and reduce the amount of light by about a third of a stop.

ELECTRICAL CONTROL AND DISTRIBUTION IN THE STUDIO

The requirements of television have stimulated the development of many highly efficient lighting systems, with elaborate dimmer boards equipped with preset electronic memories. For schools and small production companies, the most economical grid system consists of ordinary 1½-inch gas

4-63 A simple grid system constructed from 1 1/2-inch gas pipe. (Photo by author)

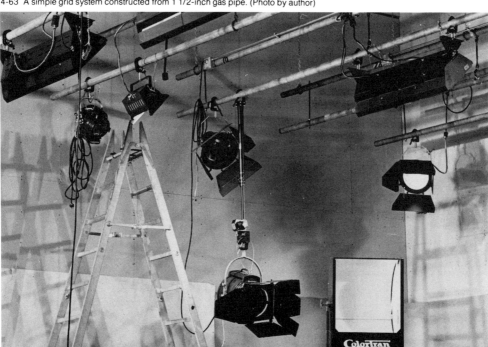

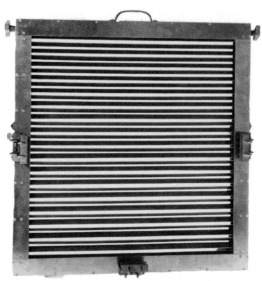

4-64 A shutter. (Courtesy of Mole-Richardson Co.)

pipes, suspended from the ceiling, with outlet boxes along the pipes, spaced about one every 4 feet. A simple breaker box can serve as the switchboard. Each outlet should be on its own 20-amp circuit and have its own switch in the breaker box. Convenient spacing of the pipes is about 4 feet apart. When building a grid and buying lights, much time will be saved by making sure to order all compatible plugs.

A variety of portable dimmers are available in many sizes and capacities, some with remote-control devices. One must be careful when using dimmers with color film productions, as varying the voltage will change the color temperature of the light. If a mid-scene dimming is required when using color film, it should be done with a purely mechanical shutter that operates like a venetian blind.

LIGHTING PROCEDURE
AND RIGGING ORDER

It goes without saying that the cameraman (director of photography) must be familiar with the script. He will talk it over with the director, determining the mood, time of day, etc., of each scene. At this stage, close cooperation with the art director and set designer is invaluable. Before he does anything, the cinematographer must know the size and shape of the sets, the number of actors and extras, and all the color schemes of the sets and costumes.

Once the set is erected, the gaffer will rig the lights according to the cameraman's direction. The set walls and backdrops can be lit before the actors arrive. Practical lights,

since they are props as well as light sources, will also be prepared. The key lights, fill lights, back lights, and kickers can be hung in likely places, but they will not be focused in their final settings until the actors arrive and the director blocks the scene.

During the blocking, the cameraman cooperates with the director in lining up the shot and marking camera and actor positions. When the blocking is over, the real lighting starts. In professional studios the actors usually take this opportunity to go off and either rest or practice their lines, leaving the cinematographer to light the scene with stand-ins. This is why it is important to mark each actor's position on the floor. The incident meter is especially vital when lighting without stand-ins.

First the key lights are positioned and adjusted to the proper levels. Second come the fill lights, then the back lights and/or kickers. It often happens that one light may serve several functions. For example, one actor's key light may be another's kicker.

When the lighting is completed the first full rehearsal follows for cast, camera crew, sound crew, special effects, etc. After this rehearsal any necessary changes will be made before more run-through and the actual shooting.

THE LOGIC OF LIGHTING

Unless the production is intended to be unrealistic, the lighting will generally follow the logical scheme of the natural light sources within the scene — windows, practical lamps, candle flames, fireplaces, etc.

The most common of these is the window. If a window is visible in a daylight scene, we might have strongly backlit curtains or an illuminated backdrop, either painted or photographic. (For a realistic effect of bright daylight, these backdrops should be about two stops brighter than the faces in the key light.) Because this window is the logical source of light, the general direction of most of the key lights will therefore come from the direction of this window. We may also want to introduce the window-pattern shadow on the opposite wall by using a cutout in an ellipsoidal spotlight, or by using a shadow-forming device such as a flag in the path of a Fresnel.

Practical lamps in the scene look best if they are two to four stops brighter than the face. Here a dimmer is useful in obtaining the right level. The practical lamp can even be used as the key light, in which case you will need a strong bulb. The camera side of the lampshade may have to be shaded in order to maintain a two- or three-stop difference between the face and the lampshade. To do this we could place a scrim between the bulb and the lampshade, or use a neutral density gel cut to fit the inside of the lampshade. Still another method would be to cut out the back of the lampshade and allow the bulb to shine directly upon the actor's face. The rest of our lighting must also simulate the light supposedly coming from this practical.

To further illustrate this, let us consider the similar example of a candle flame. The candle flame is a very weak source,

and therefore it must be supplemented with artificial light. When faced with candles or other weak sources some cinematographers will use low illumination to make the candle seem brighter compared to the face. For example, say the key is 400 foot-candles. In comparison, the candle appears dim. If the key is reduced to 100 foot-candles, the candle will seem brighter in relation to the key light. Keeping the flame against a dark background will help.

In lighting the scene in figures 4-65 to 4-70, our key lights must appear to be coming from the candle. To maintain a realistic effect, no fill lights are used (or very little with color film). The circle of candlelight on the table can be simulated by a Fresnel with a snoot pointing directly down from above (figure 4-67). Two 500-watt baby Fresnels are used as key lights. This is called a "back cross" because the paths of the key lights cross behind the actors (figure 4-65).

The two key lights are angled so that the shadows of the candle do not fall upon the actors. Barndoors are used to keep the woman's key light off the man's back and vice versa. For a realistic effect, these two key lights are positioned at about the same level as the candle flame. The candle should not cast a shadow across the table because it supposedly is the only source of light. Therefore the bottom barndoor of each key light is raised until the key no longer illuminates the top of the table, thus removing the candle shadow (figure 4-66).

4-65 A "back cross" of key lights.

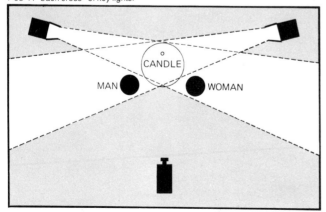

4-66 The bottom barndoor of each key light is raised until the key no longer illuminates the top of the table, thus eliminating the candle shadow.

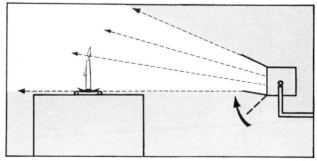

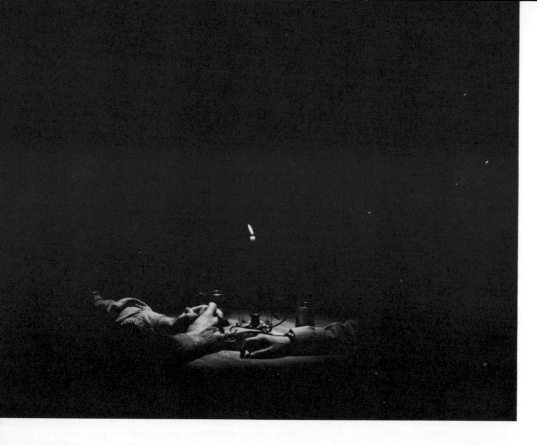

4-67 The circle of candlelight on the table can be simulated by a Fresnel Baby, with a snoot, pointing straight down from above.

4-68 The candlelight on the faces is created by two key lights in the back-cross fashion.

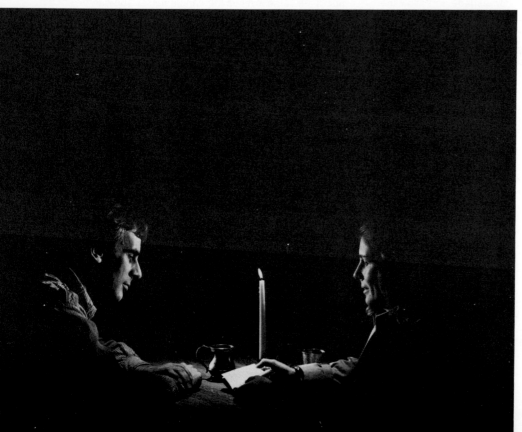

4-69 A bit of back light is added to separate the actors slightly from the background.

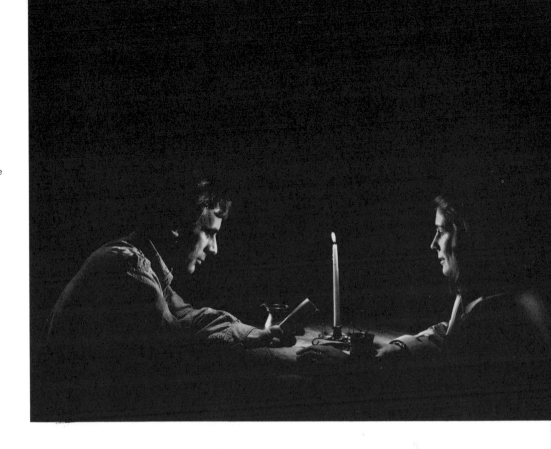

4-70 A window pattern (supposedly coming from the moon or a street light) is used to show the back wall slightly. (Series of photos by Roger Conrad)

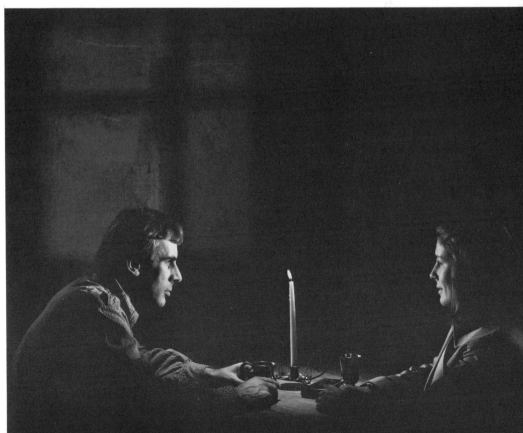

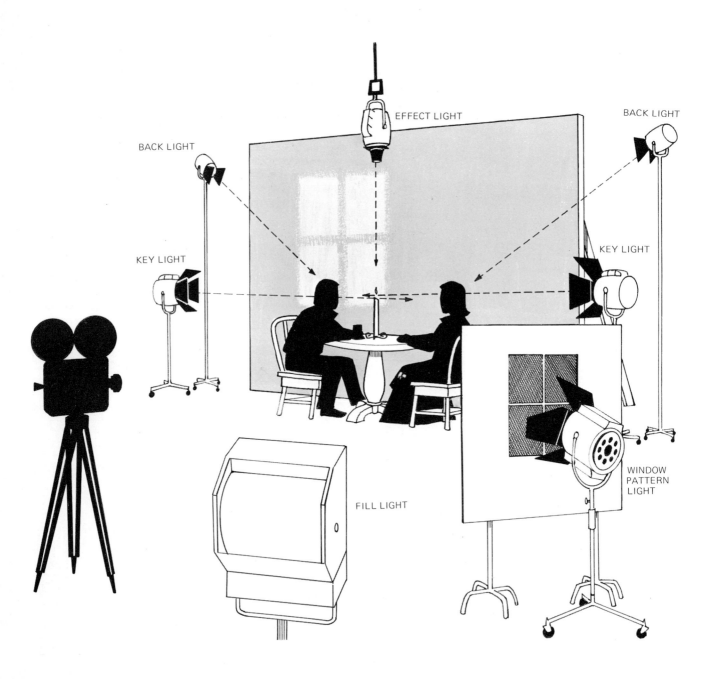

EFFECT LIGHT

BACK LIGHT

BACK LIGHT

KEY LIGHT

KEY LIGHT

WINDOW PATTERN LIGHT

FILL LIGHT

4-71 Lighting scheme for the candle effect. Fill, from the soft light, would be used if the scene had been shot in color.

In this particular scene there is no logical reason for back lights, but we may use them with great discretion to separate the actors slightly from the background (figure 4-69). These minor violations of logic are acceptable as long as they remain subtle.

Now in looking at the scene as we have lighted it so far, we notice the large black void behind the actors. It would be nice to break up the area and perhaps see the back wall. To illuminate it flatly might make it uninteresting and would certainly be in conflict with the shadowy depth created by the rest of the lighting. By simulating a window pattern cast on the back wall by moonlight, we can break up the monotony of the large black area and show the back wall (figure 4-70). The effect is created by using flags to shape a square some distance from a Fresnel. A Fresnel is chosen for its distinct shadows. A scrim is placed on a century stand near the flags and crisscrossed with gaffer's tape to obtain the shadows of the window's crosspieces. One could also use an actual window frame, perhaps with venetian blinds, mounted on a century stand.

If shooting color film, it might be effective to put amber gels over all sources that are supposed to be coming from the candle, and a pale-blue one over the source of the moonlight window pattern.

Thus we finish lighting the candle situation. This is just one of many ways we could have approached it. Probably no two cinematographers would have lit it the same way. However, the one thing most of their techniques would have in common is logic. Each light performs specific tasks. If a given effect is not realistic, yet is still needed (in this case the backlights), it is very subtle. But each light has a reason for being used.

Another difficult variation of this is an actor *walking* with a candle. In this case he may be illuminated by a hand-held Fresnel (such as an inky-dink) with a snoot. A dimmer could be used to achieve the flicker effect.

When working with a large candle or a lantern, there is the possibility of hiding in it a small bulb (operated by battery or a hidden cable).

For imitating larger fire sources, such as fireplaces, a flickering effect can be cast on the subjects by moving a fringed flag in the light beam or by reflecting the light from a rotating drum covered with wrinkled orange tinfoil.

When an actor is switching a practical lamp on or off, our lighting must react simultaneously. The practical switch can be connected to the lighting circuit, or the electrician can rehearse the movement with the actor. In the latter case it helps if the actor partly covers the switch with his hand and turns it with a smooth movement.

Frequently sets create problems that the cinematographer must overcome in order to obtain the best visual result. For example, a medium shot of a person in bed may create a lighting problem if the linen is white. Here we don't want the white sheets to be too much brighter than the face. Therefore the light should be controlled so that the face is illuminated, but the light on the sheets is reduced. There are several ways. When using small Fresnels, such as inky-dinks, it may be sufficient to spot the lamp and use the barndoors to limit the beam width. With larger instruments we may need other shadow-creating accessories, such as flags and fingers. If only a slight reduction is necessary, we can use a large scrim on a flag stand, some distance from the lamp, with a cutout portion in the shape of the face. This problem should have been at least partly remedied through cooperation with the art director, who could have ordered a low-reflectant material for the sheets. However, when using borrowed locations and props the cinematographer must do his best with what he has.

There are many less obvious situations that require such control. For example, the upper portions of interior walls should be softly shadowed for more realism and better composition. This is easily done with a barndoor or a flag.

One of the most common lighting problems arises when the scene requires an actor to move toward or away from his key light. If we wish the light levels to remain the same throughout the scene, we use half-scrims on the front of the light. Because the intensity of the lower part of the beam is reduced by the half-scrim, the actor's illumination level will remain the same as he moves throughout the area.

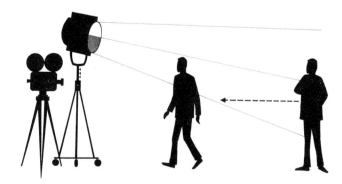

4-72 A half scrim is used to equalize the illumination as the actor moves closer to the light.

Another difficulty is that our lights may create unwanted shadows, the most common of these being *multiple* shadows of people and objects and the shadow of the sound boom. Generally we try to keep the actors several feet away from the walls, especially if the walls are light-colored, which makes the shadows more visible. Shadows on the floor are generally less noticeable. Sometimes having two shadows from a single person is unavoidable, but three shadows become distracting and unrealistic. The crossing sound boom casts *moving* shadows and is most objectionable. We can try to position our lights so that the boom shadows fall outside the frame. If the key light is causing a boom shadow on the back wall, it can be eliminated by using a flag or barndoor to remove the key light from the wall without removing it from the actor. The wall is then illuminated by another light. The cinematographer needs a lot of cooperation and understanding from the sound man, who may be able to help by changing the boom position or using some method other than a boom mike. One advantage of soft lighting is that this problem becomes less critical.

DEPTH

Most of the time the cinematographer is trying to recreate a three-dimensional reality on a two-dimensional screen. This depth can be controlled through the manipulation of many variables: shapes and volumes, scales and distances, color and light, movement (subject and camera), and lenses (perspective). An understanding of these variables is essential to all artists involved in visual arts. Most of them are the direct responsibility of other members of the production team, such as the art director, set designer, makeup artist, and film director. The director of photography, or cinematographer, is involved in the coordination of all of them, but he concentrates on his own contribution, the lighting.

For individual subjects, depth can be accentuated by back and side lighting. This highlights prominent features, leaving the rest in shadow. The three-dimensionality of the set can be augmented by using pools of light, separated by dark objects or areas. For example, a long hallway has more apparent depth if only a few parts of it are lit with many shadow areas in between. When shooting color, the depth will be further expressed as chromatic separations, thus adding to the three-dimensionality. Conversely, black-and-white lacks this advantage, therefore black-and-white films are harder to light than color because more time and care must be invested to obtain

a three-dimensional image. With color film color gels can sometimes be used over light sources to enhance the depth. For example, the actors can be lit with warm tones and the background with slightly cooler colors.

TEXTURES AND SHAPES

The texture of a rough surface is best accentuated by lighting from the side or back. The texture is revealed through many small shadows. Because sharp shadows will be most effective for this purpose, a hard light source is used. Conversely, if we wish to smooth out a surface (such as a face), a soft frontal lighting would prove most advantageous. As shape and texture are expressed by shadows, designers sometimes have shadows painted on their sets to create a desired physical appearance, such as in *The Cabinet of Dr. Caligari.* The early Disney animation films, such as *Snow White and the Seven Dwarfs,* gain much depth and realism through the use of dramatic lighting achieved by meticulously painted shadows that move with the characters.

When dealing with shiny surfaces, it is essential to remember the high school physics principle that the angle of incidence equals the angle of reflection. In situations where it is impractical to change the light, perhaps the surface can be tilted or moved. In the case of a hanging mirror or picture on a wall, a matchbox can be placed under one corner to alter its plane.

Curved, shiny surfaces such as car bumpers or bathroom fixtures represent a greater problem. Like any shiny surface

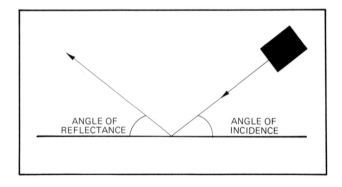

4-73 The angle of incidence equals the angle of reflection.

they can be toned down with dulling spray, available from most photographic and art-supply shops. In emergencies, soap and other substances have been used.

In the case of water surfaces, a back-lit reflection may be desirable, especially at night.

Often the "texture" is not a surface, but a substance suspended in the air. Rain, fog, dust particles, steam, and other such elements can be seen best when back-lit. For the effect of an aura or halo one might suspend gauze in that area of the scene. If the background is dark, the gauze can be back-lit for the desired effect. Barndoors, flags, etc., will be used to limit the area illuminated by this particular back light.

Of all the shapes in nature, the human face is the one that interests us most in cinematography. Every face is different and may require a different treatment. The shape and size of the nose and depth of the eye sockets are perhaps the most challenging elements of the subject's face. A long nose shadow can be ugly, and to diminish it we move the key light to a more frontal, medium-height position. To prevent deeply seated eyes from appearing as dark cavities we can lower the key light or use a soft fill light positioned close to the camera lens. An eye light (discussed earlier) will fill in the eye sockets and give the eyes a sparkle. A small Fresnel light such as an inky-dink makes an excellent eye light. Similar procedures may be needed to eliminate shadows created by a wide-brimmed hat.

Through placement of lights we can also control the facial contour. Frontal lighting will portray the face as more round than with three-quarter back lighting. An excellent homemade tool for studying the effect of different key-light positions is made by attaching a hooded light bulb to the end of a 3-foot rod. By moving this device around the subject we can observe how the key light models the face from various angles.

Many portrait photographers have long realized that human faces are rarely as symmetrical as they appear. There is usually a small side and a large side. Given his choice, the portrait photographer would usually rather photograph the smaller side because the result is more complimentary. However, in cinematography the cameraman doesn't often have this choice. The side to be photographed is most often dictated by the director's staging and the needs of the scene.

The proportions of the face can also be changed by various camera positions. A heavy chin will be diminished when photographed from above with the light favoring the upper part of the face. A *longer* lens (50 to 100mm lenses for 16mm film) is usually used for closeups because it does not exaggerate the nose. Alternatively, a wide-angle lens would be used to exaggerate a feature. The cinematographer will often do a great deal to improve an actor's appearance without the actor realizing it. For example, he might quietly ask an actor with protruding ears to look a bit more to the side, instead of directly into the camera. This slight repositioning hides one ear and makes the other appear to lie flat against the visible side of the actor's head.

In trying to modify the appearance of a face, the cinematographer should closely collaborate with the makeup man. Makeup is an excellent tool for accentuating or hiding facial contours.

Reflections from eyeglasses may betray the presence of film studio lights. It is most objectionable when the glaring reflections hide the actor's eyes, interfering with the audience's ability to see his full performance. Using empty frames, with the glass removed, is an easy but unrealistic solution. Normally the glass *should* have some shine. Some cameramen prefer the actors to wear flat surface glasses in place of normal convex lenses. These "plane" glasses will not reflect so many light sources but at certain angles may unfortunately shine with their full surfaces. This problem has to be carefully watched during the rehearsals and lighting angles may have to be adjusted to minimize this glare.

I have mentioned only a few techniques of dealing with textures and shapes. The subject is infinite. Combined observation and practice is the best way to acquire a sense of how to handle them.

STUDIO LIGHTING

More and more film makers are shooting on location rather than in the studio. Location shooting saves money on studio rental and set materials and gives greater authenticity and realism. Nevertheless, the film studio still offers some very real advantages: full control of the environment and weather, an overhead lighting grid, extensive electrical power (including, in bigger studios, DC current for the use of arcs and for quiet operation of incandescent lights), ideal sound quality control, a smooth and level floor, set construction (flexible ceiling heights and removable walls and floors), and so on. One advantage that is unique to the studio is the possibility to attain the abstract situation called the limbo effect. To create the limbo effect (apparent infinite space), the studio must be

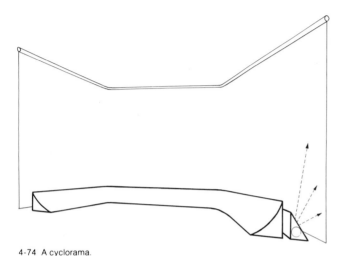

4-74 A cyclorama.

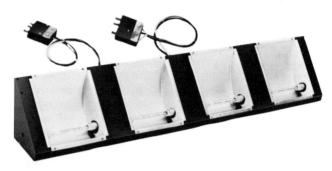

4-75 A quartz cycstrip. (Bardwell & McAlister, courtesy of F & B Ceco of California, Inc.)

equipped with a cyclorama. The "cyc" can be a permanent installation, such as those made out of plaster, or not so permanent, made out of a plastic or cloth material stretched from the floor to the grid. A wedge-shaped "foot" is used to merge the curtain invisibly into the floor. This wedge may be positioned away from the curtain in order to hide the cyc strip lights. Other cyc strips will be hung from the grid. The object is to illuminate the floor and wall evenly, creating the illusion of infinite space. Therefore, for smooth lighting the cyc strips should not be too close to the cyclorama. To obtain the full limbo effect of the subject suspended in a white void, we don't want any shadows on the floor. To achieve this we use all diffused light, such as several large soft lights on the subject. Another excellent diffused source is a large lightweight Dacron screen stretched above the scene and illuminated from above by several powerful lamps. Whatever type of instruments are used, the light should come from all sides in order to achieve the shadowless quality.

The studio can also provide a *black* limbo effect. In this case the cyclorama and floor will be black and we will not have to light the cyc. Black surfaces still may reflect a certain amount of light. To keep the light off the back wall we may use a controllable light such as a Fresnel spotlight or ellipsoidal spotlight. The lamp is equipped with barndoors and placed in either a three-quarter-back or side position. This keeps shadows off the back wall and the back stage floor. If fill light is necessary it should be weak enough so as not to illuminate the background. These three things should be remembered when trying to eliminate shadows from dark-colored floors and set walls: the fewer lights, the fewer shadows; softer lights create less distinct shadows but are more difficult to control; and finally, shooting from a low angle tends to eliminate the floor altogether.

When lighting a black limbo effect, our eye may mislead us into thinking the background is too visible. A spot meter is invaluable in giving the number of stops difference between the faces and the cyc, enabling us to determine whether the latter will be visible on the film. In most cases six stops difference should be enough to render the background black.

LOCATION LIGHTING

The studio provides the ideal lighting situation, but the director may see greater advantages in location shooting. There, limited working space and insufficient power make the cinematographer's job more difficult, but the results are often more interesting.

The first problem is power. Most modern houses in the United States have a total supply of 100 amps. This power is distributed into several circuits, each with its own amperage limit, which is usually 15 or 20 amps. Each circuit may go to a different part of the house. Suppose the bedroom is on a circuit with a 20-amp fuse. From the wall sockets on this circuit we can use a maximum of 20 amps. It is wise to remember the equation: watts = amps x volts. Therefore, amps = watts ÷ volts. For example, say we are using two 1000-watt lamps. Added together they make a total of 2000 watts. To find out how many amps are required, we divide 110 volts into our 2000 watts. This yields approximately 18 amps.

Therefore, we can use up to 2000 watts in this 20-amp circuit. A 2-amp margin is allowed for safety. There is also a shortcut method useful when the voltage is 110. Total watts divided by 100 gives the approximate amps, with a margin of safety.

In Great Britain and other European countries the voltage is usually 220 to 240 volts. In this case, our 2000 watts divided by 240 volts would equal a little over 8 amps. So when the voltage is greater, the same lamps will require less amperage. However, European houses generally have a lower total amperage and the fuses are also of lower denominations. For example, 13 amps is a common circuit. The exact electrical situation varies from country to country and from district to district, and will also depend on the age of the house.

Trying to get more than 20 amps out of the 20-amp circuit will cause fuses or breakers to blow. The wires in the wall are not designed for a higher amperage, and if the circuit is overloaded, the wiring may overheat and start a fire. Fuses and breakers are safety devices designed to turn the circuit off if it becomes overloaded. Therefore, simply installing a larger-capacity fuse or bypassing the breaker switch is dangerous.

If you need more than the maximum amperage of the circuit, you can use extension cables to bring power in from another circuit, possibly in a different part of the house. We can find what outlets belong to which circuits by turning the breaker switches on and off or unscrewing the fuses. Such extension cables should be heavy enough to carry the expected amperage load. A #12 cable will carry up to 2000 watts and is therefore a standard cable for such a location. A #8 cable should be used for the same load if the distance is longer than 100 feet.

To help overcome power limitations, professional film crews usually employ the services of an electrician. He will bypass the circuit breaker switches or fuses and use a distribution box of his own. He takes power from the incoming line after it has passed the main house fuse. Extension cables of the proper capacity run from his distribution box to the lights. This eliminates the hassle of crisscrossing cables from room to room and the worry about blowing fuses. Bypassing the breakers without the aid of a qualified electrician is dangerous and illegal, but it is often done.

If the total power requirement exceeds 80 amps, the law further requires you to contact the local power company and have the power especially laid in from the street. Sometimes the voltage on location may drop slightly, especially in the peak hours of electricity consumption. A drop of 10 volts will cause a 100° K drop in color temperature. Usually the lab can correct minor variations, but for extremely critical work, a voltage meter can be a useful tool in lighting operations. The voltage is measured at the end of the extension cable.

The second limitation encountered when filming on location is space. The amount of available working space will dictate the size and placement of the lighting instruments. The low ceiling and lack of a grid forces the cameraman to place lights closer to the subjects. This creates two problems: hiding the lights and achieving an even illumination. First, the lights must be kept out of the field of view. Therefore, smaller instruments and ingenious mounting devices are required. Because of their higher output and smaller size, quartz lamps (especially the open reflector types) will be used more often than they were in the studio. Inky-dinks and babies will be the most useful Fresnel lights on location. The main mounting devices will be compact, lightweight lamp stands. In addition, a temporary gridlike structure (such as a polecat) will permit mounting lights very close to the ceiling without using a floor stand that might otherwise be visible in the picture. This temporary grid could be of stronger construction for supporting larger instruments. Gator grips, Gaffer grips, and Mitee grips are useful in attaching lamps to doors, fixtures, furniture, etc. (See illustrations on page 126.)

The other space problem is that the close positioning of lights will create an uneven illumination and will be uncomfortable for the actors. Whenever space permits it is preferable to use a more powerful light from farther away in order to even out the light. This is not always possible. A very even illumination can be achieved by using bounced light. If a light is pointed at the wall or ceiling, the reflected illumination will be evenly distributed, resembling a daytime interior effect. In color photography this procedure may be inadvisable, as the color of the wall will change the color of the light being bounced from it. Therefore the most professional approach is to use parasols and reflective sheets (either pure-white or silver). Silver surfaces have the highest reflectance and do not change the color of the light. One of the cheapest and most easily available silver sheets is the so-called "space blanket" sold in many sporting-goods and surplus stores. Space blankets are not only highly efficient reflectors, but also protect the walls and ceilings from the hot lights. However, even with a space blanket the lamps should be positioned at least a few feet away from the reflecting surface.

When trying to create a night interior effect the cameraman uses only a little bit of bounced light for overall fill and depends more heavily on practicals and directional lights such as Fresnels and open reflector quartz lamps supporting the practicals.

After power and space limitations, the third major location problem is dealing with mixed color temperatures, most often daylight from the windows mixing with tungsten light from the lamps. Actually the best solution is to block out the window entirely, saving the difficulty of mixed light and eliminating continuity problems caused by changing sun or weather conditions. If the window cannot be avoided, it is possible to use a daylight emulsion (or a tungsten emulsion with a daylight conversion filter), in which case the artificial lights will need to be equipped with dichroic filters or blue gels to convert them to daylight color temperature. The more com-

4-76 Gaffer grip. (Courtesy of Berkey Colortran, Inc.)

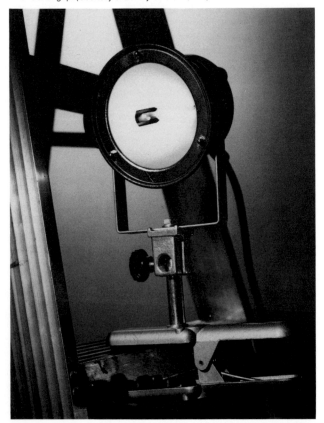

4-77 Mitee grip. (Courtesy of Berkey Colortran, Inc.)

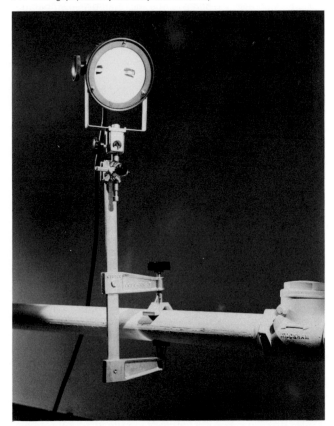

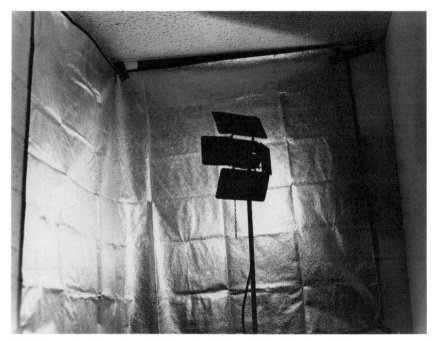

4-78 A "space blanket" used as a reflective surface for bouncing light. (Photo by author)

mon solution is to use a tungsten emulsion and cover the windows with a #85 window gel to conform the incoming daylight to the 3200° K balance of the film. For simply converting the color temperature, the self-sticking gel is most convenient. However, it is optically poor. When a landscape, etc. is visible through the window the higher-quality gel sheets should be used.

In any case, especially if the window is visible one may also have to use a neutral density window gel, reducing the outside light level to keep it within an acceptable brightness range with the interior illumination. Window gels are available that combine the neutral density filter with a #85. When using a neutral density window gel, the exterior might be visible, but one may lose the sharp shadow patterns cast by the sunlight coming directly through the window, falling on the set and objects in the scene. To recreate this sunlight at exactly the desired brightness, an arc or other powerful lamp could be placed outside, shining in through the window.

EXTERIOR LOCATION SHOOTING

When planning to shoot an exterior location scene, a reconnaissance trip is essential. On such occasions a magnetic compass should be on hand so that sunlight directions can be predicted for different times of day. The shooting order can then be planned according to the sun's movements. If you know in advance which side of the street (or whatever) will be in sun or shadow at a given time, you can plan the shooting accordingly.

During the actual shooting, the scenes should be blocked so that the shadows are always in correct continuity. For example, if the master shot is done in the morning and the closeups are not completed until late in the afternoon, the director should "cheat" the actors' positions so that shadow directions and backgrounds will match the master scene as closely as possible.

Another vital item to investigate before shooting outdoors is

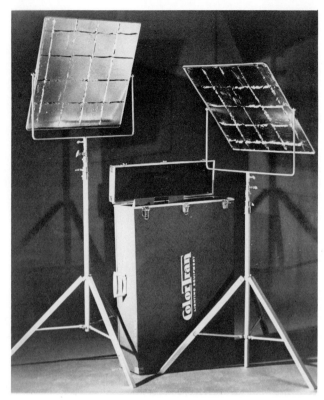

4-79 A reflector board kit. (Courtesy of Berkey Colortran, Inc.)

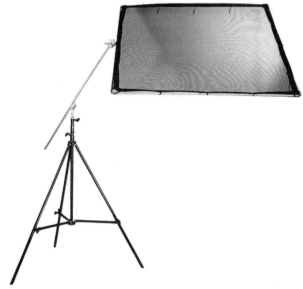

4-80 Butterfly scrim. (Courtesy of Mole-Richardson Co.)

the availability of power. This applies to reconnaissance of interior locations as well. How much power, and how far away are our primary questions. Secondly, we must note whether adapter plugs will be required. If the existing system employs fuses, we should note their sizes and arrange to have some spares on hand while shooting.

Exterior lighting is principally aimed at reducing the harsh contrast created by sunlight. When shooting in sunlight, the sun automatically becomes our key light. The sky and surrounding surfaces provide a certain amount of fill light, but rarely enough, especially for well-lit closeups. A 2:1 ratio of key plus fill to fill light is excellent for most daylight scenes. To the untrained eye this may appear to be too much. Nevertheless the result usually appears quite natural on the screen.

The simplest source of fill light is a silver reflector board. Reflectors come in different sizes with surfaces of different textures. They are usually silver but are also available with gold surfaces for imitating sunset light. Reflectors are usually mounted on stands and positioned to reflect the sunlight to the subject *from above eye level* so as to imitate sky light.

Positioning it from below will cause an unnatural and often unacceptable appearance. Reflectors should not be hand-held, because any movement during the take, caused by wind or the person holding it, may spoil the shot. It is best to have the reflector securely mounted to the stand with someone there to steady it in case of wind. This same person will have to reposition the reflector often to allow for the movement of the sun.

On windy days or in restricted locations, reflectors are sometime impractical. In such cases artificial light is often needed. The light will have to be intense in order to function as a fill light in the sun. An arc light is strong enough to supply outdoor fill light to a large area, but the expense of arranging an adequate power supply is often prohibitive. The modern solution is the use of lamp clusters such as the Mole-Richardson Molefays and Molepars or Colortran Mini-Brutes and Maxi-Brutes. On overcast days these lights are bright enough to raise the overall light level or even to imitate the sunlight over small areas.

Another method of reducing outdoor contrast is to diffuse the sunlight with butterfly scrims. Butterflies come in all densities, including solid black for complete shadow. Unfortunately, these devices are much affected by wind.

OUTDOOR LIGHTING FOR SPECIAL CONDITIONS

On an overcast day the light is very diffused and therefore may be excellent for shooting color film. We must remember, however, that the brightness range between the sky and the landscape will actually be *greater* on an overcast day than on a sunny day. A graduated neutral-density or even a cutout blue filter might be used to reduce the contrast and obtain a more pleasing picture.

Sometimes the weather conditions render a picture dull or flat. For example, scenes on white sand or snow have a great deal of soft shadowless illumination, created by the reflection from the surrounding white surfaces. Similarly, fog or mist will reduce contrast, especially when the subject is farther away. Such scenes may appear shadowless and dull. Depth can be increased by placing some dark object in the foreground.

Forests and flowing or static water often appear flat in long shots taken in midday sun. But if photographed when the sun is lower in the sky, they will appear much more alive. The best hours will depend on the season and the geographical location.

Sunrises and sunsets are difficult to expose. This rule of thumb seems to help. For sunsets, use a spot meter to read the sky right next to the sun (but not the sun itself) and expose it two stops less than this reading. For example, if the sky next to the sun was f/5.6 then the scene would be shot at f/11. When filming a sunrise, use the spot meter to read the glowing sky just next to the place the sun is about to appear and then underexpose three stops. For example, if the glowing sky reads f/5.6 just before the sun appears, then the sunrise should be exposed at f/16. It is also worth noting that sunsets are generally more beautiful than sunrises, and it is possible to film a sunset in reverse and use it for a sunrise. But care must be used to avoid betraying the trick. One Hollywood film crew needed a sun rising out of the ocean. They filmed a West Coast sunset in reverse. Audiences couldn't help but notice that all the breakers were going backward. When filming sunrises, especially, a reconnaissance trip is essential to determine exactly where the sun will appear.

SHOOTING NIGHT SCENES

A night effect is not achieved by simple underexposure. Most of the objects will be dark, but given objects will be correctly exposed and some points may in fact be quite bright. The night appearance is really achieved by creating many dark shadow areas in an otherwise correctly exposed scene. Therefore night is suggested by using a generally high contrast ratio with little or no fill light.

Night-for-Night

The most convincing night scenes are shot at night. As usual, the logic of the lighting will have to follow the practical light sources in the scene, such as street lights, campfires, or the moon. In addition, we must consider the audience's preconceived notions about the appearance of night light. Night light looks best if the key light sources come from the side or back and usually from a low angle, creating many long shadows. Night lights in reality are usually small sources, and therefore it is best to use hard lights so that the shadows will be appropriately sharp. There is also a popular notion that moonlight is pale blue, and therefore, when shooting color, pale-blue gels would be put over any sources supposedly coming from the moon. We can suggest depth by lighting selected separated areas, to obtain pools of light with shadow in between. Another technique, especially useful with buildings and city streets, is to wet down the area with water, obtaining high-contrast textures that reflect the lights. When shooting night-for-night scenes, the actors' costumes should be of lighter tones to separate them from the dark sets.

Day-for-Night

For the sake of expediency and greater visibility, night scenes can be shot during the day. The main objectives are to darken the sky and increase the contrast. The shadows can be increased by blocking the scene so that the sun comes from a three-quarter back position. Mornings and evenings are the best times because the low angle of the sun creates more and longer shadows. As contrast is essential to the night effect, it is best to shoot on a clear day with strong sunlight.

The night appearance will be achieved by the use of filters and a slight underexposure. When shooting black-and-white, filters can be used to deal with the number-one problem in day-for-night: the overbright sky. If the sky cannot be avoided, it can be darkened by using a red filter, like #23-A or #25. Because this also removes blue skylight filling in the shadows, it creates a high-contrast picture with overbright faces as well as rendering the sky black. A combination of a #23-A (red) with a #56 (green) will correct the flesh tones. Of course in order for a red filter to darken the sky the sky must be blue. When shooting toward the sun the sky may not be blue enough for the red filter to have effect. Here a graduated neutral density filter might be used.

The majority of cameramen underexpose black-and-white day-for-night by 1½ to 2 stops.

Black-and-white day-for-night can also be shot on infrared black-and-white film. This will give a very convincing appearance of moonlight in long shots and an adequately dark sky, but closeups are risky, as the infrared film may penetrate skin or clothing, showing blood veins, blemishes, and undergarments, and even bringing out a beard from below the skin's surface in spite of a close shave. For these reasons, infrared day-for-night should be limited to long shots. Labs are often unreliable in processing infrared film. When shooting color day-for-night, the sky will have to be darkened with either a graduated neutral density filter or a polarizer. To obtain the effect of blue moonlight, many cinematographers use a tungsten-balanced emulsion *without the #85 filter*. To reduce the bluishness it is often replaced by a #81EF alone or in combination with a #CC20G to improve the flesh tones. Or a Wratten #2C filter can also be used to remove the ultraviolet light, and make the picture slightly less blue. For an even warmer effect than with a #2C, a Wratten Aero-1 light-yellow filter could be used. One could also shoot the scene with correct color and have the lab introduce a blue cast later in printing. The latter technique allows for precise control of the amount of blue. Most cinematographers agree that color day-for-night scenes should be underexposed by 1½ to 2½ stops and later printed lighter. However, the lab can do many things to enhance a day-for-night effect, and one should work with the lab men, consulting them about the best filters and proper amount of underexposure.

Incidentally, for long shots the effect of a lighted window can be simulated by placing a reflector board in the window and adjusting it so that it reflects the sun directly toward the camera.

Dusk-for-Night

Perhaps the most difficult, yet visually most rewarding, night scenes are shot at dusk. During this very short period of twilight there is still enough light to see the shadowed details and the horizon, yet the lights from windows, etc., appear realistically bright. The blue light from the sky acts as a gentle fill light (just the right color).

Although long shots are fairly simple, the time element makes acting scenes difficult when shooting dusk-for-night. The twilight period is brief, and so the actors and crew must be well rehearsed. The lights for the foreground action should be properly filtered for color and equipped with sets of scrims to allow for quick light-intensity changes. First, set up any practical lamps, making them as bright as possible. Determine their brightness with a reflected light meter. Let us say they should be f/8 for the emulsion used. We want the practicals to be three stops brighter than the foreground action. Therefore if the practicals are f/8, the foreground action should be f/2.8 (three stops more exposure than the practicals). The scene is exposed at f/2.8. As the sky light fades, the artificial light will have to be increased to maintain the faces at f/2.8, and therefore we start with the lights scrimmed so that the light can easily be increased by removing the scrims. There will be three takes. The first will be taken when the sky is the same as the faces (in this case f/2.8). The second will be taken when the sky is one stop darker than the faces (f/2). The artificial lights are increased to compensate for the fading sky light so as to keep the faces at f/2.8. The third take comes when the sky is two stops darker than the foreground. One of these three takes should yield the proper result. Any closeups will have to be taken later with only artificial light. Dusk-for-night shooting has yielded some of the most beautiful "night" scenes ever on the screen.

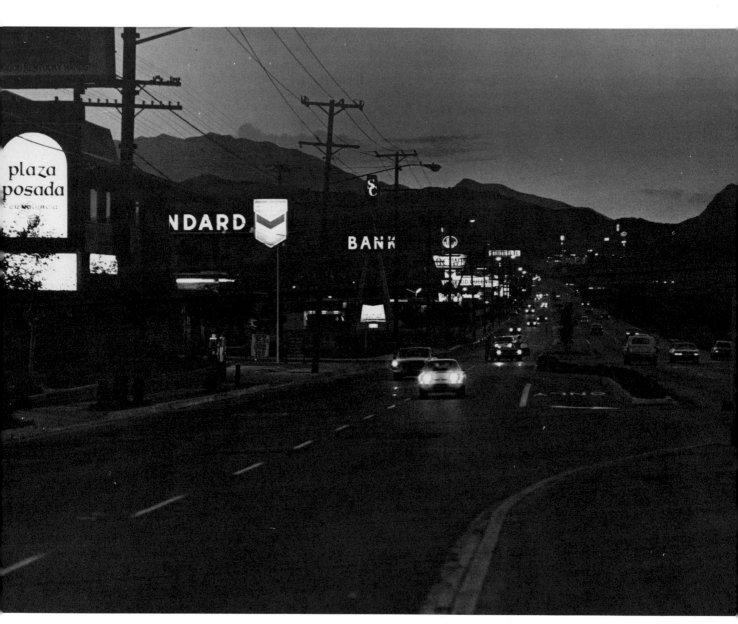

4-81 Dusk-for-night effect. (Photo by author)

CHAPTER 5
PICTURE QUALITY CONTROL

Up to now we have been analyzing the different aspects of cinematography as separately as possible. Yet the final aim is the total coordination of these many elements to create the image on the screen as it first existed in the film maker's mind.

The photographic quality of a film has a broad range of possibilities, from naturalistic to stylized to abstract. By manipulating the color, composition, image quality, and lighting we are able to evoke the atmosphere of a given period, place, or time or suggest a state of mind or impression. Cinematographers may imitate the paintings or etchings of a given period and culture or perhaps constantly introduce a visual effect that will complement the mood of the film. A classic example of such an application is John Huston's film *Moulin Rouge,* in which cinematographer Oswald Morris used the color schemes and compositions typically found in paintings by Toulouse Lautrec to create the atmosphere of the Parisian cabarets of the late nineteenth century.

Whatever artistic concept is employed, the cinematographer must be in full control of his technology in order to ensure success. This chapter will explore techniques of image quality control, using the basics introduced in previous chapters.

HARD AND SOFT

The most complex aspect of picture quality is the hardness or softness of the image. It is a function of contrast and definition. More contrast and higher definition create a harder picture. In black-and-white, high definition is *generally* one of the prime objectives, yet on rare occasions, soft diffused pictures are desired. Color reversal emulsions, on the other hand, tend to yield a hard appearance, and we are almost always trying to desaturate color, softening the picture, by lowering the contrast and sometimes the definition. In most cases, we do not want to loose definition and therefore first try to soften the color picture by reducing the contrast.

As discussed in the chapter on lighting, the amount of fill light and the direction of the key light will influence the contrast range. Contrast is reduced by using more fill or by key lighting from a more frontal position. In addition, contrast is affected by the tonality and reflectance of the subject. To reduce contrast, the colors of costumes, sets, and makeup should be made subtle, perhaps even a bit pastelled.

When shooting negative film, the contrast can be increased by pushing or decreased by underdeveloping. This does not equally apply to reversal films. Excessive pushing of any film will also cause changes in color rendition. The increase of grain is usually undesirable, and so pushing is not always advisable as a means of altering contrast.

There is more definition at the higher f-stops, because of the increased depth of field. This will result in higher contrast, leading to a harder picture. By using a neutral density filter to reduce the light, we can film at a wider f-stop. This will result in a shallower depth of field. The important areas can now be in sharp focus within the depth of field, while the rest of the scene is softened, which also lowers the contrast. Therefore a wider f-stop is more complimentary for closeups.

Backgrounds can be softened or reduced in intensity by suspending a lightweight gauze material between the actors and the background. Different densities and colors of gauze and different lighting patterns (back light, side light, etc.) will vary the effect.

Long telephoto lenses are inherently somewhat soft, not only because they have less depth of field than a normal or wide-angle lens, but also because the distance to the subject is usually greater, allowing for more atmospheric diffusion. Because the telephoto image seems brighter and less contrasty, it often appears to be overexposed. When extensive telephoto work is done, one should use a fairly contrasty emulsion or obtain higher contrast in the development or printing.

Filter placement may reduce definition, depending on the type and placement. A glass filter on the front of a lens (especially on a longer lens) will slightly soften the picture unless the filter is optically perfect. To avoid this one might use a gelatin filter behind the lens. When using wide-angle lenses the opposite is true. Any retro-focal lens (this includes wide-angle and zoom lenses) shorter than about 12mm may have its optics slightly upset by a filter placed behind the lens. This is especially true of wider angles, such as 9.5 to 95mm zoom lens at a wide-angle setting or any fixed-focus retro-focal lens, like the 5.7mm. Some extreme wide-angle lenses are so wide that it is difficult to mount a filter on the front, and so some are designed with a filter slot in the middle of the lens, where the optics will be less affected.

In color film, the most important function of lowering contrast (softening the picture) is to desaturate the color, which would otherwise be harsh. Old lenses that do not have an anti-halation coating scatter some light, slightly fogging the film, thus desaturating and pastelling the color. Some cinematographers spend much time shopping around for old lenses, but there is an easier way of achieving almost the same effect. Harrison low-contrast screens reduce contrast and desaturate color with practically no loss in definition. This also eliminates the problem of color rendition not matching between two old lenses. The best filter value to use will depend on the contrast in the subject. Harrison double fog filters from #1/8 to #2 could also be experimented with to find the best effect. Harrison regular fog filters might be used, but they will create halos around highlights and slightly reduce the definition.

Diffusion filters will reduce definition and are therefore not preferred for desaturating color.

Individual cameramen have developed desaturation techniques of their own, including the use of glass filters with textured or patterned surfaces. At times sets have been filled with real smoke or fog to obtain an effect.

A slight overexposure will wash out and desaturate color film, but this is a somewhat risky way of doing it.

Post-flashing or post-fogging is a laboratory technique used mainly for Ektachrome EF to reduce both contrast and color saturation.

COLOR RENDITION

With color, a vital concern is maintaining consistency and avoiding mismatches. The cinematographer must be wary of factors that might influence the color continuity. The color of the face in closeup should match its color in the long shot. Color variables could be introduced at several stages. When using many lenses, their color qualities should be the same. If the lenses are not color-balanced, they may create differences between shots that cannot be corrected in the lab. Even the most expensive lenses could cause this problem if they are not matched. Replacing several primary lenses with one zoom lens assures constant color rendition. On the whole, zoom lenses tend to be slightly warmer in their color rendition than primary lenses. These differences between lenses are *usually* so minimal that it is not worth correcting them with filters. If a slight correction is necessary, it is usually best left to the lab.

Different emulsions will have different contrast and color characteristics. That is why EF is usually post-fogged when it must be cut into Ektachrome Commercial. The latter has low contrast and the EF looks more like it after the post-fogging. But above all, try not to intercut these two film stocks within the same scene.

Different emulsion batches of the same type of film stock may also have some slight color differences. Because of this it is always reassuring to shoot an entire production on film from the same emulsion batch.

To keep track of any color variations it is somewhat academic but effective to shoot a color test chart at the beginning of each roll. This will help the lab technicians to correct the color when printing. Tests should be accompanied by a report indicating any unusual effects, such as a bluish color cast introduced as a night effect.

There are many situations when color variations are intentionally introduced by using lens filters and colored gels over the light sources. For example, when lighting for the candle effect, we might have used a light-yellow filter over the lamps creating the supposed candle light. In the same example, a pale-blue gel might have been used to color the window pattern supposedly created by moonlight. Another common effect is the use of a sepia filter over the lens to simulate the color of old etchings. When such effects are created, the lab should be notified so that the technicians do not try to correct the color rendition back to normal.

One can shoot through just about any optical medium, but for better uniformity and definition it is advisable to use gels. Camera filters are not available in all colors. However, gel manufacturers produce a wide variety of light-source gels that can be experimented with. However, bear in mind that their optical quality is well below that of camera filters.

In many cases filters are used to improve upon the natural colors of the scene without introducing a noticeable artificial cast of their own. If we wish the sky to appear in a deeper shade of blue, we might use a graduated blue or a graduated neutral density filter. When using tungsten emulsions a similar result will be achieved with a graduated #85 filter that leaves the top of the frame clear and therefore uncorrected, yielding a deep-blue sky.

Sometimes a gel is cut to match the horizon line and aligned in front of the lens so that it covers only a given area. For example, a blue gel might be cut so as to cover only the sky portion of the picture. When aligning a gel cut to match some object in the foreground, such as a wall or side of a building, the lens should be set at the f-stop to be used in the shot. This is to make sure that the depth of field does not bring the edge of the filter into focus enough to be noticeable.

We should qualify the generally accepted notion that the #85 filter corrects daylight to 3200° K. This is generally true in the United States, where the average daylight is of warm sunny quality. But when shooting on overcast days or in northern Europe where the daylight tends to be more blue, the #85B is the proper filter for converting the daylight to 3200° K.

Toward sunset the color temperature drops off, eventually becoming very reddish. As it decreases the #85 filter may be replaced by the #81EF, which gives half the value of the #85. At one point near sunset the color temperature may be close or equal to incandescent light (3200°K), and in such instances no filter is required. Any artificial lights should be corrected to match the changing daylight, using color gels.

When shooting with a daylight emulsion, the #85 filter is of course not needed. Therefore when faced with an overcast bluish day, a Wratten filter #1A (sky-light filter) could be used to "warm up" the colors.

Close cooperation with the lab is essential to achieving high quality color. For feature films the lab will often assign a technician to the production. He will view the rushes, write reports to the cameraman, and visit the studio to go over the rushes with the director of photography. This is rarely done for smaller independent productions or student films, yet for any film maker it is essential to establish a personal contact with at least one technician in the lab. Don't hesitate to use the lab as a source of advice on the emulsion you are using or on how to achieve the visual effects you need. In most cases the lab will be only too happy to help you in any way it can.

Occasionally a lab will balk at some unusual effect. Every lab cares about its reputation for maintaining high professional standards of picture quality control. Therefore you may have trouble convincing a lab to do unusual, out-of-the-ordinary work. The most common example is a large lab refusing to push film more than two stops because it doesn't want its name associated with the degraded quality of film that has been excessively pushed. In such instances the smaller, lesser-known labs prove more flexible.

All labs will do minor color corrections and density changes. Often the film is shot in anticipation of a complementing lab service. For example, one might slightly overexpose the original, expecting to print it down later to the proper density level. This particular technique can be used to desaturate the color.

ACCUMULATIVE ERRORS

At times a cinematographer may seem to give too much attention to minor and purely technical details. For example, some cinematographers insist that the f-stop be set by first opening it to the widest aperture and then closing it down until reaching exactly the correct setting. This is done just in case there is a little bit of "play" in it. It can be argued that the difference between doing it this way and turning to the desired setting from a smaller aperture would be very minimal. But the reasoning behind such meticulous care is that such minor errors accumulate. For example, say the f-stop calibrations are very slightly off. There might also be a very minor inaccuracy in the light meter. Two minor inaccuracies may reinforce each other and amount to a significant error. For this reason, cinematographers insist, whenever possible, on using the most consistent methods.

MAKEUP

Today the trend is toward using little, if any, makeup. However, it is usually helpful to use some. A light application will actually enhance the skin tones and make them appear more natural.

The skin normally secrets an oil, which will cause a very subtle glare. Without makeup, an actor may appear to have an overwhite face, which looks neither healthy nor natural. A light covering of basic makeup, usually pancake, will darken the skin and eliminate glare. On film the actor will appear quite natural.

In addition, the makeup can be used to improve the actor's physical appearance, covering blemishes and pimples that would otherwise distract the audience. Darkening the skin can give the actor a suntanned look. It also makes the eyes and teeth look brighter by comparison. Furthermore, for some reason, color films tend to introduce a greenish appearance into areas containing scattered black points, such as an actor's five-o'clock shadow. Makeup will prevent an actor's beard from appearing greenish. For a natural result, makeup should be applied at least an hour before shooting to allow the natural moisture of the skin to work through it. To eliminate glare, it is often repowdered just before each take.

Because color rendition varies between emulsion types, the makeup may also differ, depending on the emulsion used. (This applies to black-and-white as well.) The color rendition — or tonal rendition in the case of black-and-white — will also be influenced by the filters used. In establishing what shade or type of makeup looks best for a given character, it is often a good idea to shoot tests.

CHAPTER 6
SOUND RECORDING

Beginning film makers frequently underrate the importance of obtaining good original sound. They think that if the original recording is at least audible, it's good enough. They forget that the original recording will be re-recorded many times and put through many generations, each slightly deteriorating the quality before it reaches the screen. If the original recording was poor, the film sound track will suffer greatly. For this reason, the original recording should strive for excellence. Only the best professional equipment and techniques should be used if the final sound track is to be of high quality.

SYNCHRONOUS SOUND

There are two popular methods of maintaining synchronous sound: mechanically and electronically. The first, called "single-system," employs a single-perf film stock with a narrow magnetic track laminated to the edge of the film. Many cameras can be easily adapted to single-system sound by inserting a modular recording head into the film compartment. The sound signal from the microphone goes through a portable control unit and then into the camera, where it is recorded onto the magnetic stripe on the film. Magnetic sound

is usually recorded 28 frames ahead of the picture, but this varies between designs. After the film is processed, the original can be viewed (with sound) on a magnetic projector. When time permits, the sound can be transferred from the original mag stripe to a separate piece of magnetic film for editing and mixing. This allows the editor freedom in arranging the sound. If the sound is not transferred, then any time a cut is made, the sound from the first 28 frames will be lost because it is left on the other side of the cut. If the sound is instead on a separate piece of film, this cutting problem is avoided. Single-system sound is mainly used by news cameramen who must quickly obtain sound footage, ready to air right away.

"Double-system" sound offers higher quality and greater flexibility. It electronically interlocks the camera with a tape recorder. The two are coordinated by means of a 60-Hertz sync tone. "Hertz" means cycles per second. 60 Hertz applies to the United States, where the power is 60 cycles per second. In Europe, where the power is 50 cycles per second, the sync tone is also 50. Some countries use 25 and some use 100. The sync "pulse" must match (in cycles per second) the power used to transfer the sound from the magnetic tape to magnetic film.

A sync tone oscillator is built into the camera. It generates a

60-Hertz tone when the camera is running at exactly 24 frames per second. (In Europe the combination is usually 50 Hertz and either 24 or 25 fps. European television stations broadcast film at 25 fps, as this speed is more compatible with the 50-Hertz power.) While the camera is running this sync tone will change as the speed of the camera varies. The sync tone signal and the dialog are recorded onto the ¼-inch magnetic tape on separate tracks of the tape. The recorded sync tone expresses the net effect of all the variables: change of camera speed, tape-recorder speed, tape stretch, tape slippage, etc. When the sound track is then transferred to 16mm magnetic film, the sync tone recorded on the tape will control the speed of the playback tape recorder to obtain a sound track that will exactly match the picture.

The common method of obtaining double-system sound has been to connect the sync tone device in the camera with a cable running to the ¼-inch tape recorder. A more advanced method utilizes highly accurate crystal controls. With crystal sync the camera speed is held constant at exactly 24 fps by one crystal control while another regulates the sync tone device, which in this case is in the tape recorder. The advantage of crystal sync is that because of the high accuracy of the crystal controls there is no need for the cable connecting the camera to the recorder.

SLATE AND BLOOP

Having established synchronous speeds, we still must provide sync marks on both picture and sound so that the two can be matched up. This is traditionally achieved through that well-known symbol of film making, the clapper board, or slate. The scene and take numbers are written on the slate *and* voiced by the assistant, who then claps the board hinged to the slate. This provides identification marks on both the sound track and the film, telling which scene and take is being shot. Later, the "clap" on the track is aligned with the frame on which the slate closes and the film is in sync.

In situations where the use of a clapper board at the beginning of a shot would disturb the subject (such as when filming wildlife or children or in cinema verite) a "tail slate" is used. At the end of the take the camera and the recorder are left running and the assistant "slates" the take as before. The only difference is that the clapper board is held upside down to inform the editor that it is a tail slate. The assistant

should say "tail slate" and then give the scene and take numbers.

Many modern cameras using the sync tone system are equipped with a "blooping" device. This device automatically flashes a light inside the camera, thus fogging a few frames of film. Meanwhile, it triggers a "bloop tone" that is recorded onto the sound track. Later the two can be synced up by aligning the fogged frames with the bloop sound on the track. When the camera is *connected* to the recorder, the bloop is controlled through the cable. However, in cordless crystal-sync operation, either a clapper board must be used or the camera can be equipped with a small radio transmitter that activates the bloop in the recorder. In any of these cases, each take must still be identified — both picture and sound — to tell the editor which shot goes with which sound take.

RECORDERS

There are only a few excellent ¼-inch tape recorders for sync-sound operation. The industry's favorite is the Nagra. Other fully professional recorders include the Arrivox-Tandberg, the Stellavox, and the Perfectone. Low-budget producers may prefer the less expensive Uher 4000 adapted for sync sound recording.

The current trend toward greater portability has led to the development of the miniaturized Nagra SN, which uses ⅛-inch tape and is small enough to be hidden in an actor's pocket. (See illustration on page 138.)

MICROPHONES

Microphones are classified two ways, first by structure and second by reception pattern. These are the more common structures:

Dynamic microphones are the most durable type. Because they employ a strong magnet, it is advisable to keep them away from magnetic tapes and recorders.

Condenser microphones (also called electrostatic or capacitor mics) require power from either a mic battery or the recorder, in order to operate. They are somewhat more fragile and generally more expensive than most dynamic mics. Many sound men recommend them as the highest-quality design available.

Crystal or *ceramic* mics are often used with mag-stripe

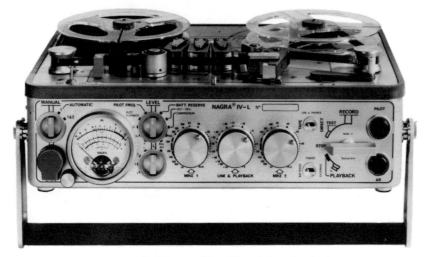

6-1 Nagra IV-L 1/4-inch tape recorder. (Courtesy of Nagra Magnetic Recorders, Inc.)

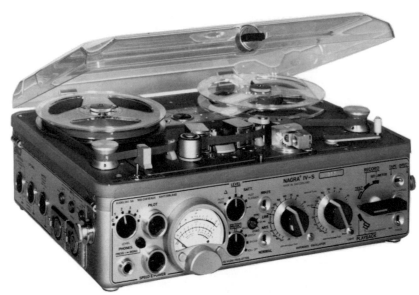

6-2 Nagra IV-S 1/4-inch tape recorder. (Courtesy of Nagra Magnetic Recorders, Inc.)

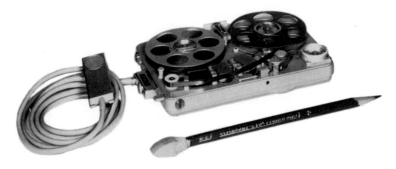

6-3 Nagra SN 1/8-inch tape recorder. (Courtesy of Nagra Magnetic Recorders, Inc.)

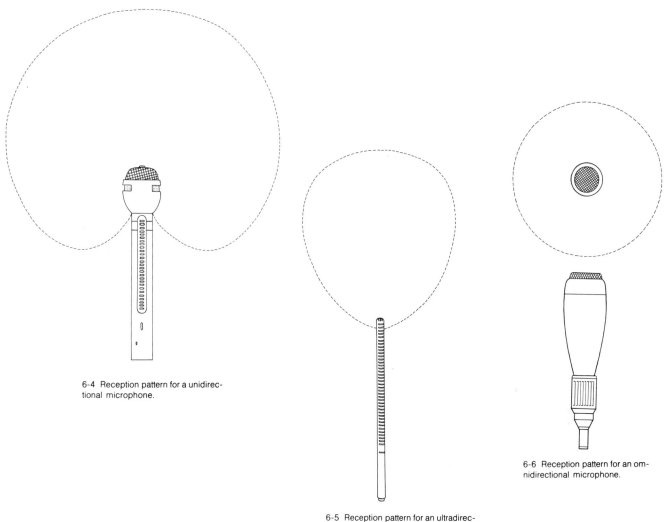

6-4 Reception pattern for a unidirectional microphone.

6-5 Reception pattern for an ultradirectional microphone.

6-6 Reception pattern for an omnidirectional microphone.

projectors for adding commentary. They are small in size but do not pick up extremely high or low frequencies and are therefore rarely used for professional sound shooting. Further, their inherent electrical characteristics make them incompatible with professional motion-picture recorders unless special adapters are used.

Ribbon mics are also rarely used for motion-picture work. Outdoors they are affected by wind or shaking, and their bidirectional characteristic makes them awkward in the studio.

Classifications by reception pattern are as follows:

Unidirectional mics are those most often used in films. They favor sound sources coming from a particular direction. The levels fall off away from the axis, thus eliminating unwanted sounds. As a sound source moves away from the axis the high frequencies are the first to vanish.

Ultradirectional or *"shotgun"* mics have a very important application in film work. They are bigger than unidirectional mics and highly directional, making them more selective in their reception. The long narrow reception pattern makes them especially suitable for outdoor shooting, where there is usually more background noise to be avoided.

Omnidirectional mics (sometimes called "nondirectional") have a wide angle of acceptance, picking up especially low frequencies from every direction. They are fine for recording background sound effects and for group discussions where the mic must remain stationary.

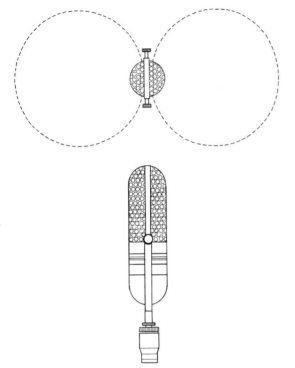

6-7 Reception pattern for a bidirectional microphone.

Lavalier or chest microphones are designed for one purpose only; picking up a speaking voice. Lavaliers should be hung around the actor's neck or in some other way held against the chest. Lavaliers are designed to favor high frequencies in order to compensate for the overabundance of low frequencies originating in this area. For this reason they should always be placed against the chest. Lavaliers eliminate the need for a sound boom and keep the mouth-to-mic distance constant. The localized pickup tends to eliminate ambiant (surrounding) noise. Therefore lavaliers can sometimes be used in conjunction with a noisy camera. Unfortunately, they may be susceptible to "cable noise," caused by the cable rubbing against the actor's clothing or the floor.

Bi-directional mics are rarely used in film because of their awkward pickup pattern.

Microphone designs differ in their sturdiness, and therefore mics will have to be selected after considering the physical demands of the location. The dynamic mic is quite strong and will withstand a considerable amount of mistreatment, but all other designs are sensitive to shock. All mics should be kept in padded cases for protection. All microphones (including the dynamic) will suffer when exposed to water, and so when filming rain or snow sequences in which the mic might get wet, a rain screen should be used. Microphones and amplifiers can also be easily damaged by loud noises such as gunshots or explosions. Only specially designed equipment should be used around high-intensity noises.

OTHER EQUIPMENT

High-quality earphones are necessary for the sound man to evaluate the recording characteristics and sound quality. The earphones must be compatible with the recorder in use.

Because the best microphone position is generally above and in front of the speaker, there is usually a need for some sort of a boom. Depending on the production needs and budget, the boom could be anything from a broomstick to a sophisticated studio boom (such as a Fisher or Mole-Richardson). In any case, the microphone must be mounted so that it does not directly touch any hard surface. It can be suspended by rubber holders, or, *in emergencies only,* taped directly to the pole with a piece of foam rubber in between.

For outdoor filming, a wind screen is a necessity. This usually consists of a foam-rubber cover that slips over the microphone to protect it from direct contact with the wind. It is often used indoors as well on the theory that it certainly doesn't hurt.

The mic and sync cables are sensitive and require considerable attention and care. There is a set way of coiling them to avoid the constant twisting of the delicate fibers. Kinks must never be pulled out. They should always be carefully untwisted.

Opposite:
6-8 The proper method of coiling sound cables. A: The first loop is normal. B & C: The second loop is given an inside twist. D: The third loop is normal. And so on, alternating a twisted loop with a normal loop.

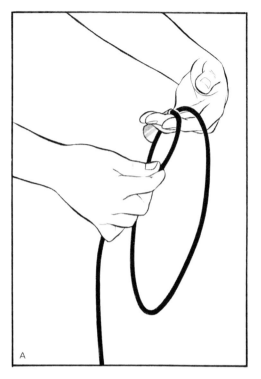

A

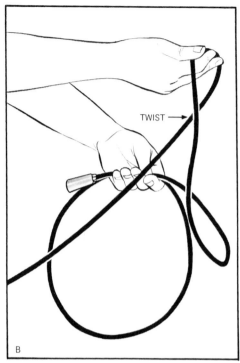

TWIST →

B

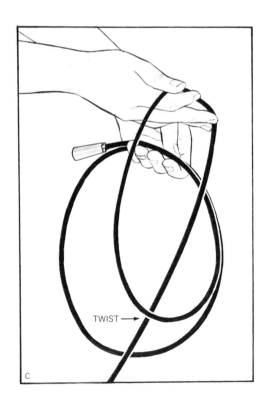

TWIST →

C

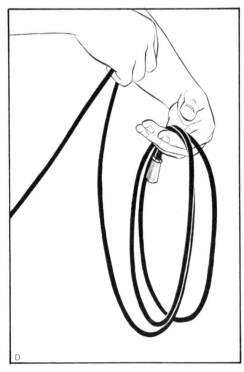

D

141

MAINTENANCE OF SOUND EQUIPMENT

Like the camera, the tape recorder must be checked before use. The most important parts to be examined are the magnetic head, the transport mechanism, the bias oscillator, the amplifiers, and the switch and cable connectors.

The most common problem is the magnetizing of the heads. The recording and playback heads should be demagnetized regularly. This must *never* be done by using the bulk degausser for tapes. A small head demagnetizer should be used on a regular basis, such as after every ten hours of use or after the head has come within the field of any magnetic material, such as a dynamic microphone, a powerful electric motor, or metal tools of any kind, such as screwdrivers, wrenches, etc.

Dirt is frequently left on the head by the passing tape. It should be removed, using a liquid head cleaner. Rubbing alcohol is not recommended, because it has additional ingredients designed to please the skin but not recording heads. When cleaning, *never* scrape the head with any hard instrument.

Care must be taken not to jar the head or it may become misaligned. If the head is out of alignment the high frequencies will be the first to disappear. Never attempt to realign the head yourself unless you have had experience doing it before.

Recorder troubles often manifest themselves on the sound track. A wow or flutter effect is usually caused by a faulty transport mechanism advancing the tape at an uneven speed. Hums and hisses can be caused by a faulty amplifier but could also have their source in some nearby electrical disturbance. Such things as current in a close-by power line, or even a radio station, can occasionally be picked up by the mic cables, acting as antennas. They might also be received through the tape recorder's AC power supply. When filming at a campus, a carrier-current radio station can be a real headache. For these reasons, it is always a good idea to have batteries on hand when depending on AC power to run the recorder. If a hum is present, the first thing to do is move all the mic cables around. If they are picking up the hum, their movement may eliminate it. It should always be kept in mind that the hum might be acoustical, generated by some audible source nearby. Fluorescent lights are notorious for this, and microphones must be kept clear of them. Better still, the fluorescent lights should be turned off. Refrigerators are another common source of room noise. Because we are used

to them they are frequently not noticed until the recording is played back. Crackling noises are usually due to faulty connections. If the tape recorder is left in the hot sun it may overheat, causing it to hum or in some other way operate improperly. Therefore, whenever filming in extremely hot conditions, try to keep the recording equipment cool.

CARE OF TAPE

Equally important to the maintenance of the recorder is the care of the tape. Tapes should be stored away from strong magnetic fields (including dynamic microphones). Neither should they be exposed to extremes of temperature and humidity. Room temperature and a humidity of about 30 to 70 percent is acceptable.

When reels of recorded tape have been stored and not played for six months or longer, they should be rewound before playing back.

For professional recordings, use only *new* (never used) high-quality tapes. Before recording, some sound men degauss (bulk erase) all their tapes even though new, just in case they were partly magnetized during storage or transport.

Whenever traveling with magnetically recorded materials, try to carry them with you, especially when traveling by air. If the materials must travel in the baggage compartment, make sure an airline official does not X-ray them or subject them to strong magnetic fields that might erase or damage the recording. Whenever traveling with or mailing tapes, indicate the contents on the outside of the package and make sure it can easily be opened for inspection.

OPERATION OF TAPE RECORDERS

Some recorders have a choice of tape speeds. The standard in the film industry is 7½ ips (inches per second) for dialog. At this speed a 5-inch reel — which is the most commonly used size — runs for about 16 minutes, which comfortably matches the 400-foot magazine of 16mm film usually used with self-blimped sound cameras.

When threading up a new reel of tape, the first thing to do is to put a voice identification at the beginning of the tape. Include the following: production title, production number, recordist, tape roll number, and date. This same information will also appear on the sound report sheet and on the tape box, in addition to the recorder number, the type of tape, and the speed at which the tape was recorded. After the voice identification, a reference tone is recorded onto the tape for about ten seconds. This reference-tone oscillator is built into many professional film tape recorders. The tone is used by the sound technicians in setting the volume for the transfer.

Depending on the job at hand, we can set the volume control at either automatic or manual. Professional sound men agree that using the manual volume control yields a definitely superior recording. The automatic setting records a less distinct sound with a higher level of background noise. However, there are often situations, such as in cinema vérité, where there is no time to worry about sudden volume changes. In these trying situations the sound quality is sacrificed in favor of flexibility and the automatic setting is used.

When using the manual control, volumes are set ahead of time during a rehearsal. The most serious distortions in sound recording are caused by overloading, which in practical terms means that the volume setting is too high for the subject and the VU (volume-unit) needle is constantly exceeding its optimal range. Such recordings sound harsh. Manual volume levels are set in conjunction with placing the microphone.

BASIC ACOUSTICS AND MICROPHONE PLACEMENT

Generally, we try to place the microphone as close to the subject as possible, depending on the design of the mic. If the microphone is farther away, the recording level has to be set higher, and a higher recording volume raises the background noise. To avoid this, try to place the mic closer so that a lower volume level can be used. Perhaps have the actor speak up.

Generally, the best microphone placement for voice recording is slightly above and in front of the performer's face, within arm's reach. The mic should usually be pointed directly toward the actor's mouth. One exception might be in the case of an actor or actress with a sibilant voice, which can be favorably modified by pointing the microphone slightly to one side, losing the high frequencies. A sound boom is used to hold the microphone just out of the frame, in proper position. If the actor turns or another person starts speaking, the mic must be rotated to keep it pointing directly into the speaker's mouth. Otherwise there will be a considerable change in voice quality. Using one mic, turned back and forth between

speakers, may at first seem difficult, yet it is in practice not that hard. It yields considerably better sound quality than using a stationary bi-directional mic. It is also easier than using *two* microphones, one for each actor, although two microphones are sometimes used, but usually only in cases where the actors are separated by distance or set walls or if for some other reason it is difficult to use one mic turned alternately between them. In documentary work two or more lavalier mics are often used simultaneously.

As the study of acoustics is an enormous field, we will confine our discussion of it to only a few practical hints. There are different microphone designs for speech and music, although many are excellent for both. The demands of music require a frequency response broad enough to record faithfully the wide range of instruments without overloading. Condenser mics are excellent for this purpose.

The shape of the room and the shapes and textures of the furnishings will influence the room's acoustical quality. A large room with hard smooth surfaces such as concrete walls, glass, linoleum floors, etc. will cause the sound waves to reverberate for a long time, creating a "boomy" or "echo-y" atmosphere. With longer reverberation times, speech or music becomes blurred as successive sounds overlap. In the studio, sound-absorbing surfaces can be used to deaden the sound to the proper degree. The sound shouldn't be overdeadened or it may become dull. The ideal reverberation time differs from subject to subject.

On location, the sound conditions are generally too live (boomy). The best temporary treatment is the use of blankets and rugs. Spread them on the floor under the microphone, hang them *a few inches from* each wall, and drape them over any hard surfaces such as table tops. Another thing to avoid is a pair of parallel surfaces on either side of the microphone. Whenever possible, the mic should be positioned so that its axis runs diagonally through the room. Otherwise, a standing-wave effect may occur — the sound waves bounce from side to side, sometimes canceling, sometimes complementing each other.

When filming an announcer or recording narration, a few simple steps should be followed: If the mic is on a table, cover the table with a blanket. If the mic is on a stand or hand-held, the announcer must not cover it with his script or the high frequencies will be lost. The announcer should try to keep his mouth at a constant distance from the mic and not turn away, such as to glance down at his notes. Similarly, if the mic is not directly in front of his mouth he must not turn his head suddenly *toward* it or the unexpected rise in volume may cause distortion.

SOUND PERSPECTIVE AND PRESENCE

The sound and picture perspectives should match. For realism, if an actor appears far away in the picture, he must not sound as though he were close. Similarly, the sound quality must fit the location. For example, a huge cathedral should have a rather live, "echo-y" sound. It should not have the relatively dull presence of a carpeted living room. These rules, like any others, are often broken for creative reasons.

To preserve the same atmosphere throughout an entire scene the sound man will record a length of "room tone" to be used on the sound track over any silent footage, or to back up dialog replaced after shooting. Even if silent footage is not to be used, the room tone should be recorded, as it is often invaluable to the sound-editing and mixing technicians who may use it, for example, to fill in for some unwanted noise occurring between lines. The room tone should always be recorded for every location, with actors, props, equipment, etc., all exactly the same as during the scene.

Other "presence" tracks may also be recorded, such as street sounds that will later supposedly be coming from a set window, etc.

CAMERA NOISE

The sound man is frequently fighting a noisy camera. Many self-blimped cameras are not quiet enough for closeup work, especially in confined areas. There are also nonblimped cameras available with sync pulse. Padded covers, called "barneys," are available for these cameras, and they reduce the sound somewhat but should never be expected to render these cameras as perfectly quietly as, say, a well-maintained Arri BL. There is *no way of filtering out camera noise* during mixing. Therefore when using a noisy camera, steps should be taken to reduce the noise while shooting. Noise can be decreased by using a blimp, shooting through a window, or, when filming outdoors, using a longer lens and shooting from farther away. The sound man can also help to avoid camera noise by using a unidirectional or a shotgun mic, or perhaps a localized mic such as a lavalier.

DIALOG REPLACEMENT

Often because of poor recording conditions, such as airplanes, traffic noise, interferences, or partial equipment failure, it is impossible to get a high-quality track on location. In such cases the producer may save time by going ahead with the shooting, recording an unusable track. This "guide track" will be recorded in sync and will later be used in a mixing-and-dubbing theater when those lines of dialog are "dubbed" by the actors. The guide track is played with the picture while the actor watches and listens to recall his exact delivery. The film is run again and the actor delivers his line in sync with the picture. This process is expensive, and so everyone hopes all will go well on location and dialog replacement will not be necessary.

CHAPTER 7
CUTTING AND LAB WORK

After the film is shot and taken out of the camera it does a lot of traveling, first to the lab, and then to the cutter or his assistant. Along the way to the release print there are many different processes, procedures, and optional routes available. To take best advantage of them, the competent cutter is thoroughly familiar with laboratory services and capabilities. Because the technical cutting and lab work must be so coordinated, the two subjects are treated here in the same chapter.

SUBMITTING MATERIALS TO THE LAB

Labs require information sheets with *all* submitted materials. The information must be as explicit as possible. Time and care must be taken to fill out the form completely to ensure that the material receives *exactly* the work intended for it. The information should usually include:

Name of the company or individual
Purchase-order number
Account number at the lab
Production title
Production number
Roll number
Type of film being submitted
The job to be done:
1. If the raw footage is to be post-flashed, indicate this *first* in a very visible manner.
2. If test footage was shot on this roll, indicate where and how much.
3. Indicate whether it is to be developed. When submitting *already developed* material, indicate it to avoid a second development.
4. If the film is to be pushed in processing, give the ASA index at which it was exposed.
5. If it is to be printed (as with dailies), state whether the print is to be:
   A. Black-and-white or color
   B. One light or corrected
   C. Single or double perf
   D. Whenever possible, insist that the original edge numbers be printed through.
   Usually a "Negative Report Sheet" is also submitted, stating which takes are to be printed and giving their location by footage.

Indication of any suspected breaks or sprocket damage

Instructions on where to send the print
(Perhaps it is to be held for a pick up. Also indicate whether the original is to be held in the lab vault or returned.)

Mark whether the print is to be put on a core or a reel with can or case

Finally, if you are working with one particular lab technician who is familiar with you and your project, send the order to his attention. This is a lot of information, but each item is vital to the fast and efficient execution of the work.

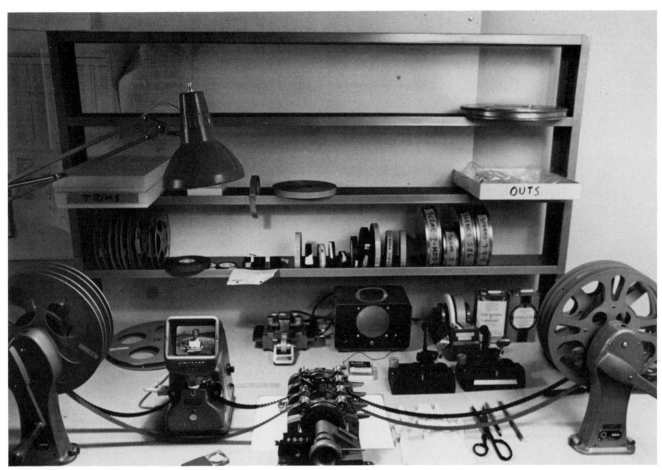

7-1 An editing table with basic equipment. (Photo by author)

EDITING-ROOM EQUIPMENT

The most basic editing equipment consists of rewind arms, reels, synchronizer, sound reader, viewer, a tape splicer, and an editing table with a light well. Use plastic reels for sound.

When storing film, to economize on reels, the film is wound onto a plastic core that uses a "split reel," which comes apart, allowing the core to be seated in the center. Another indispen-sable piece of equipment is the film bin, where the footage being worked on can be separated and each shot convenient-ly hung on a separate peg. Film bins can easily be home-made.

It is not a recommended practice, but if necessary an action viewer may be used for very careful viewing of originals. It must not be permitted to scratch the film. The Zeiss Ikon Moviscop is one of the safest viewers available.

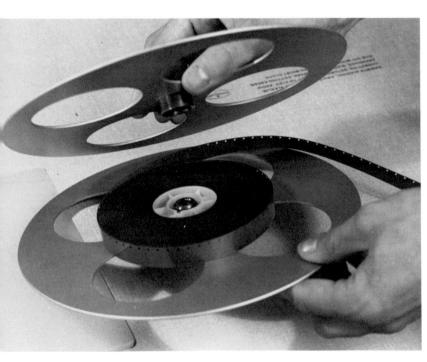

7-2 Split reel. (Photo by author)

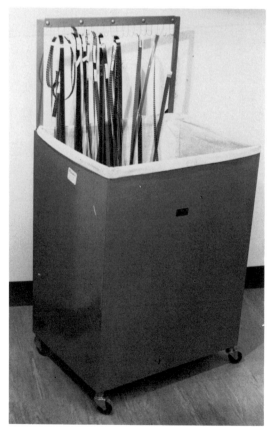

7-3 Film Bin. (Photo by author)

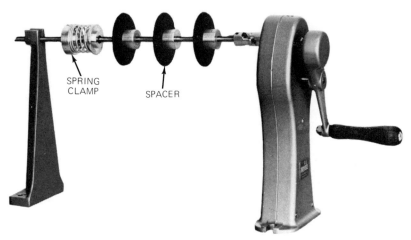

SPRING
CLAMP

SPACER

7-4 Moviola rewind with spring clamp and spacers to hold four reels in position. (Courtesy of Magnasync/Moviola Corp.)

7-5 Parliament Guillotine tape splicer. (Photo by author)

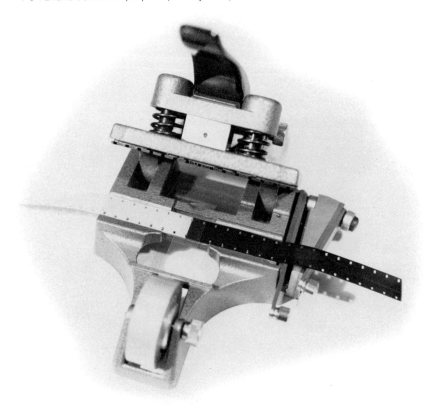

The synchronizer and rewinds should be of the four-gang type (capable of running up to four rolls of film in sync at once). All reels must have centers of equal size, in order to keep a constant tension on all rolls when winding two or more strips through the synchronizer at once.

Tape splicers are always used for editing the work print and sound. Unlike cement splices, tape splices can easily be taken apart without losing a frame. This allows the editor to make a mistake or change his mind. He may intercut the film in many ways before finding the version he likes best. There are two basic types of professional tape splicers. The Parliament Guillotine splicer uses clear, very thin tape without sprocket holes. The splicer punches the holes after the tape is applied. The second type (such as the Revisquick Tapesplicer) uses sprocketed tapes to provide a cleaner splice. Both types are available in either straight-cut or diagonal-cut models, straight for picture and diagonal for sound cutting. Splicing tape is applied to both sides of the film to facilitate movement through projectors and editing machines. For sound, it is applied only to the base side. Film with tape splices will not be accepted for printing by the lab, as the tape will not only show on the print but also possibly jam or clog in the printer.

For splicing the original, cement splicers are used. They

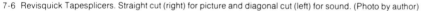

7-6 Revisquick Tapesplicers. Straight cut (right) for picture and diagonal cut (left) for sound. (Photo by author)

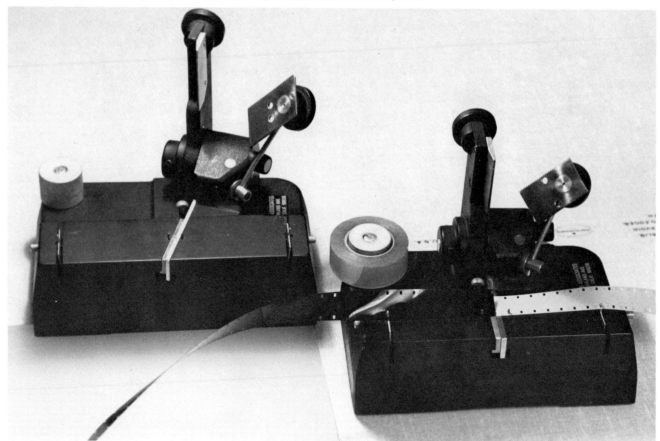

are usually "hot splicers" that warm the cement as it dries, producing a fast strong join. A small scraper is provided to remove the emulsion from one of the pieces of film so that the base of one piece can be glued directly to the base of the other without the emulsion in between. The fastest and best hot splicers are foot-operated. They are usually too large and expensive for individuals or small organizations, but the laboratories often use them. When operated by a professional, these large machines make excellent splices. For this reason many film makers allow the lab do the final splicing of the original.

Hot splicers can be either "positive" or "negative," depending on the width of the overlap. The positive type is used mainly for repair jobs on release prints, as it has a wide 1/16-inch overlap. The negative type has a narrower 1/32-inch overlap and is the kind used for splicing original.

For serious film making this equipment must be supplemented with an editing machine. There are many designs, all of which fall into two categories: vertical and horizontal. The Moviola is the best-known brand of vertical machine, and other machines are often called moviolas. It can be equipped with extra sound or picture heads. The horizontal editing machines were developed in Europe, where they have been used extensively for many years. Recently, this type is gaining popularity in the United States. Apart from the imported designs, moviola manufacturers are also making their own version. The advantages of the horizontal design include a large bright screen and quiet operation. Some models have facilities to project the picture onto an even larger screen.

Entire editing rooms, including equipment, can be rented from some laboratories, studios, etc. When reserving such a place, it is wise to make certain the room is equipped with everything that will be needed and that the facilities are clean and in good repair.

Apart from editing equipment there are many small items that are needed: grease pencils (usually red and yellow), felt pens, scribes, spools, cores, a can of cement and dispensing bottle, empty film cans and blank labels, 1/4-inch masking tape, log books and paper, rubber bands, white gloves, tissue paper, a demagnetized film punch and scissors, a demagnetizer, white leader, black leader, academy leader, and "fill" leader for the sound track, which could be of any color.

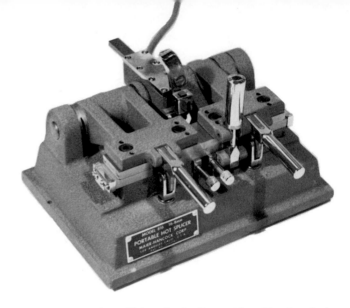

7-7 Maier-Hancock portable hot splicer for 16mm and 8mm. (Photo by author)

7-8 Moviola vertical editing machine with picture (right) and sound (left) heads. (Courtesy of Magnasync/Moviola Corp.)

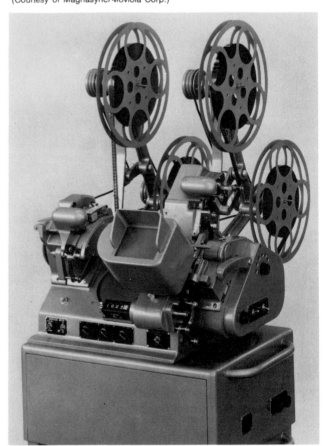

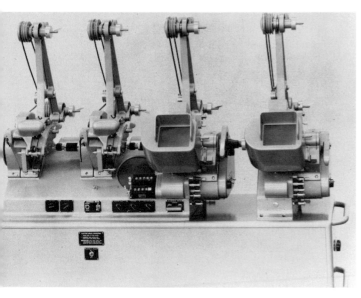

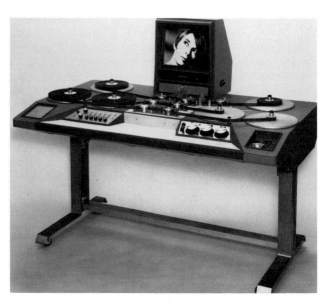

7-9 Multiple-head vertical Moviola with two sound and two picture heads. (Courtesy of Magnasync/Moviola Corp.)

7-10 Moviola Console Editor ("Flat Bed"), horizontal editing table with one composite sound/picture and two sound heads. (Courtesy of Magnasync/Moviola Corp.)

7-11 Steenbeck ST 6000 16/35mm Six Plate (one composite sound/picture, two sound heads) horizontal editing table. (Courtesy of General Enterprises, Inc.)

7-12 KEM Universal, including eight plates, which can be used for 3 picture/1 sound track, 2 picture/2 sound tracks, or 1 picture/3 sound tracks. Equipped with composite sound/picture capability. (Courtesy of KEM Hollywood, Inc.)

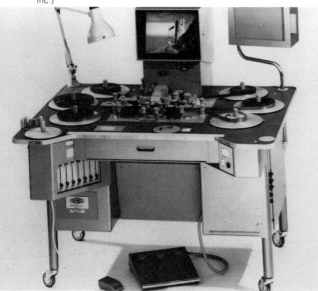

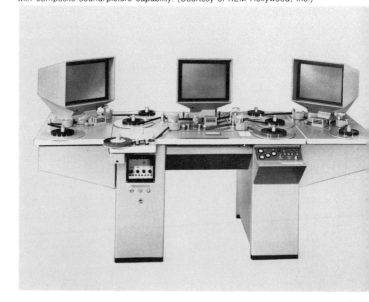

DAILIES

The camera original is very sensitive to scratches. *Under no circumstances should the original be projected.* Scratches in the emulsion are impossible to remove. Any film maker projecting his originals, looking at them on a viewer, or in any way risking scratches can expect to pick up irreparable damage.

To protect the original, the lab makes a print called "dailies" or "rushes" that is screened by the director and the producer along with the cinematographer. This daily print is later given to the editor, who edits it together to make the "work print." When the work print is completed, the delicate original is carefully cut to match it. To facilitate this operation, the edge numbers (sometimes called "key" numbers) printed every half foot on the original must be printed through onto the dailies. If the negative cutter does not like working with the small edge numbers (they are sometimes difficult to see) or if the film does not have edge numbers, as in the case of Kodachrome II, matching ink edge numbers should be printed onto both the original and the dailies.

Dailies can be either "one-light" or "timed." Cameramen prefer one-light dailies. In this case, all the footage is printed at the middle of the printer light scale so that the cameraman can see exactly how he exposed the original. For timed dailies, the lab corrects the density in each shot, making the dailies look better but preventing the cameraman from evaluating the original exposure. Timed daily prints should only be ordered when, as in some amateur productions, the film makers do not plan to get release prints and the dailies will be the final product.

When shooting color film one can save money by ordering black-and-white dailies.

Dailies can also be printed on Eastman Direct MP, auto-positive (also called direct positive film). This is a unique black-and-white film stock that develops a positive image in only one development. It has a very high resolution but lacks uniformity, and therefore it is used only as an inexpensive stock for making dailies or work prints from reversal emulsions.

When delivering dailies, some labs automatically keep the original filed in their vault until otherwise instructed. When picking up or receiving the originals from the lab, they should immediately be checked to make sure they were all returned. Occasionally the lab will misplace a roll. The chances of finding it are poor if the loss is not reported immediately.

After making sure that all the original has been returned, it should be taken out of the lab's cardboard boxes and put into metal cans and labeled with the roll numbers and edge-coding numbers.

SYNCING UP DAILIES

After receiving the rushes from the lab and the magnetic film from the transfer service, the sound takes are "synced up." This is usually done on a synchronizer with magnetic sound head, but can more easily be done on an editing machine with picture and sound heads, such as a moviola. The bloop or clap on the sound track is located and marked. Then, on the picture, the place where the film was flashed or the clapper board closed is located and marked. Then the picture and sound are locked into the synchronizer. In the case of the slate, they should be placed opposite each other. With blooping systems the coordination varies and the literature should be consulted. For example, one system starts the bloop on the last fully flashed (clear) frame. At any rate, the picture and sound are now locked into the synchronizer and should be in sync. After winding ahead to the next take, it is frequently found that because the tape recorder is usually started before and stopped after the camera, there will be more magnetic film than picture film. This excess of sound film will be removed making sure that the identification of the next sound take, before the clap, is left intact. Whenever editing picture and sound, professional editors do all their splicing on the *left* side of the synchronizer. In this way, as the film is wound from left to right, through the synchronizer, the editor knows that everything on the *right* of the synchronizer (the finished side) will always be in sync and he has only the left side to worry about.

After syncing up, one should order the lab to print corresponding ink edge numbers on both the picture and magnetic film. This is because when the intercutting starts, the slated frames will be removed. The corresponding numbers printed every foot along the edge of the picture and sound track are a convenient method of maintaining sync.

LIBRARY FOOTAGE

There are stock-footage libraries that offer shots of various locations and events. A film maker can sometimes buy stock footage cheaply when it would be too expensive or even impossible, as in the case of historical footage, to shoot it himself. The price involves the printing cost, plus royalties based on the amount of footage used in the final film. One disadvantage is that library footage will be several generations away from its original negative and therefore of less than excellent quality. Furthermore, it may be well known to audiences, due to previous overuse. Stock footage is often bought *before* the shooting so that sets can be designed and action staged to match the stock footage, so that the two will more easily intercut. The library footage must also be of the same wind as the footage used in the rest of the film. For example, if your film is all B-wind, then you must order B-wind library footage. All the stock footage should be bought before the editing begins.

LOGGING

All footage (sound, silent and library) should be logged. This involves writing down the original edge numbers with a short description of the action. As edge numbers appear every half-foot, frames will usually have to be counted in order to establish the exact beginning and ending of each shot. Although logging is a very tedious job, in the long run it usually saves time and often money as well. For example, an accurate log book enables you to look up the exact length of a given shot when planning overlaps for dissolves. Without it, you would have to look at your original, thus exposing it to unnecessary hazards, see figure 7-13.

ASSEMBLY

Once the logging is complete, the next step is usually to assemble the scenes into *approximately* the order indicated in the script. In the assembly the cutter will often use a grease pencil to make sync marks on the sound and picture within each take and then remove the slates. Although the edge numbers will indicate sync, the more visible grease pencil marks are convenient when working quickly. After removing the slates, each shot together with its sound track is clearly labeled and hung in the film bin or stored on a core. When the shots are all in approximate order, they are spliced together, leaving in alternative takes. No intercutting is attempted. Head and tail leaders are added to both the picture and sound rolls. Some editors label all sound rolls with one color of grease

pencil and all picture rolls with another color, for example, red for picture and yellow for sound. When working quickly, this tells them immediately which roll is which.

Often a picture will be assembled scene by scene as the editor works a day or a week behind the film crews. The early scenes may already be assembled while the last scenes are being shot. It is often a good idea to start editing as soon as possible. If the editor discovers he needs a given shot it is less expensive if the cast and crew is still shooting and do not have to be specially reassembled for one or two shots. The assembly is often viewed by the director, the producer, and the editor to decide which takes are to be used and how to intercut the footage.

ROUGH CUT AND FINE CUT

The next step, called the rough cut, will fit the shots more closely together, inserting closeups into master shots, etc. The rough cut may go through many forms and stages with numerous changes in between.

All "out-takes" and "trims" (whole shots and bits of film not to be used in the final version) *must be saved* and filed in an orderly manner. As an editor works on a film he may change his mind many times before he finishes, and so he does not throw any footage away. Professional editors will save pieces as small as *one frame*.

The fine cutting follows, in which the work print is "locked down" to its finished form. The work print is now complete. The sound, however, is still on a separate roll and contains dialog and perhaps a few sound effects only.

SOUND EFFECTS

The sound tracks are now assembled. Apart from the dialog there may be several more sound tracks with effects, music, and narration. When ordering from sound-effects libraries, one must be *very specific*. For example, if a motorcycle sound effect is needed, every possible bit of information should be included, such as the manufacturer of the cycle; its size, displacement, and horsepower; a description of its age and condition of repair; and what it is doing — whether starting, accelerating, cruising and at what speed, etc. Of course, whenever possible it is good to record your own sound effects at the location where the footage was shot. If the

LOG SHEET

COMPANY CURVA Productions
PRODUCER Alfons Chwiej
PROD. TITLE "To Be Alive is Illegal"
PROD. NO. 2001
LOCATIONS John's house ← Hallway & Living room

CAMERA ROLL NO. 7
PREFIX J1/26 19 & 20
LAB ROLL NO. 412 BW 10
LAB ORDER NO. 212619

CODE NO.	EDGE NO.	NOTES	SC/TK	DESCRIPTION
B 0004 - 030	J1/26 19739-791		1 - 1	JOHN ENTERS Hallway, looks, SEES MARY. - (Mary poor)
B 00031 - 050	19792-836		1 - 2	Same. (John forgets line)
B 00051 - 080	19872-927		1 - 3	SamE. (good)
B 00081 - 089	19969-20002		1A - 1	C.U. JOHN - gives lines
B 0099 - 165	20006-140	MOS	1B - 1	C.U. Mary - reacts
B 0166 - 228	20346-469		2 - 1	LIVING ROOM - John & Mary ENTER. Fair
B 0229 - 285	20470-512		2 - 2	SAME - JOHN very good look - Mary good.
B 286 - 299	20513-532	MOS	2A - 1	C.U. Mary reacts - poor
B 0300 - 314	20533-543	MOS	2A - 2	C.U. Mary reacts. very good
B 0315 - 325	20544-550	NO SLATE	2 X	John Falls on Roller Skate better
B 0326 - 350	20551-569 END of roll	TAIL SLATE	2B - 1	John Falls on Roller Skate ?

7-13 Sample log sheet.

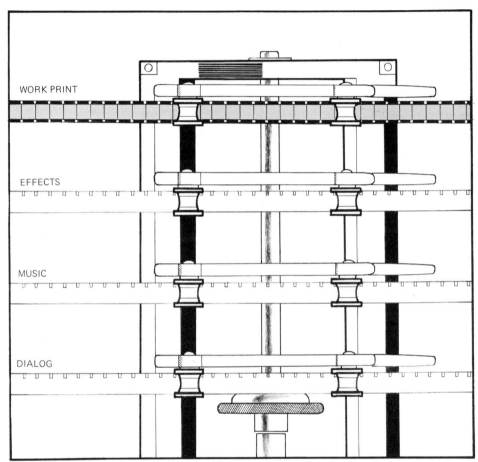

WORK PRINT

EFFECTS

MUSIC

DIALOG

7-14 Sound tracks and work print assembled in a synchronizer.

sounds are picked up *during* the actual filming, this further eliminates the problem of syncing them up, although the sound mixer does lose the ability to balance the effects relative to the dialog.

MIXING

The various tracks will eventually be assembled. This could be done on a multi-sound-head editing machine or a synchronizer and later mixed onto one piece of magnetic film during the re-recording session. There should be no splices in or close to sections of music, as this might cause a wow. Whenever preparing sound it should be spliced with *white* splicing tape to provide for easy location of the splices. Single-perf white or yellow leader is used to space the contents of each track in areas where there is no sound. The white or yellow color also helps to locate visually various sounds. Instead of white leader, some low-budget producers use old out-takes, etc. Whatever is used for spacing, it *must* be spliced in "base up" — unlike the sound film — so that the emulsion of the spacing footage does not rub off onto the

RYDER SOUND SERVICES, INC.

1161 NO. VINE ST.   HOLLYWOOD 38. CALIF.

RERECORDING LOG

Date_____

Effects Editor		Producer			Production		
Track No. Dialogue	Track No. FX 1	Track No. FX 2	Track No. Music	Track No.	Track No.	Track No.	
Reel No. 1	Reel No. 1	Reel No. 1	Reel No. 1	Reel No.	Reel No.	Reel No.	
10 Pop	10 Pop	10 Pop	10 Pop				
			12				
	20 Traffic under						
			25 Fade				
28	Jaws						
		32 Horn					
		45 Car pass					
		50					
		70 Car pass					
		83					
85	85						
			90				
			150				
- more -	- more -	- more -	- more -				

7-15 Re-recording log (mixing cue sheet). (Courtesy of Ryder Sound Services, Inc.)

sound heads. It is also very important that the spacing footage be the same pitch as the magnetic stock. That is, the sprocket holes must be spaced the same for both. Otherwise, the mixing equipment may jam, chewing up your track and causing expensive delays during the mixing. Furthermore, no grease-pencil marks should be left, because their markings tend to come off and collect on the magnetic head. A pencil with a very soft lead is excellent for marking the magnetic track, and it can be erased easily.

In preparing tracks for the final mixing session, it is absolutely necessary to make precise cue sheets for the sound mixer. This will indicate what the various tracks are and where they are to come in or out, the changes of relative levels, and a description of the action. The room-tone track (explained in

Chapter 6) may be an additional track or it could be "looped" by splicing it head to tail so that it runs continuously, over and over. This loop is often ¼-inch magnetic tape. Throughout the mixing session it can be brought in at any time. Sound services usually offer a variety of "stock" room tones, although it is preferable to record one's own at the actual location.

A "sync pop" (often called a "blip tone") is placed at the head of each track opposite the number two of the SMPTE leader on the work print. During the mixing session, the sync pops are used to check sync. As the film and tracks are projected, the pops should sound exactly together and opposite the number two. The pops consist of one frame of sound tone spliced into each track. Prerecorded sync pops are available on tape with an adhesive backing and can be stuck onto the surface of the tracks.

Dubbing sessions are very expensive, and therefore the better prepared one is, the faster and cheaper it will be. *Always consult the sound-mixing lab about their particular requirements* regarding cue sheets, leader lengths, cue marks, etc., so that no time is wasted during the session. Make sure that all your splices are strong so that you will not be delayed with breaks. The film will be projected during the mix, and so if the work print is in poor condition, you might make a special dubbing print from the A-B rolls, or a so-called "slash print" that is made directly from the work print. To make sure the film is fully ready for mixing, it is often useful to have an "interlock" or "preview" session in which the film and all tracks are run together in sync in the mixing theater with the technicians present. Many sound houses will allow reduced rates for preview sessions.

BASIC LAB EFFECTS

When making first-trial and release prints there are four basic optical effects normally offered by the labs at no extra charge: fade-outs, fade-ins, dissolves, and superimpositions.

A fade-out is a gradual darkening of the image until it becomes black. The printer light is gradually diminished as the film is being printed. A fade-in is just the opposite, a gradual lightening of the scene from black to normal. For this the light is gradually increased while printing. When these two effects occur simultaneously they make a dissolve, where one scene gradually disappears as another scene appears in its place. This is sometimes called a "cross-dissolve" or "lap-dissolve." It is done in two printer operations. The first scene is printed until the beginning of the dissolve and then faded out. The raw stock is then rewound and run a second time. The printer light is out until the beginning of the dissolve, and then the second scene is faded in over the same place that the first one was faded out. Fades and dissolves can differ in length depending on the type of printer being used at the lab. Therefore, the standard lengths vary. The lab should be consulted for their specific capabilities.

Superimposition is achieved by printing two scenes over the same piece of film. This usually starts by fading a second picture in over the first. The two are then seen together for a period and one of them is faded out. It is much like an extended dissolve. Frequently, "burn-in" titles are superimposed over a live-action background. When a project is filmed on reversal original, the burn-in "supers" are usually also shot on reversal. They are white letters on a black background, and when superimposed, they make white letters over the background footage. Instead of white, the letters could be colored. To ensure that the letters will be visible, the area of the background over which they are to appear should be dark. The letters themselves should be either very white or, if colored, highly saturated.

When the original is negative, many complications arise. When preparing supers for a film shot on negative, the lab should always be consulted for their recommendations.

The title card is not always shot on the same stock as the rest of the film. The lab should always be consulted when the original is negative, but there are recommended stocks for shooting burn-in supers when the original is reversal:

When the original is black-and-white reversal: Kodachrome II has very deep blacks making an excellent super with no "bleeding" (see Glossary). Ektachrome EF 7242 also provides enough contrast for titles. 7362 High Contrast Positive (reversal) is a print stock that offers a very high contrast. Because it was designed as a print stock, it has a relatively low speed. Tests should be made to determine the best ASA to use (usually about ASA 12). When titles are for black-and-white reversal production, they can be prepared as black letters on white background and shot on 7362 to be processed as negative.

When the original is color reversal: Kodachrome II with its excellent deep blacks is the best. Ektachrome 7242 is also very good. If the letters are colored, the colors should be well saturated for the best effect. Also the shot over which the title is supered should be dark. No color will super over a white background without becoming almost completely washed out.

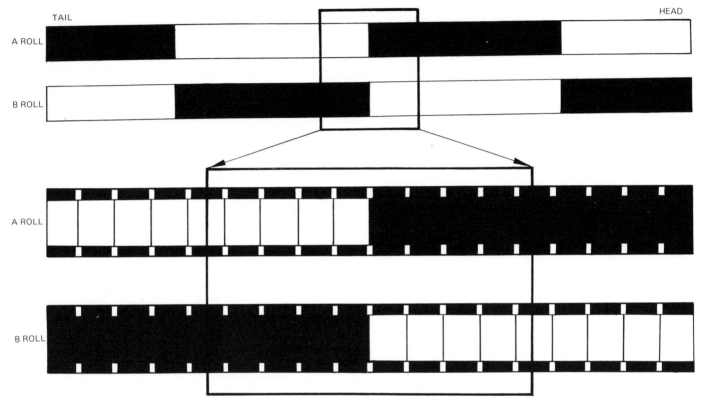

7-16 A-B roll checkerboard technique.

A-B ROLLS

Cutting the original into "A-B rolls" that relate to the work print is called "conforming." The A-B roll "checkerboard" technique is used only in 16mm film. A-B rolls may be used in 35mm as well, but mainly to provide the overlaps required for dissolves and superimpositions. The splices in 35mm fall entirely between frames and therefore don't show. In 16mm film, however, the splices overlap part of one frame and are therefore visible when projected. So, in 16mm, A-B rolls have the additional purpose of achieving invisible splices by using the checkerboard technique.

Before the conforming can begin, the work print must be "locked down." That is, all shots must be cut to the exact final length that will appear in the finished film, with all anticipated optical effects marked with a grease pencil. Dissolves and superimpositions require the two adjacent shots to overlap each other in the A-B rolls. Therefore, to maintain sync, the full lengths of the original shots *will not appear in the work print*. Remember that the length of the dissolve represents the two scenes *overlapped*. You cannot physically overlap the two shots of the work print as they would jam in the equipment. Therefore, the two scenes are cut and spliced together in the middle of the dissolve and it is understood that each scene extends into the other. For example, a 48 frame dissolve in a work print will show 24 frames of each shot.

When planning the lengths of dissolves, we must be sure that the original is long enough, by checking in the log book.

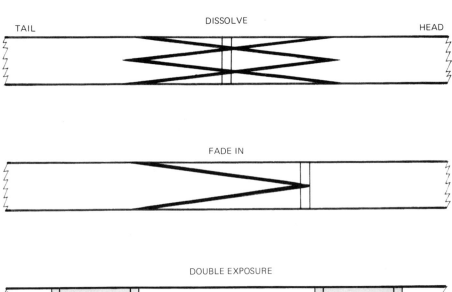

DISSOLVE
TAIL   HEAD

FADE IN

DOUBLE EXPOSURE

EXTENDED SCENE

UNINTENTIONAL SPLICE

7-17 Work-print marks.

7-18 Dissolve in
checkerboard technique.

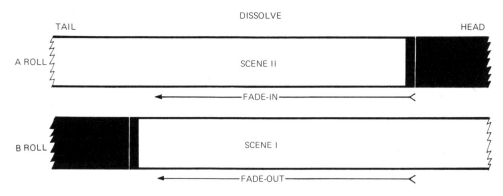

DISSOLVE
TAIL   HEAD

A ROLL   SCENE II

FADE-IN

B ROLL   SCENE I

FADE-OUT

NAME W. VOLO TITLE "Sticky Build-up"

COMPANY GABLOTA Films PROD.NO. 521

ADDRESS #3 Santa Anna St. EDITOR BACON

Valencia, Calif EDITOR'S PHONE 255-1405

91355 TYPE OF ORIGINAL 7252 and

PHONE 255-0789 7242

FT	FR	A ROLL	B ROLL	C ROLL	SOUND
00	00	Print Start	Print Start		Edit Sync
08	02	F.I. - 24			
09	24		F.I. - 24		
13	31		F.O. - 24		
16	18		F.I. - 24		
22	09		F.O. - 24		
27	39	F.O. - 48	F.I. - 48		
32	21	F.I. - 24	F.O. - 24		
41	36		F.I. - 48		
106	30		F.O. - 12		
113	16	F.O. - 48			

7-19 Sample cue sheet showing location and lengths of effects.

A-ROLL

BLACK LEADER

| PRINTER | START | TITLE PRODUCER FOOTAGE | A-ROLL FILM TYPE | HEAD |

2 FT. — 5 FT. 26 FRAMES — 6 FEET

B-ROLL

BLACK LEADER*

| PRINTER | START | TITLE PRODUCER FOOTAGE | B-ROLL FILM TYPE | HEAD |

OPTICAL TRACK

CLEAR TRACK

* *

| PRINTER | START | TITLE PRODUCER FOOTAGE | TYPE TRACK & WIND | HEAD |

2 FT — 5 FEET — 6 FEET

| EDIT | SYNC | MAGNETIC TRACK | HEAD |

SYNC POP

A-ROLL - TAIL

| TAIL | A-ROLL TITLE FILM-TYPE PRODUCER FOOTAGE | | |

BLACK LEADER

2 FEET — 4 FEET — 5 FEET — 2 FT.

B-ROLL - TAIL

| TAIL | B-ROLL TITLE FILM-TYPE PRODUCER FOOTAGE | | |

OPTICAL TRACK - TAIL

| TAIL | TYPE TRACK & WIND TITLE PRODUCER FOOTAGE | | |

CLEAR TRACK

2 FEET — 4 FEET — 5 FEET & 26 FRAMES — 2 FT.

7-20 Standard head and tail leaders.

*If SMPTE Academy Leader is used, it would come in place of the black leader on B-roll. Naturally, the track and A-roll would be extended by an equal amount so as to maintain sync.
**"Printer sync" indicates synchronization in the printer. Therefore, "printer sync" for an optical track includes the 26-frame advancement of the sound needed when projecting release prints. The "edit sync" on the magnetic track indicates that the 26-frame advance has not been made and the lab will advance the magnetic track accordingly.

A cue sheet should be made, indicating the location and length of each effect. The location is given as the distance from the "printer start" frame on the head leader to the beginning of the effect.

If the budget permits, one could submit the untouched originals along with the finished work print and cue sheet to a professional negative cutter, allowing him to do the actual conforming. Otherwise, the editor will conform the originals himself. Even if the editor performs this task, he will usually not make the actual splices himself. He will mark where they

should come and leave them for the lab to do. There is usually a small charge for this service, but the stronger, cleaner splices offered by the lab are worth the expense.

Before beginning to conform the original, the leaders are usually set up. SMPTE universal leader could be used. When SMPTE leader is used, it is customarily placed on the B-roll, 5 feet and 26 frames after the "printer start" (see figure 7-20). The first shot of the film will then be on A-roll. Tail leaders will later be prepared for the end of each roll.

When marking A-B rolls, all information must be written in

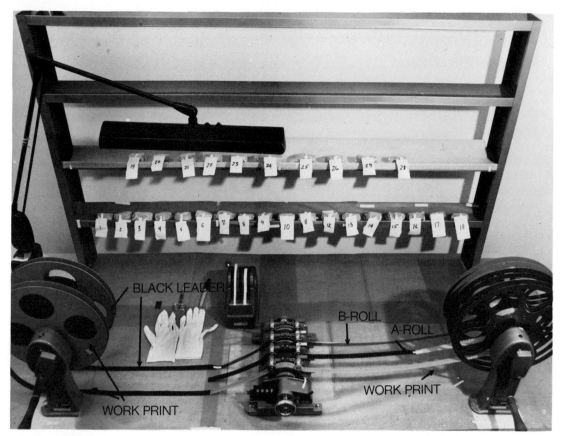

7-21 The editing table, prepared for assembling the original into A-B rolls. Note the original broken down by "takes" and numbered according to their order in the work print. (Photo by author)

india ink — never grease pencil. Anything else may come off or be smeared all over the picture. Also, the lab will often clean the film with high-frequency sound waves before printing. India ink does not come off in this process.

As you begin to assemble the A-B rolls you will appreciate the meticulous preparation of the log book and the orderly storage of the rolls of original. This gives you the exact location of each shot in the original. Before beginning, you will go through the work print and list the edge numbers of each shot that was actually used. Next, take this list and mark these shots in the log book.

When you have finished, for any given roll of original, the log book will show which takes were used and where they will appear in the finished film. For example, original roll number two might contain the shots appearing 1st, 9th, 13th and 21st in the work print. Using the log book it will be easy to remove just those shots from the roll or original and place them in order with a minimum of wear on the original.

You are now ready to begin conforming.

The first thing to do is to "sterilize" the editing room. Tape clean paper to the top of the editing table and the floor around it, especially at each end of the table. Remove all tools from underneath the film path. "Scrub up" and put on white editing gloves.

BREAKING DOWN THE ORIGINAL

Take the first roll of original, *tail out.* Look in your log book to see what takes were used from this roll. Carefully remove each such take, *in its entirety.* Keep everything from camera start to camera stop. You will trim or divide it later. Wind it *tail first* onto a clean core. This way it will be *head out* on the core, ready to be wound directly onto your A or B roll. Now wrap it in tissue paper and label it, giving its number according to its appearance in the work print. Place it on the shelf. Continue this process until all the *chosen* takes have been removed and arranged *in consecutive order.*

ASSEMBLING THE A-B ROLLS

On the right rewind you will need three take-up reels with equal hub diameters. On the first "gang" of the synchronizer, the work print is positioned *base up*. On the left rewind, or on a separate "horse," place a roll of black leader. Next, the head leaders for A-roll and B-roll are placed in the synchronizer, *emulsion up* and in sync with the work print. Their heads are wound onto the second and third reels on the right rewind. Now you are ready. See figure 7-21 on page 162. Although some budget-minded film makers perform the original cement splicing themselves, I prefer to scribe and temporarily tape my originals, allowing the lab to make the permanent cement splices. This service is well worth the usually reasonable price. The location of a future splice is indicated by two marks, one on either side of the nearest sprocket hole. These marks are scribed (scratched) into the

dark border of reversal emulsions or marked with india ink in the clear border of negative emulsions. Scribing can be done with the corner of a razor blade or the point of a push pin and marking with a Pentel marker. Now the excess is trimmed away, leaving at least an 1½ frame margin. When trimming this excess to be extra alert and make certain to trim it on the correct side of the scribe mark or you will destroy something you need to use. Once trimmed, the two pieces to be joined are exactly overlapped and taped so that the future splice lines exactly coincide.. The sprocket holes must be aligned so that the overlap will move easily through the synchronizer. One must always use the modern paper tape which when pulled off, will leave no trace on your original. When using such tape it is customary to tape everything left over right.

7-22 When the actual splices are left to be done by the lab, the splice line is indicated by scribe marks scratched into the emulsion on the edge of the film as seen here. The excess is then trimmed away, leaving a 1 1/2-frame margin.

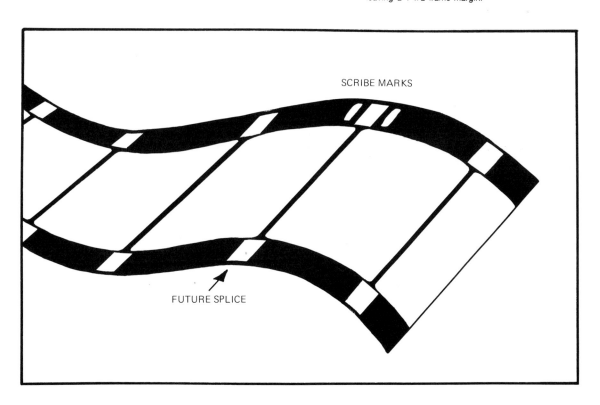

SCRIBE MARKS

FUTURE SPLICE

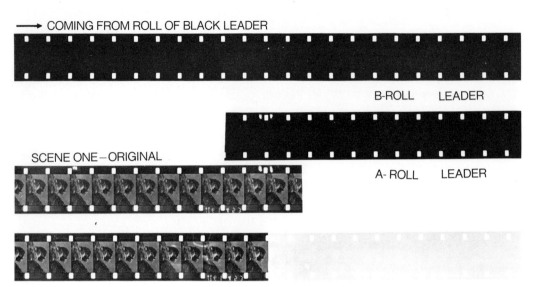

B-ROLL   LEADER

SCENE ONE — ORIGINAL

A- ROLL   LEADER

7-23 The first scene (original) is aligned with the work print so that the original edge numbers are in sync. Scribe marks are made to indicate the splice line. (Photo by author)

WORK PRINT

Let us say your first shot is an A-roll. We will leave the black leader extending from B-roll. Take scene number one from the shelf and match its edge numbers to those on the work print. Lock them into the synchronizer so that they are in sync. Scribe the scene one original on either side of the sprocket hole opposite the first splice in the work print. Cut off the unwanted portion before the first frame, leaving 1½ frames before the future splice line. Next, on the A-roll leader, scribe the sprocket hole opposite the first splice and trim it leaving the 1½ frame margin. See figure 7-23 above. Tape the two pieces of film (the first scene overlapping the A-roll leader) so that their scribe marks exactly overlap each other and their sprocket holes are aligned. See figure 7-24 below.

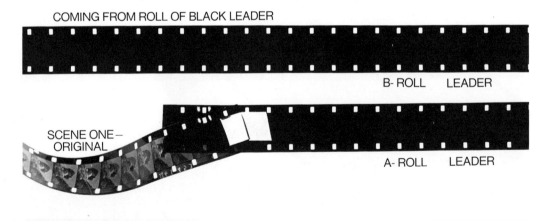

COMING FROM ROLL OF BLACK LEADER

7-24 Scene one is taped to the end of the A-roll leader so that the scribe marks overlap. Notice that the tape does not extend into the picture area to be used. It is kept on the black leader side of the splice line so that it touches only the black leader and the 1 1/2-frame margin. (Photo by author)

B- ROLL   LEADER

SCENE ONE— ORIGINAL

A- ROLL   LEADER

WORK PRINT

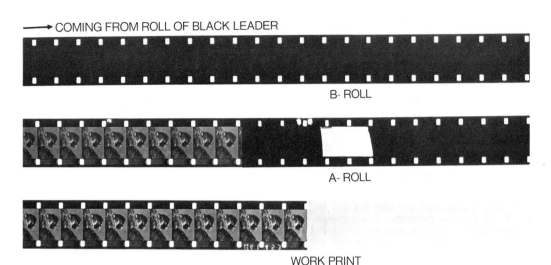

COMING FROM ROLL OF BLACK LEADER

B- ROLL

7-25 The first shot, scribed and taped to A-roll. (Photo by author)

A- ROLL

WORK PRINT

At this point we have the first scene scribed and taped to A-roll. Its edge numbers are in sync with those of the work print. We have black leader opposite this on B-roll. See figure 7-25, above. Now we wind in sync ahead (film moves to the right) until we come to the end of the first scene in the work print. Here the second scene will be placed on B-roll and the black leader will be joined to A-roll. To do this, find the splice between scene one and two in the work print. Opposite this splice put scribe marks on the end of the scene one (on A-roll). Trim the excess from A-roll leaving the 1½ frame margin. Also scribe the black leader on B-roll opposite this splice. This leader is coming from a large supply roll on your left. You cut it from B-roll and scribe and tape it to A-roll at the end of scene one. See figure 7-26 below.

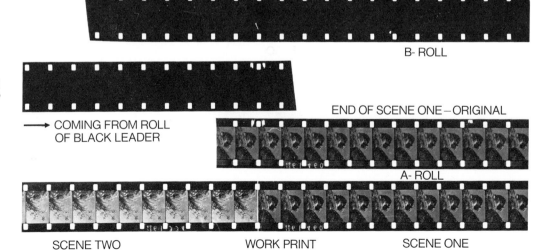

B- ROLL

7-26 After the end of scene one, the black leader is removed from B-roll and scribed before taping to the end of scene one on A-roll. (Photo by author)

COMING FROM ROLL OF BLACK LEADER

END OF SCENE ONE—ORIGINAL

A- ROLL

SCENE TWO   WORK PRINT   SCENE ONE

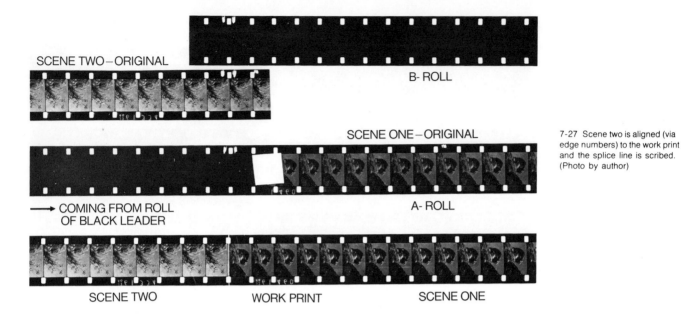

SCENE TWO—ORIGINAL

B-ROLL

SCENE ONE—ORIGINAL

7-27 Scene two is aligned (via edge numbers) to the work print and the splice line is scribed. (Photo by author)

→ COMING FROM ROLL OF BLACK LEADER

A-ROLL

SCENE TWO   WORK PRINT   SCENE ONE

Now take down scene two. Match its edge numbers to those of the work print. Scribe the sprocket hole on the original that coincides with the splice in the work print. See figure 7-27 above. Overlap and tape it to B-roll. Scene two is now on B-roll. Black leader is opposite it on A-roll. See figure 7-28 below. You are now ready to wind ahead, in sync, to the end of scene two where you will put in scene three. As you work, be constantly checking to make certain your edge numbers are always in cync. Keep repeating this cycle, except when

dealing with dissolves or supers to be discussed next. When cutting negative original, fades must also be handled differently

In passing, we should note that single sprocket original will *only* fit *base up* on a normal synchronizer. Therefore when conforming, you are forced to back the film out of the synchronizer and turn it over in order to scribe the *emulsion side.* This is somewhat awkward. This is *one* reason that single perf film is usually avoided in the camera original, work print and all other steps until the relase print.

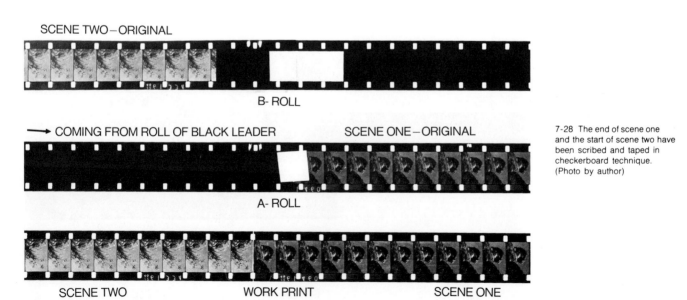

SCENE TWO—ORIGINAL

B-ROLL

→ COMING FROM ROLL OF BLACK LEADER   SCENE ONE—ORIGINAL

7-28 The end of scene one and the start of scene two have been scribed and taped in checkerboard technique. (Photo by author)

A-ROLL

SCENE TWO   WORK PRINT   SCENE ONE

Dissolves

Dissolves must be very clearly indicated on the work print so that you don't forget one of them and A-B roll it like a straight cut. Some labs require that the center of the dissolve be scribed. See figure 7-18.

Superimpositions

Supers are cut much like dissolves. The important thing is to give good timing instructions, especially indicating which image you want to be more visible. To indicate the super in the work print, small sections of the shot to be supered are cut into the work print at the beginning and end of the area over which it will be superimposed. When possible, these sections should contain edge numbers to help the editor find the original before conforming.

Fades

With reversal originals, fade-outs and fade-ins will be indicated on the work print and cue sheet but do not require any other special treatment. However, in the case of negative original, the fade-out and fade-in sections must have transparent leader (in case of color made from the same negative stock) on the opposite roll. When a fade-out is followed by a fade-in, *both* of the original shots should appear on *one roll* with the clear leader on the other.

Lengths of Effects

For fades and dissolves, some labs require a few frames of extra overlap. For example, a 34-frame overlap might be required for a 24-frame dissolve. Similarly, different labs will offer their effects in different lengths. For example, the shortest dissolve possible might be 16 frames with other specific limited lengths available, such as 24, 48, 64 and 96. Other labs may offer different lengths in between. Before even the work print is edited, the editor should have consulted with the lab to find out what lengths are available.

Minimum Spacings

The minimum distance between effects is dictated by the length of the effect and the printer used. If the printer fades out in 24 frames, it will require 24 additional frames to open back up. Usually a few more frames are required as a safety margin. Therefore, if A-roll fades out in 24 frames, there must be at least 24 frames before the next shot on A-roll. If the shot on B-roll is less than 24 frames, the next shot on A-roll will start dark and lighten as the fader finishes opening. There are two common ways of dealing with this. One *could* use a C-roll, an additional roll like the A-roll and B-roll. The extra expense of running the third roll is often not desirable, unless the C-roll has more than one purpose. Additional rolls are always possible, and some films (frequently experimental) use A,B,C,D, and E-rolls, although there could be even

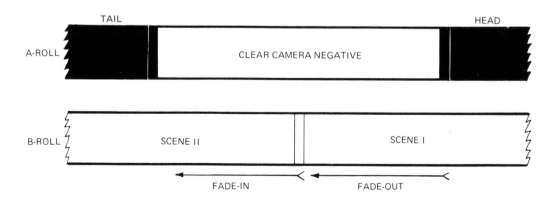

7-29 When conforming *negative* original, clear leader (or clear camera negative, in the case of color) must be placed opposite any fade-ins or fade-outs. (This does not apply to dissolves in negative.)

more. If money is not plentiful and the problem only occurs once, the solution is frequently just to splice the shot onto the same roll as the shot before, so that in the above example, A-roll fades out and then the next two shots are on B-roll. The splice will be visible, but it saves the expense of a C-roll.

SUBMITTING THE ORIGINALS TO THE LAB

The A-B rolls should be submitted to the lab on cores, wrapped in tissue paper and placed in a can or box. A precise cue sheet and the finished work print should be included. The lab will again require the same information as listed at the beginning of this chapter.

ANSWER PRINT

The first print made from the finished A-B rolls is called the "answer print" or "first trial" print. It is like a release print, except that its primary purpose is to get the errors worked out before running off the release prints destined for theaters and wherever. This first trial print could be silent, although it is usually a "composite" ("married") print — that is, it carries a sound track. See figure 7-32.

The first trial print is more expensive than later release prints, because all the effects, timing, and color corrections must be set up for the first time. At the lab the "timer" views the A-B rolls on a special electronic apparatus to evaluate the color balance and density. He notes which scenes require minor color balancing and decides what density corrections might be made. It must be understood that the lab does not correct the original exposure. However, the lab can modify the overall density. For example, suppose a scene is very badly overexposed. Without correction it would appear in, say, two or three slightly different densities, such as white (clear) and *very* light gray. The difference between these shades is minimal, meaning there is barely any contrast left. The lab can lower the overall density of this image, repositioning those slightly different densities closer to the center of the range, instead of at the bright end. For example, what was white and light gray before would now be represented as two very similar shades of gray, but the contrast range will not have increased. It *must* be understood that the lab cannot re-create tonal differences that existed in the scene but which were not recorded by the film because of incorrect exposure.

The color and density modifications, along with the fades, dissolves, and supers, will all be programmed onto tapes that will control the printer while the print is made.

When the first trial is ready it is viewed by the film makers with the timer present. Some corrections are usually necessary. They are taken into account and another print is then produced. This could repeat itself several times until the producer is satisfied. If the print is unsatisfactory because of mistakes or oversights made by the lab, then the customer can usually insist on and get a replacement print, free of charge.

When submitting your A-B rolls to the lab, be sure to specify what kind of answer print you want, whether for television transmission or screen projection. This is very important, as the color bias in the case of color prints and the contrast range in the case of either black-and-white or color will be different for each. If a color television print is projected onto a screen, it will appear bluish. A television print also generally has less contrast.

MASTERS AND DUPES

Having at last obtained a satisfactory print, we are now ready for release printing. If only a few prints are desired they can be made directly from the A-B rolls. However, if it is intended to have many prints made, it is the normal procedure to make an intermediate negative copy and print from it rather than from the precious originals. In some cases, especially when greater numbers of prints are required, it is *cheaper* to do release printing from a negative.

If the originals are negative to begin with, a "master positive" will first have to be made. Then, from the master positive, a "dupe negative" is printed, which will be used in making the release prints. If the originals are reversal, an "inter-negative" can be made right from the A-B rolls.

CONTACT PRINTING AND GENERATIONS

Most lab work involves "contact printing." That is, the original and print stock come together, emulsion to emulsion, while the print is made. Because of this, with each succeeding generation the film will alternate its wind.

1st Generation B-wind	2nd Generation A-wind	3rd Generation B-wind	4th Generation A-wind
Reversal A-B rolls	Answer print, release prints, or inter-negative	Release print	
Negative A-B rolls	Answer print, release prints, or master positive	Dupe negative	Release print

If for some reason you wish to make a print with the same wind as the material it was printed from (A-wind from A-wind or B-wind from B-wind), it will have to be optically printed instead of contact-printed. Optical printing is less common and more expensive than contact printing.

It should be restated that A-wind and B-wind depend only on emulsion position. Do not confuse them with A-B rolls. On B-wind film, the lettering reads correctly when the observer is looking through the base; that is, the emulsion is on the side away from the viewer. A-wind, on the other hand, reads correctly when looking at the emulsion side. Whether a film is single- or double-sprocket has nothing to do with it at this stage.

Single-sprocket film is not as easily manipulated as is double-sprocket film during the editing. Therefore, single-sprocket film is usually avoided until the final release prints with sound. Except under certain circumstances, such as when using single-system sound, the camera original, work print, and all intermediate negatives are usually double-sprocket.

SOUND ON RELEASE PRINTS

Sound can either be electroprinted or optically printed onto the sound track of a release print. Electroprinting optically records the mag track onto the film. Alternatively, we could make a high-quality "sound negative" on a separate piece of film, and then print the sound onto each release print. For fewer prints, electroprinting is cheaper; however, often the quality control is higher in the negative process. The initial expense of the sound negative makes the second method more expensive for only a few prints, but it is cheaper in the long run if many release prints are to be made.

When making release prints from inter-negatives or dupe negatives it is customary to provide a sound negative. Be sure to order the sound negative with the same emulsion position (A-wind or B-wind) as your picture negative. That is, when printing from an A-wind inter-negative, order an A-wind sound negative. Otherwise the sound will have to be printed through the base, resulting in a loss of high frequencies. (See illustrations on pages 170, 172, and 173.)

Schemes of Printing 16mm Color Prints from 16mm Camera Originals

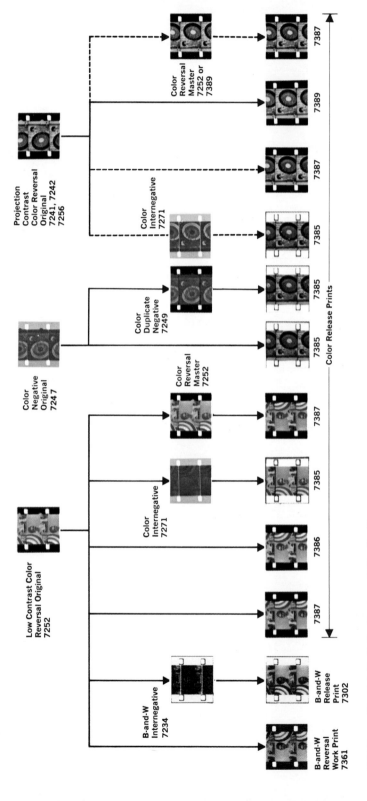

Low Contrast Color Reversal Original 7252

Color Negative Original 7247

Projection Contrast Color Reversal Original 7241, 7242 7256

B-and-W Internegative 7234

Color Internegative 7271

Color Duplicate Negative 7249

Color Reversal Master 7252

Color Internegative 7271

Color Reversal Master 7252 or 7389

B-and-W Reversal Work Print 7361

B-and-W Release Print 7302

7387   7386   7385   7387

7385   7385

7385   7387   7389   7387

Color Release Prints

7234 EASTMAN Fine Grain Duplicating Panchromatic Negative Film
7241 KODAK EKTACHROME EF Film (Daylight)
7242 KODAK EKTACHROME EF Film (Tungsten)
7249 EASTMAN Color Reversal Intermediate Film
7252 EASTMAN EKTACHROME Commercial Film
7247 EASTMAN Color Negative Film
7256 KODAK EKTACHROME MS Film
7271 EASTMAN Color Internegative Film
7302 EASTMAN Fine Grain Release Positive Film
7361 EASTMAN Reversal Duplicating Film
7385 EASTMAN Color Print Film
7386 EASTMAN EKTACHROME Reversal Print Film
7387 EASTMAN Reversal Color Print Film
7389 EASTMAN EKTACHROME R Print Film

NOTES

1 Where special effects are to be included, originals may be edited in "A" and "B" rolls. Where a color intermegative or color reversal master is employed, the special effects can be introduced at this stage.

2 The choice of printing system depends on a number of factors, including the types of printing and processing equipment available, the physical and chemical processing requirements for each film, and certain economic considerations. As a result, certain compromises may have to be accepted.

3 The dotted lines indicate less preferable methods (from the standpoints of excessive contrast build-up or reduced definition).

C-1 Courtesy of Eastman Kodak.

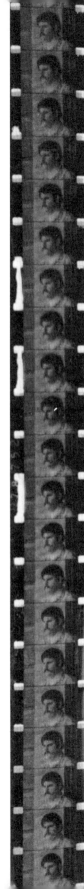

7-31 Repairing torn sprocket holes. Perforated splicing tape is applied to both sides of the sprocket-hole area, without overlapping into the picture. The excess tape is then trimmed away with a razor blade. (Photo by author)

PRINT DAMAGE

Some labs offer services designed to conceal scratches. When "wet gate" prints are made, both films are submerged in a liquid during the exposure. The liquid fills in scratches in the base so that the light is not refracted and the scratches are less visible. This will only diminish scratches in the base. There is no way to repair deep scratches in the emulsion.

If old or damaged footage is to be given to the lab for printing, the lab should be notified that it may be in poor condition. There are many precautions that can be taken to ensure its gentle treatment. For example, it can be "waxed" so that it will move more easily through the projector gate. If the footage is to be printed, the lab might alert the technician to run the printer somewhat slower than normal and to be especially alert to stop the printer should a break occur.

Torn sprocket holes can be repaired with many techniques. One method that seems to work well is to use sprocketed tape over only the area of the torn sprockets. The picture area is left as clear as possible. If the tape is applied so that the *right* side of the tape fits over the sprocket holes on the *left* side of the film, the excess tape can be trimmed away with a razor blade, leaving the sprockets reinforced. The overlap into the picture area is minimal. Although most labs usually refuse to print films with tape splices, some labs will accept films which have been repaired in this fashion.

There are many techniques and services available for print repair. Some laboratories specialize in salvaging damaged prints. One should consult a reputable lab for their recommendations.

7-30 Film with torn sprocket holes. (Photo by author)

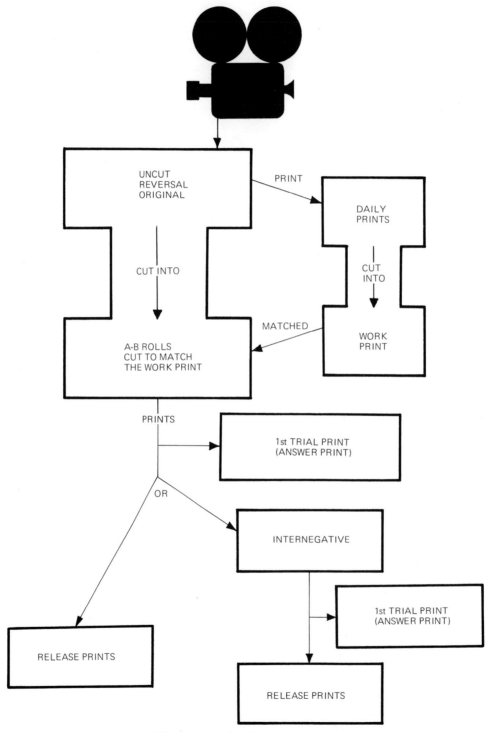

7-32 Flow chart for films shot on *reversal* original.

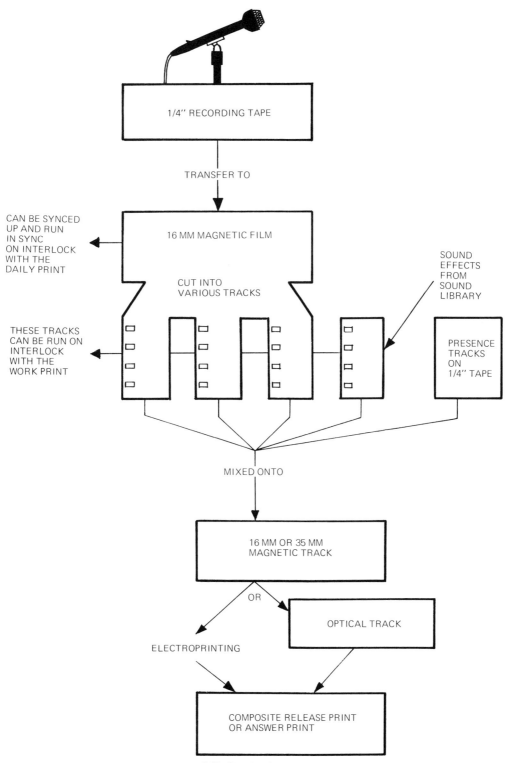

7-33 Flow chart for sound.

CHAPTER 8
THE BASICS OF OPTICAL PRINTING

The optical printer is almost as old as film making itself. In recent years experimental film makers, aided by more flexible lab techniques and new film stocks, have created a new art form with almost limitless possibilities. Due to the great variety of effects available in optical printing, film makers often end up developing their own techniques. In this chapter we will try to introduce enough of the basic principles so that the student can begin to experiment on his own. Then, near the end of the chapter, we have some specific examples, given to help the reader understand how these rather complicated techniques can be coordinated.

BASIC OPTICAL PRINTER FUNCTIONS

The optical printer's most basic function involves a rephotographed-image technique. It differs from contact printing in that a lens is introduced between the image being photographed and the raw stock. Because the lens reverses the image, the film in the projector side must move from bottom to top to keep the photographed image right side up. Both the camera gate and the projector gate must have good registration to assure perfect steadiness. Otherwise, images

combined through several printer runs would appear to vibrate slightly in respect to each other.

There is no effective way of calculating exposures for an optical printer. Tests must be run. The best test is to get some Kodak test film, print it on reversal, and compare it to the original. Most optical printers have an adjustment that will dim or brighten the light. However, this should be kept constant because a change in voltage will vary the color temperature. The best results are obtained if the f-stop is kept constant at a given setting about the middle of its range and the exposure is controlled with a set of neutral density filters.

The basic printer functions are:

1. Fade-outs, fade-ins, lap-dissolves, and superimpositions (multiple exposures), similar in effect to the normal optical transitions performed by the lab during contact printing from A-B rolls. However, the optical printer offers much greater control over the lengths and rates of these effects.
2. Freeze-frame (the action stops and remains on one frame). That frame is arrested in the printer gate and continuously printed onto consecutive frames of film stock. On low-budget productions a freeze-frame can be achieved without an optical printer by stopping the frame in the gate of a moviola

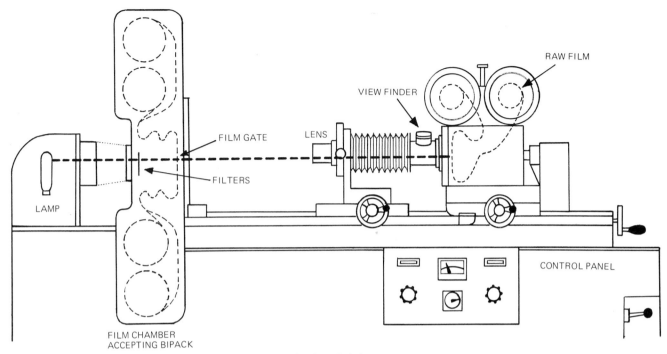

8-1 An optical printer.

and filming it with a camera. This technique is not officially to be recommended, yet it has yielded some usable results. A similar effect can be used to extend footage without the appearance of a freeze-frame. To achieve this we might print three consecutive frames over and over, back and forth. This avoids the stillness of a freeze-frame because the grain and such things as leaves, etc., may move slightly. Of course, any movement by an actor will spoil this effect.

3. Stretch printing. By printing every second frame twice, the action is slowed down. This is commonly done to convert footage shot at 16 fps to 24 fps. Of course, by skipping frames, we can speed up the action.

4. Change in composition. New frame limits can be established within the limits of the old frame — for example, obtaining a closeup from a medium shot.

5. Zoom effect. A *gradual* change of the frame limits will create a zoom effect that did not exist in the original footage.

6. Printing without changing the emulsion position, such as obtaining a B-wind print from B-wind original.

7. Reverse printing. The image can be turned around so that left becomes right.

8. Transition from black-and-white to color. Gray tones can be introduced into a color picture. If a fine-grain black-and-white positive is made from the color original, the two can then be superimposed. The amount of gray can be controlled or even faded in or out, making the picture go from color to black-and-white, etc.

9. Optical transitions. The limitless varieties of optical transitions, such as "wipes," "push-offs," and many others are too numerous to be described here.

10. Bi-packing. We have already discussed double exposures in which two pieces of film are individually printed one at a time onto a third. Instead of printing them one at a time, we could instead "bi-pack" them. That is, we could overlap them and hold them together in the printer gate while they are exposed onto a piece of raw stock. The effect of bi-packing is quite different from that of double exposure. When bi-packing, the densities (shadow areas) will add up, whereas when double-exposing the light (clear) areas will add up. The effect of bi-packing can be judged by looking at two pieces of film overlapped against the light. Bearing in mind that dark areas will dominate, reversal materials shot especially for bi-packing should be as light as possible. Otherwise, the image resulting from the bi-pack may turn out to be almost black. The opposite is true about film shot for superimposing. In double-exposing ("supering"), the *transparent* areas add up,

and therefore when shooting film for superimposition, the two images should be shot so that light areas do not overlap, washing each other out.

11. Matting. This is probably the most important optical-printer function. Matting means blocking out a certain area of the frame. This is done by bi-packing the original film with a piece having a high-contrast silhouette image that blocks out an area in the shape of that silhouette. This blocked-out area can be filled in with another image in the second run. Many optical-printer operations depend on this two-part process, which usually involves many additional intermediate steps to be discussed later. Some of the more basic effects made possible by matting include split-screen, inserting a picture into a prop television set, and adding a background behind a studio foreground; there are many others.

GENERATIONS, PRINT STOCKS, AND PROCESSING

In addition to different printer operations, there are many related factors and variables that must be understood before one attempts any serious work on the optical printer.

Optical-printer effects are often achieved through many print generations. If color accuracy and the original contrast are of importance, one should avoid too many generations and rather keep as close as possible to the original.

Whenever printing through many generations, a common source of confusion is the changing of emulsion positions of the prints. The wind alternates between A-wind and B-wind with every successive contact-print generation. Whatever manipulation we go through, the final wind (emulsion position) has to match the wind of the A and B rolls into which it will be incorporated.

The optical-printer camera will usually be loaded with a camera original raw stock (such as ECO) rather than with a print stock. This is because *usually* (depending on the job at hand) the camera stock provides better grain and contrast characteristics. Furthermore, almost all 16mm optical-printer work is shot on reversal camera emulsions, with one exception.

Occasionally, a "negative effect" is desired, in which case a negative stock would be used in the optical-printer camera. If Eastman Color Negative Type 7254 (a camera stock) were used, we would end up with the orange cast inherent to this film. The orange cast disappears in prints but is very visible in the negative. To avoid this one should use Eastman Color Print Stock Type 7385, which does not possess the orange bias. It represents the image in "negative colors," i.e., complementary to the actual colors.

Most labs will process a black-and-white reversal stock as a negative. As you remember from Chapter 2 on film stocks, when reversal is processed, at one stage it is in negative form. If the processing is stopped here and the film "fixed," the reversal stock will yield a negative image. Because this alters the developing procedure, the ASA exposure index changes and one should ask the lab for the adjusted ASA to be used when shooting reversal film to be processed as negative. Color reversals cannot be processed as negative, because the colors are brought out in the second development. If the process was halted after the first development, there would be no color.

Many film makers have experimented with unusual developing techniques and used them to enhance their work. These very specialized and experimental processes are rarely offered by the labs, and therefore some film makers try to have their own small processing machines, such as for 400 feet of film. Hand-operated 100-foot processing tanks are also available.

One of the most interesting processing techniques that can be done with one's own developing machine is solarization. This is a rather intuitive and unpredictable process, requiring many tests to determine the best processing times, etc. The best black-and-white stock for solarization is Eastman Fine Grain Sound Recording Negative #7375. This stock is very slow and can be handled in the darkroom with a yellow safe light. The exposed film is only partially developed, and then washed in water. Next, the film is exposed to normal room light. The intensity and duration of this exposure is determined by tests. The film is then immersed in a dilute developer, and with the safety light it is observed until the image comes out to the desired intensity. Finally the film is washed and fixed.

Although this method works well for black-and-white, color solarization is even less predictable. Optical-printer techniques of "high-contrast manipulation" (discussed below) are much better suited to achieving unusual color effects.

Another possibility available to a film maker who owns his own processing machine is the ability to add color to black-and-white film through toners or color-coupler developers such as Develochrome, made by the FR Corporation. An interesting effect results from coloring a piece of film with a household dye, which imparts an overall color to the image.

One can also experiment with immersing original into hot water to cause a "reticulation" effect, that is, a uniform texture of fine cracks like the grain of leather. Different textures could also be obtained by introducing a texture screen, either photographed or drawn onto a piece of clear film and then bi-packed with the original in the printer.

HIGH-CONTRAST MANIPULATION

Contrast manipulation is at the heart of the more complicated optical-printer operations that employ matting techniques. Eastman High Contrast Positive #7362 (a black-and-white print stock) is commonly used as an intermediate step for matting. It provides extremely high contrast. Any given density in the original will be represented (on 7362) as either deep black or clear (white), with very few gray tones in between. After printing through two or sometimes three generations of 7362 there will usually be no midtones. The density at which this rapid drop-off occurs can be controlled by varying the exposure in the printer. This two-tone characteristic of 7362 can be used in many ways.

As we print our black-and-white original onto 7362, by controlling the printer light we control the "drop-off" point, that is, the density level that will divide black from clear in the high-contrast print. To illustrate this, consider a face. In our black-and-white original the nose is brightest (clearest). From there the density gradually increases along the cheek until the ear, which is in complete shadow. By reducing the printer light, we could give it only enough light to make the nose turn white (clear) in the print, leaving the cheek completely black. With gradually higher printing lights the clear area in the print would be gradually extended into the cheek. Thus by controlling the density at which the high-contrast drop-off occurs, we also control its *location* in the picture.

Let us apply this to a practical example. Let us say we would like to introduce two colors into a picture of a man's face. (See figures 8-2, C-2.) We wish the highlights to be solid blue and all the shadows to be red. The original black-and-white negative is first printed onto 7362 High Contrast Positive, *developed as negative*. From this negative 7362 print we make another 7362 print, also processing it as negative, resulting in a positive image. (A negative of a negative forms a positive image.) We have gone through these two generations in order further to increase the contrast. By this third-generation 7362 print, the contrast should be extreme, showing only black and clear. From this another 7362 print is made and processed as negative. It and the third-generation print will be used to make the final print.

Thus, each was *processed as negative* so that we end up with a negative and a positive showing the same high-contrast image. We are now ready to combine them. Both the negative and the positive are printed onto the same piece of reversal color stock. In the positive 7362 print, the highlights of the man's face are clear and the shadows are black. Therefore if we print the positive with a blue filter, the highlights will be blue and the shadows will be left untouched for the moment. Next we rewind the raw stock and print over it again, this time printing the negative through a red filter. In the negative, the shadows are clear and the highlights are black. Therefore, this second pass will fill red into the shadows, leaving the highlights, previously colored blue, alone. The result is a high-contrast blue-and-red face.

This is a relatively simple operation, and does not require an optical printer. It could have been done with all contact printing. In matting situations, the unique value of the optical printer is its ability to bi-pack. Suppose, in the above example, that instead of orange and blue we wanted to use *two pictures*. Say we wish to have all the highlights contain clouds, while in all the shadows of a man's face, a rock surface would show through. To do this we would have bi-packed the clouds with the positive during the first run. On the second pass, footage of the rock surface would be bi-packed with the negative. This would put rock surface in the shadow areas, while leaving clouds in the highlights.

Another interesting application is a multicolored outline effect. (See figures 8-3, 8-4, C-3.) From the black-and-white original we make several high-contrast 7362 prints, but they are printed at graduating printer lights. This will yield a different black-and-white cut-off point in each print. From each of these prints we make another 7362 print, again processed as negative. This (the third) generation will have positive images. From each of these prints yet another 7362 print is made, all processed as negative. Now if prints from the third generation are bi-packed with fourth-generation prints that descended from the adjacent lower density, the result will be a fringe. If prints from the third and fourth generations are bi-packed in this fashion and each pair is printed through a different color filter, the result will be a multicolored image.

Another effect (called "phasing") is achieved by using a high-contrast positive and negative of a subject, using several generations of 7362 as described earlier. The positive and

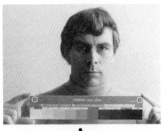

8-2 High-contrast color-separation effect. Successive generations of 7362, processed as negative, are used to increase the contrast. Then, by printing the third generation through a blue filter, and then the fourth generation through a red filter, a high-contrast color-separation effect is created. (Photo by author)

**ORIGINAL
(1ST GENERATION)**

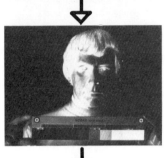

2ND GENERATION

3RD GENERATION

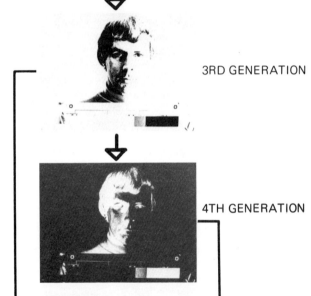

4TH GENERATION

BLUE FILTER   **RED FILTER**

C-2 High-contrast color-separation effect. (Photo by author)

negative are then bi-packed. Normally this would result in no image, each one canceling out the other. However, if they are bi-packed out of phase (out of sync by one or two frames), any movement will show up as an irregular shape along the fringes of the object. The rest of the frame will be masked out. This shape, of course, could be colored with a filter.

Another popular manipulation is the "Rorschach" effect. (See figures 8-5, C-4.) This is a symmetrical repetition of the same image in both halves of the frame. It is named for the psychological testing device made by staining a piece of paper and folding it in half to produce identical imprints on both sides of the fold. The simplest way to achieve this on film is to print the original onto the raw stock twice, once correctly and once sides reversed. If the original shows a dancer standing in the left side of the frame, the print will show the dancer there and also on the right side, symmetrically reversed. But if the dancer is in the middle, her two images will be superimposed. To achieve a cleaner Rorschach effect with no ghost images, we can bi-pack the original with a roll of clear film that is opaque over half of the frame. In a second printer run we reverse the sides of the original and print again, this time bi-packing it with a negative printed from the half-frame mask. We do *not* use the original mask reversed. Using a negative of the original mask ensures that the mask for the second pass exactly matches the area left blank in the first pass. If the same mask was used reversed in the second run, we would run the risk of a gap showing if the edge of the mask wasn't perfectly vertical and exactly in the center of the frame.

When exposing the original footage from which we will make 7362 high-contrast prints, we must consider what we intend to do, in order to know how to expose the original. For example, if we intend eventually to produce a high-contrast silhouette of a person against some background, then the original must be exposed with plenty of contrast between the man and the background, that is, the background white and the man dark, or vice versa. If we had instead made the mistake of lighting the original scene flatly, the background and certain parts of the man might have been recorded in the same shade of gray in the original, making it impossible to separate them with 7362. Therefore, the film maker exposing original to be used later for optical printing effects must use lighting, set colors, and makeup to his advantage. To take an example, say we intend to insert passing clouds or a landscape behind a person's eyes. As an intermediate step

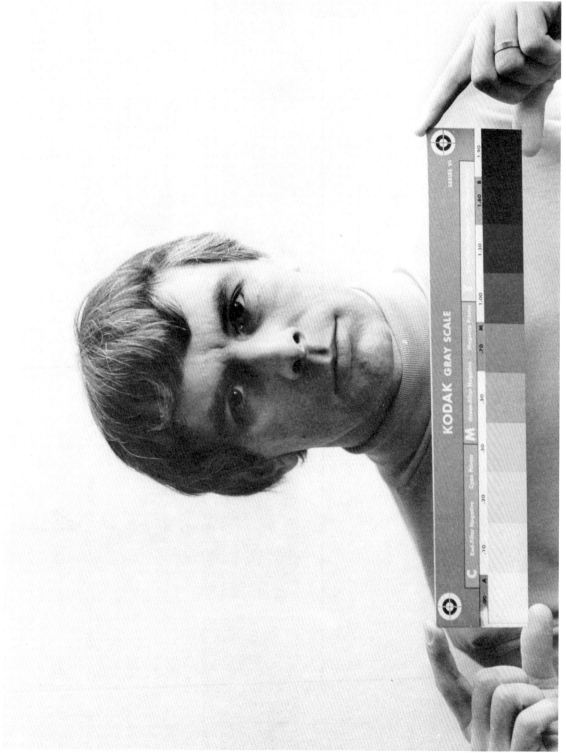

8-3 Original (first generation). (Photo by author)

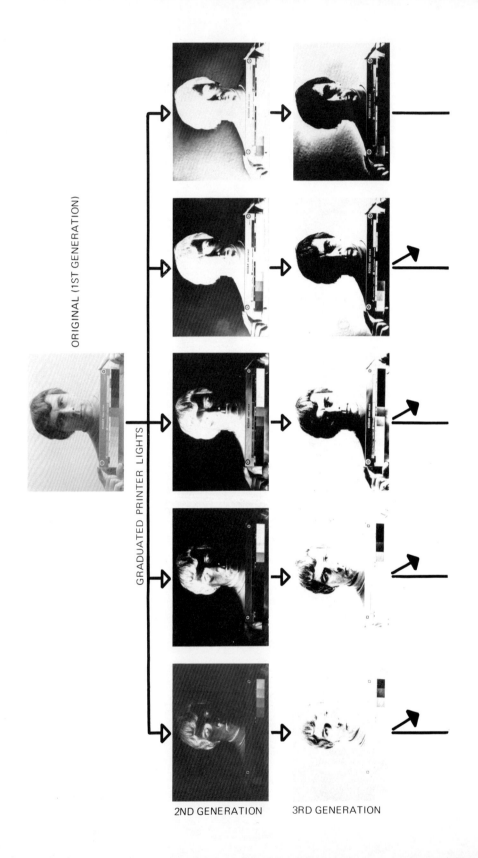

ORIGINAL (1ST GENERATION)

GRADUATED PRINTER LIGHTS

2ND GENERATION

3RD GENERATION

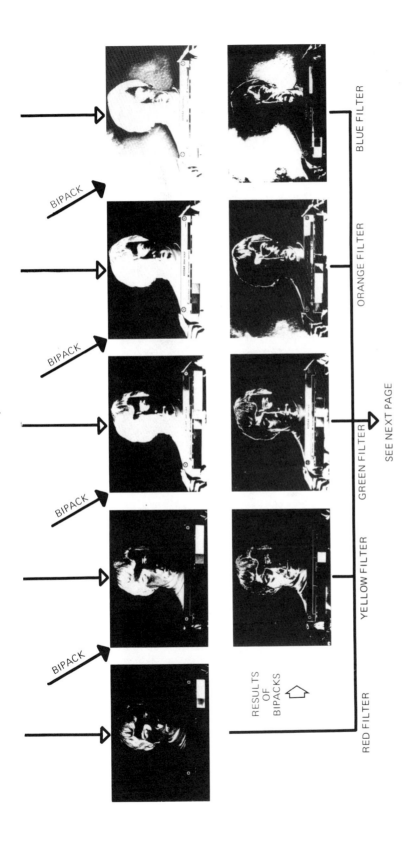

RED FILTER

YELLOW FILTER

GREEN FILTER

ORANGE FILTER

BLUE FILTER

BIPACK

BIPACK

BIPACK

BIPACK

RESULTS
OF
BIPACKS

SEE NEXT PAGE

8-4 High-contrast multicolored-outline effect. For the purpose of illustration, we show the results of the bi-packs. These show how the prints from the third and fourth generations will look when overlapped and held up to a light. The indicated prints from the third and fourth generations are bi-packed in the printer, and printed, one pair (bi-pack) at a time, through a color filter and onto color film in the printer camera.

181

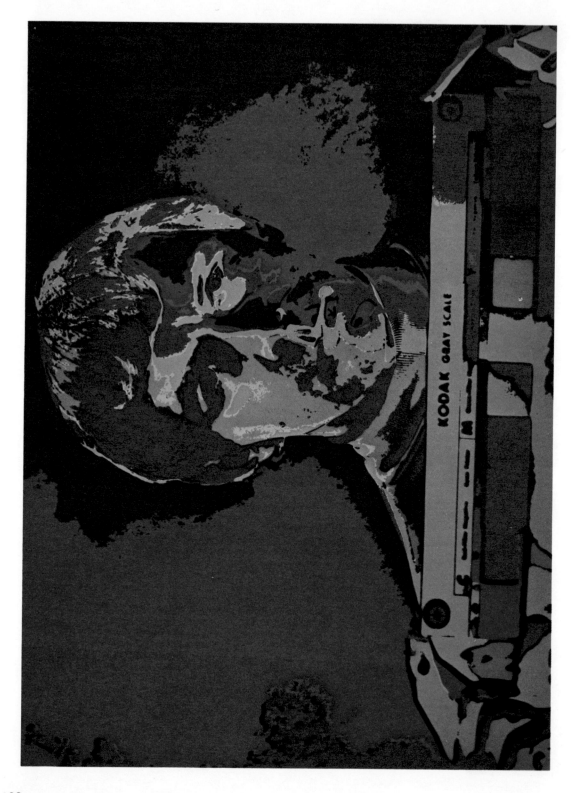

C-3 High-contrast multicolored-outline effect. (Photo by author)

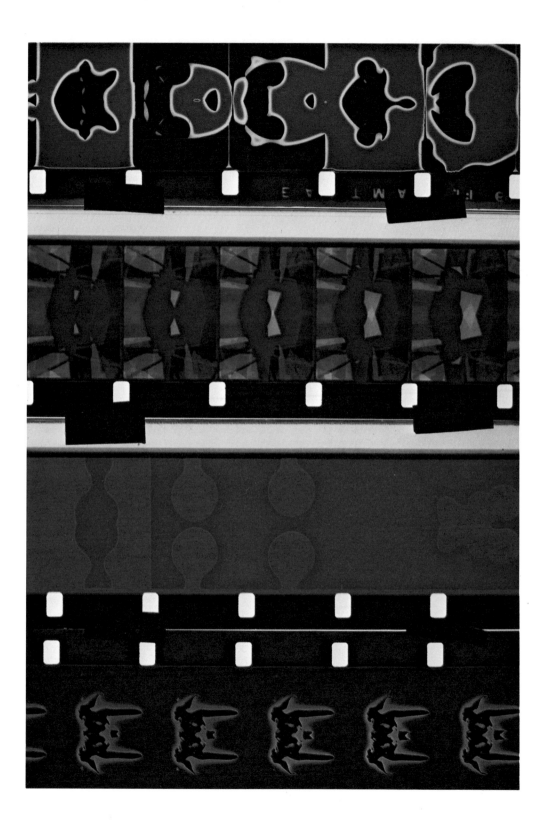

C-4 These combinations of "Rorschach" and high-contrast color effects are from a film by Pat O'Neill, titled 7362, named for the print stock used to achieve the effects. The first and fourth images were solarized and "Rorschached" in high contrast. The second one is pure animated artwork in two colors. The third is compiled from several detail shots of an oil well in motion. These shots were first superimposed and then "Rorschached." (Courtesy of Pat O'Neill)

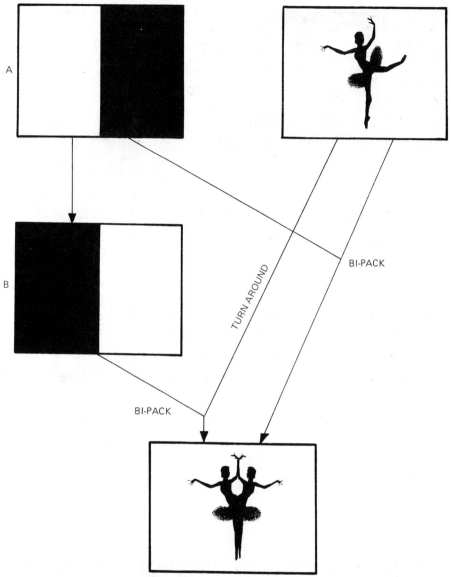

8-5 "Rorschach" effect. *A:* 7362 high-contrast mask. *B:* Complementary 7362 mask, printed from the original mask (*A*).

we would need a high-contrast image in which *just* the eye sockets are black and everything else is clear. This is easily achieved if, when we shoot the original closeup, we put black makeup over the actor's closed eyelids and then light him and the background with all soft light from the front and sides. This will wash out all the shadows and leave an image in which there is a high enough contrast between the eye sockets and the rest of the picture to obtain the 7362 prints required. One 7362 print will have the eye sockets black and the rest clear. It will block out the eyes when bi-packed with the footage of the

man's face. A negative of that 7362 print will have the eyes clear and the rest black. This will be bi-packed with footage of clouds, which will appear in the eye sockets.

AERIAL IMAGE

The aerial-image principle borders on magic and at first contact is somewhat hard to believe. To understand it, consider a normal projector casting an image onto a screen. If we remove the screen, the image is still focused at that plane in midair. Of course we cannot see it because it isn't reflected by any solid surface such as a screen or a ground glass. But if we position a camera on the other side of the "screen," opposite the projector, and focus this camera onto the "air frame" where the screen was, the camera will photograph the image formed in midair, even though there is no image-forming surface. It sounds impossible, but it works.

One such aerial-image system is available with the Oxberry animation stand. (See figure 8-6.) Here the projected image coming from below via a mirror and condenser lens is focused as an aerial image in the plane of the clear-glass artwork table. If artwork or objects are positioned on this surface and lit from above, they will be photographed with the aerial image showing through around them.

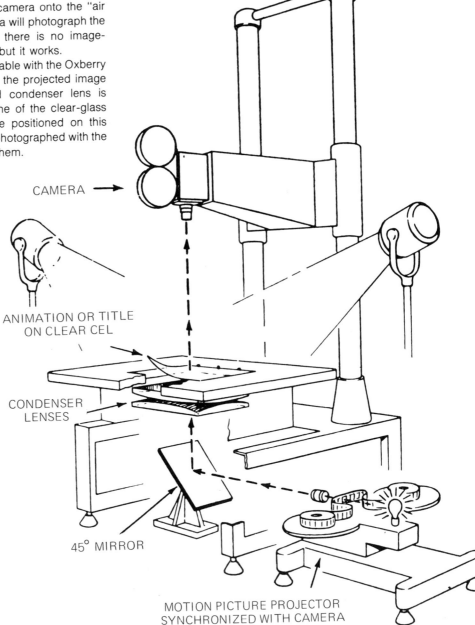

CAMERA

ANIMATION OR TITLE
ON CLEAR CEL

CONDENSER
LENSES

45° MIRROR

MOTION PICTURE PROJECTOR
SYNCHRONIZED WITH CAMERA

8-6 Oxberry animation stand with aerial image unit.
(Courtesy of Oxberry, division of Richmark Camera
Service, Inc.)

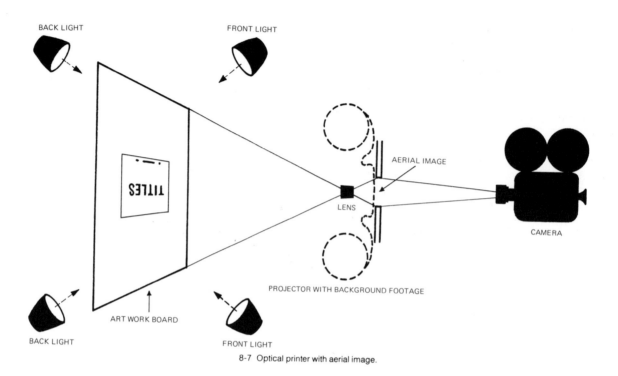

BACK LIGHT

FRONT LIGHT

AERIAL IMAGE

CAMERA

LENS

PROJECTOR WITH BACKGROUND FOOTAGE

ART WORK BOARD

BACK LIGHT

FRONT LIGHT

8-7 Optical printer with aerial image.

For example, to show animated effects against a realistic background we can draw on animation cells, leaving clear areas in which we will want background. When lit from above, the camera will see the drawings, which block out the parts of the background they cover. The light from above can be polarized so that it just illuminates the artwork. The light goes right through the glass surface and aerial image (there is nothing there to reflect it), and therefore the light does not wash out the background. Instead of drawings on animation cells we could use small three-dimensional objects.

Of the many configurations of aerial-image optical printers, perhaps the simplest is achieved by removing the lamp house from a normal optical printer and putting a lens in its place. (See figure 8-7.) An illuminated artwork area is focused by the lens to form an image in the projector gate. The lens on the optical-printer camera is also focused at this same plane. This system is less expensive as it can be set up by modifying a normal optical printer. Unlike the Oxberry, we must make two

runs. For example, if we wish special titles superimposed, on the first run background footage is put into the projector. The lettering is painted on a clear cell and placed on the artwork board, which is illuminated from behind so that the letters appear black, silhouetted against a luminous background that acts as a source of light. These letters are focused onto the film plane in the projector. Thus the camera will see the background footage in the projector gate, illuminated from behind with the black letters superimposed across it. For white or colored titles, a second pass will be made. The background footage is now removed from the printer. The back lights are turned off and the front lights are turned on so that the titles are illuminated only from the front. A piece of black cardboard is placed behind the cell so that the area around the letters will be completely black, and therefore will not affect the picture area that was earlier filled in with background. Therefore, during this second pass only the letters will be printed, fitting into their corresponding areas left unexposed in the first pass.

CHAPTER 9
INFRARED AND UNDERWATER CINEMATOGRAPHY

INFRARED CINEMATOGRAPHY

Infrared films are widely used in scientific studies and criminology. In nonscientific film making, infrared film could be used for practical applications (such as day-for-night or haze penetration) or for creating unrealistic effects. In 16mm, Eastman offers one negative black-and-white and one color reversal infrared film:

The negative black-and-white is Kodak High-Speed Infrared Film #2481, ASA 64. The code for this film in 16mm size is 16mm #HIE 430. It is available in rolls of 125 feet on 100-foot camera spools.

The color reversal is Ektachrome Infrared Recording Film #SO-117, daylight ASA 100 (with a Kodak Wratten #12 filter), tungsten ASA *about* 50 with *both* a #12 and a Kodak CC filter #50C2. For 16mm film of this type, the code number is 16mm #Sp 449. Like the black-and-white, it comes in rolls of 125 feet on 100-foot camera spools. These emulsions are thinner than normal films and so 125 feet will fit onto a normal 100-foot camera spool.

Infrared color film has three layers, one sensitive to green, one to red, and one to infrared. For scientific work a yellow Kodak Wratten #12 filter is used to remove the blue light to which *each* of the layers is sensitive. However, for artistic experimentation, other filters can be used, such as Wratten #8, #15, #K2, #23, #25, or #58. The reversal original yields an intentionally "false" color rendition. Blue sky is reproduced in its natural color, but foliage is shown as a striking red. Flowers yield various colors. Veins under the skin are visible.

Color Infrared film is rather expensive. It is also available in 35mm for still cameras. Therefore, all tests and experimentation should be done with 35mm stills in order to save money. When the tests achieve satisfactory results the actual shots can then be taken on infrared motion-picture film.

Infrared black-and-white film renditions will depend on the filter being used. With no filter, it will behave very much like a normal panchromatic film — that is, a black-and-white film that is sensitive to all colors. It is normally used with one of the following Wratten filters: #15 (orange), #25 (red), #29 (red), #70 (deep red). It is also used with infrared filters, which are usually opaque, passing no visible light (only infrared), such as #87, #87-C, and #88-A. With most of these filters the sky will be black and the foliage white.

Infrared wavelengths are longer than visible light, and therefore if the lens is filtered to pick up only infrared one must focus slightly closer than normal. (When one focuses for a closer distance, the lens-to-film distance is slightly increased.) In practice, this is achieved by first focusing normally and then turning the focus ring toward a closer setting until the image starts to go very slightly out of focus. Some lenses have a special calibration for focusing infrared. For example, the normal way of focusing a lens might be to turn the lens barrel to align the proper distance number with a black line. Next to that line there might be a red dot to which the footage numbers would be turned if focusing for infrared.

When using *color* infrared film we focus in the normal way, because color infrared is also sensitive to the visible spectrum and no infrared filters are used.

The most efficient artificial lights for use with color or black-and-white infrared films are photoflood lamps of 3400° K. Lamps of 3200° K are *almost* as efficient and have a longer life expectancy. Contrary to popular belief, heat-radiating lamps and heating devices are less efficient. However, to photograph with "invisible light" (in apparent total darkness) we should employ a visually opaque infrared filter, Wratten #87, over a 3400° K or a 3200° K lamp. A special housing is required to hold the filter away from the lamp. The filter should be mounted about 2 feet away from a 1000-watt bulb, or about a foot away when a 500-watt lamp is used. See the Kodak specifications.

For near-infrared radiation, Polaroid Corporation makes a type HR Linear Polarizer, which requires a one-stop compensation.

When calculating the exposure for infrared film, light-meter readings can only be used as a rough guide, as the selenium cells in the light meter are not sensitive to infrared light. For exteriors, when using the #29 filter with black-and-white film or when shooting color with the customary #12 filter, you can place an orange #15 filter on the light meter to obtain a somewhat better reading. Infrared exposure measurement is very imprecise because of the many variables. When in doubt, take the shot several times, varying the exposure on each one.

Storage conditions for infrared should be like that for other film stocks. Faulty storage of color infrared film will cause a cyan cast.

In the darkroom, remember that infrared is heat-sensitive and sensitive to radiation that is invisible. So turn off heaters and give objects a chance to cool, such as the darkroom light bulb.

UNDERWATER CINEMATOGRAPHY

The underwater cinematographer must be an experienced diver, and so must the entire film crew. When using actors or when filming under hazardous conditions, a safety diver should also be employed.

Underwater, the cameraman is faced with a different optical medium than above the surface. Water absorbs and diffuses the light. The intensity of sunlight decreases as it travels farther through the water. It penetrates deepest when it comes from straight above, because the more acute the angle of penetration is, the greater the effective distance the light must travel, and so the light level falls off rapidly. Therefore the best shooting time is the four to six hours in midday.

Locations must be chosen that provide shallow areas, clear water, and a high sun. Generally, uncloudy weather is also a must.

Artificial light is used as a last resort. It looks unrealistic. In addition, it fades away rapidly as it travels farther from the source, making it impossible to light large areas evenly. In some cases, where the actors have practical lights, we can logically justify uneven lighting.

Underwater lighting should be done from the sides, because frontal lighting is reflected back into the camera, creating a foggy effect. This "back scatter" is similar to what happens when you try to use your high beams while driving in a thick fog.

Power problems also add to the argument against using artificial lights underwater. Battery-powered underwater lights are hopeless, as they run down after a very short period. A small DC generator on the boat, with cables running to the lights, is a clumsy answer. The best solution is to avoid underwater lights whenever possible and try to depend exclusively on the sun. If lights have to be used, they must have a closed reflector, i.e., a piece of glass that keeps the water away from the bulb and reflector.

Measuring light levels underwater is difficult. There are differences of opinion as to the best measuring techniques. Incident readings do not account for the light that is lost on its way from the subject to the camera. (The light is absorbed by the water.) Reflected readings, taken from the camera position, are perhaps better in this respect, but they are easily influenced by bright bottoms or dark backgrounds, common factors in underwater photography. The best tool is probably a narrow-angle reflectant light meter, such as the Sekonic Marine, which features a comparatively narrow acceptance angle and has a waterproof case. Ordinary light meters can be used, if a waterproof housing is provided.

Another important consideration is color. Underwater, the colors change with increased depth, gradually becoming bluish-green. At 10 feet there are no reds. By about 30 feet orange vanishes, and 60 feet down there is nothing left but

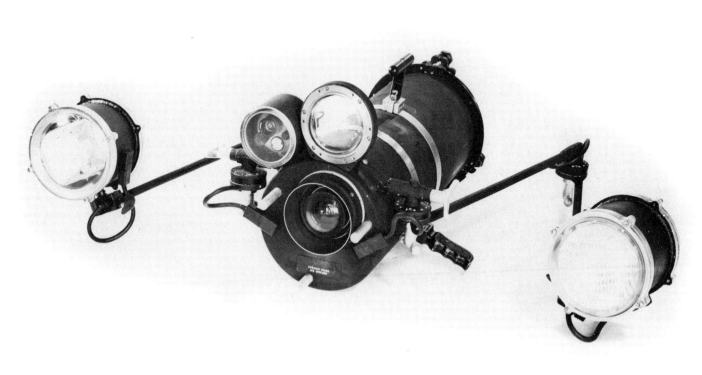

9-1 Gholson 2000 underwater camera and lighting system. (Courtesy of Oceanic Films, Inc.)

green with a bit of blue. To counteract these color deficiencies, we can use filters to favor the warmer colors. This will improve skin tones. Red and magenta CC filters of various strengths will be used, depending on the depth. When filming at 15 feet, CC.40R (red) is sufficient for *partial* correction. Partial correction will leave it more realistic; full correction may remove the underwater appearance. Pushing color film shot underwater is not advisable, as the color turns even more green.

In black-and-white, our concern is the contrast range. The water scatters and diffuses the light, thus decreasing contrast with added depth. A yellow or orange filter will improve the contrast.

Another effect the water has on light is magnification. Underwater, distances appear one-quarter closer. Therefore an object 40 feet away appears to be 30. This effect applies to both the eye and the lens. Therefore, if we *guessed* the distance to the subject, estimating by eye that it is 30 feet, and

set the focus accordingly, it would be in focus. Reflex focusing could also be accurate, but it is physically difficult to get your eye very close to the eyepiece, because of the underwater camera housing and the face mask.

Wide-angle lenses are the ones most commonly used. This allows the cameraman to come closer to the subject. There is less water between the subject and camera and the picture is therefore clearer. The standard set of lenses used on the Gholson 2000 underwater camera contains 5.9mm, 10mm, and 12mm lenses.

Underwater cameras can be either self-contained or housed. The above-mentioned Gholson 2000 is a good example of the self-contained group. It takes a 400-foot load. Another popular self-housed underwater camera is the Teledyne DBM 9-1 with a 200-foot magazine and speeds ranging from 16 to 48 fps.

Housings have been designed for many of the all-purpose

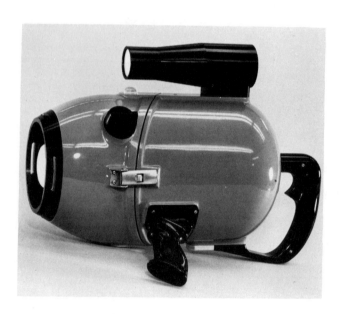

9-3 Teledyne DBM self-housed underwater camera with 400-foot magazine and speeds ranging from 16 to 48 fps. (Courtesy of Teledyne Camera Systems)

cameras, like Arriflex, Bolex, and others. Housings can be rented or bought from dealers. Many underwater cinematographers build their own.

It must be remembered that the airtight compartment requires great care to prevent humidity, which results in fungus growth or emulsion softening. After shooting, the outside of the housing should be rinsed off with *fresh* water and then the camera should be taken out of the housing (or opened, in the case of self-housed cameras) and allowed to air. While shooting, a humidity-absorbing substance is sometimes placed inside the housing as an added precaution.

The most important consideration in selecting an underwater camera is its maneuverability, which depends on the unit's buoyancy. If buoyancy can be adjusted it gives the operator many advantages. Maneuvering underwater is the opposite to maneuvering on dry land in one respect: moving shots are smooth and the cameraman can glide in any direction, but steady shots are difficult because of water movement. One solution is to increase the weight of the camera. In other cases a weighted tripod may be necessary.

Remember that everything is more difficult underwater. Communication is limited to hand signals and buzzers. There are many cumbersome problems and delays, such as air running out or crew members and actors getting cold. Therefore, when planning underwater work, allow extra time. Much time can be saved if the locations are all in shallow water, not deeper than 30 feet. Factors favoring shallow water include expediency of shooting, more light, better color and contrast, comfort (warmer water and less pressure), and less danger, especially if you are using actors who are not experienced divers.

CHAPTER 10
PRODUCTION

Unfortunately, film is a very expensive medium, and therefore the scope of any film project must depend heavily on the amount of available money. There are various ways of financing a film. You can start with an idea and shape it to the limits of your funds, or search for sufficient backing to accommodate your concept. Sometimes, with limited funds, it is better to complete a small part of the total project and use it in the search for further money. In situations where small budgets are allocated annually (such as in some film schools), it is possible to produce one or two small films each year, for a few years, planning them so that later they can all be edited together to make a feature.

Whatever way a film is financed, it must be thoroughly budgeted, if one expects to finish what is started. Otherwise, unforeseen and wasted expenditures may leave the production out of money before it is completed.

The following is a broad and rather general list of expenses to be reckoned with in film making. The list is long and includes some expenses that will not always be encountered.

Smaller productions could start with this list and scale it down to meet their needs.

I. Story
   a. Rights to the original material
   b. Screenwriter(s)
   c. Secretarial and mimeograph work
II. Producer and his staff
III. Director, assistant(s), and script girl
IV. Cast
   a. Featured players
   b. Day players
   c. Extras and stand-ins
   d. Stunt men
   e. Other costs, including a nurse or teacher for juvenile actors
V. Crew and equipment
   a. Director of photography
   b. Camera operator
   c. First and second assistant cameramen

    d. Electricians, grips, and prop men

    e. Camera and equipment rental

    f. Lighting equipment rental

    g. Miscellaneous supplies, such as replacement bulbs for lamps, etc.

VI. Sound recording

    a. Recordist, boom man, cable tender

    b. Equipment rental

    c. ¼-inch magnetic tape

    d. 16mm sprocketed magnetic film and transfer service

VII. Pre-production tests

VIII. Set costs

    a. Set designer

    b. Sound stage and set rentals

    c. Materials and construction labor

    d. Strike crew (cost of taking the sets down)

    e. Furniture, props, etc., either rented or purchased

    f. Losses or damage of borrowed or rented materials

    g. Special effects (such as fire, etc.), both rental and labor

IX. Animals and their handlers

X. Location costs

    a. Location rentals

    b. Transportation

    c. Accommodations

    d. Location scouting and advance arrangements

    e. Miscellaneous costs, such as electrical current, local permits, etc.

XI. Makeup and wardrobe

    a. Wardrobe supervisor, costume purchasing, rental, and cleaning

    b. Makeup artist and supplies

    c. Hairdresser and supplies

XII. Film costs

    a. Raw stock

    b. Development

    c. Daily prints

    d. Negative cutting

    e. First trial print

    f. Masters and dupes

    g. Optical track

    h. Miscellaneous smaller costs, such as printing corresponding edge numbers, etc.

    i. Optical effects

    j. Release prints

XIII. Editing

    a. Editor and assistant

    b. Cutting-equipment and editing-room rental

    c. Projection

    d. Materials and supplies

XIV. Music

    a. Music rights

    b. Performance rights or composer

    c. Conductor and musicians

    d. Recording stage, music mimeograph, recordist, rental and transportation of instruments, etc.

XV. Sound mixing

    a. Dialog replacement

    b. Sound effects

    c. Mixing

XVI. General

    a. Legal

    b. Taxes (payroll, sales, property)

    c. Office rental

    d. Telephone bill

    e. Accountant

    f. Insurance

    g. Miscellaneous

XVII. Contingency

In order to ensure that the film will have funds to finish, about 10 to 15 percent of the budget should be a contingency fund for dealing with unexpected expenses. With more production experience, this percentage can be decreased.

A well-developed script is essential in planning the budget. If the film idea is not your own, the first consideration is copyright. If the written material is more than 56 years old it should be in the public domain and no longer protected by copyright. For further information on researching the copyright status of a work in the United States, write to the Registrar of Copyrights, Library of Congress, Washington, D.C. 20540.

The final shooting script will evolve gradually. Step by step, the directorial approach is determined and the casting is completed. Story boards are often prepared at this stage. The final script should describe the nature of the shots, camera movements, times of day, information about the sets and props, the mood of the lighting, etc.

Very rarely will a film be shot "in order." The producer will need a breakdown showing what scenes will be shot on what day. While the breakdown is being made, the crew is also being organized. The crew will vary in size depending on the needs of the project, but it is advisable to avoid combining too many functions in one person. In documentary filming a two-man crew (one cameraman/director and one sound recordist/boom operator) is not unusual. However, for larger productions, each crew member should be able to concentrate on one job. An inexperienced director would often be wise to concentrate on the actors and not try to be his own camera operator and director of photography as well. A "proper" camera crew consists of four or more people: the director of photography (also referred to as the lighting cameraman), the camera operator, and the first and second assistant cameramen. The assistants "pull focus," operate the zoom lens, load the magazines, fill out the lab forms, and operate the clapper board. On amateur productions it is sometimes a good idea to hire at least one experienced professional, such as a cameraman, if the budget can afford it. This may save many technical errors and improve the quality of the production.

As soon as the producer has enough information to determine what equipment will be required, the studio space, rental props, costumes, and rental equipment may be ordered or reserved. When selecting lighting equipment, the producer will benefit from literature, tables, and practical experience in determining what size and how many lamps will be needed for illuminating a given area to the required foot-candle level.

LOGISTICS

All locations must be scouted on a reconnaissance trip. The choice of a location will depend on the accessibility of the area, the availability of power, the topography, the sound conditions (check air-traffic routing charts and road-traffic noise), the average weather conditions, what permits are required, the availability of local help (such as policemen to redirect traffic, electricians, catering services, etc.), and the local accommodations for the cast and crew. Travel arrangements will have to be made. When filming out of the country, passports will have to be secured; they should be applied for well in advance in case of delays. All foreign-made equipment has to be listed with serial numbers and declared to the customs authorities when leaving. This is absolutely necessary in order to bring the equipment back without having to pay customs duties.

Naturally, all the equipment used on a production should be insured. Liability insurance may also be necessary if there is any risk involved in the filming. Sometimes property owners at locations will demand that you have such insurance before using their premises.

INVASION OF PRIVACY

When shooting on location, one should know something about the laws concerning invasion of privacy that might apply to persons not under contract who appear in the film. Such participants might willingly help you while filming but then sue you later. However, if they can be persuaded to sign a simple release, the chance of a suit is reduced. The following is one type of release.

Authorization to Reproduce
Physical Likeness and Voice

For good and valuable consideration from _____ Productions, the adequacy and receipt of which is hereby acknowledged, I hereby expressly grant to said _____ Productions, or any third party it may authorize, and to its and their employees, agents, and assigns, the right to photograph me and/or make recordings of my voice, and the right to use pictures, silhouettes, and other reproductions of my physical likeness (as the same may appear in any still-camera photograph and/or motion-picture film) and/or recordings of my voice in and in connection with the exhibition and/or broadcast, theatrically or on television or radio, of any motion-picture film or tape in which my physical likeness and/or voice may be used or incorporated, and in connection with the publication in magazines, newspapers, or otherwise of any articles in which my physical likeness may be printed, used, or incorporated, and in the advertising, exploiting, and publicizing of any such motion pictures, television programs, radio programs, magazines, and newspapers. I certify and represent that I have read the foregoing and fully understand the meaning and effect thereof and, intending to

be legally bound, I have hereunto set my hand this _____
day of _____, 19_____.

_____
(Signature)

I hereby consent and agree to the above as the Parent/Guardian of _____ .

_____
(Signature)

Witness: _____
Date: _____

This is a long and very thorough version. Sometimes it is easier to get people to sign this simplified but still-binding short form:

Release Form

For consideration received, I give permission without restrictions to _____ Productions, its successors and assigns, to distribute and sell still and sound motion pictures and tape recordings taken of me for a motion picture tentatively titled _____ .

Signed _____

Date _____

Signature of Parent or Guardian _____
Witness: _____ Date: _____

Whichever release is used, after signing, the person should be given a token payment such as one dollar *in cash* (not check) to make the arrangement binding.

In some situations a similar release might be necessary from the owner of the premises to allow you to photograph his property. If the actors are not under contract it is often a very good idea to have them sign a release also. This will prevent them from suing you later, should the film unexpectedly make money.

SCHEDULING

Before shooting, the script has been broken down and a schedule drawn up showing the exact scenes to be shot each day and listing the actors, props, and sets that will be needed. Such scheduling is necessary for efficient operation and will reduce wasted time. When time is especially limited, it is wise to study each scene to determine the quickest shooting order for the various shots.

During production, the crew and cast must be kept well informed about all times, dates, and locations. Lists of phone numbers are mandatory. Professional production managers supply everyone with daily call sheets.

SHOOTING TESTS

To ensure high photographic quality, time, money, and facilities must be allocated to the director of photography for shooting tests. Tests may include emulsion characteristics, lens and camera performance, filters, color schemes of sets and costumes, lighting, makeup, and out-of-the-ordinary camera movements or special effects.

The sound recordist may also want to test certain things, such as performance of the sync system, the recorder, the mics, and cables; sound interferences, such as a radio station being picked up, etc.; and acoustics of the sets and locations.

SHOOTING

If makeup is required, the makeup man and the actors will be the first to arrive. The director will first block out the scene, marking the camera and actor positions. The lighting and microphones are then set up and the first full rehearsal follows. Any necessary adjustments are made. When the actual shot is taken the recorder and camera are started, the scene is slated, and then the actors begin. In coordinating this procedure there is usually a dialog something like this:

ASSISTANT DIRECTOR *(when everyone is ready)*: Quiet, please.
DIRECTOR: Sound.
SOUND MAN *(starts recorder and when it is up to speed)*: Rolling.
DIRECTOR: Camera.
CAMERA OPERATOR *(starts camera and when it is up to speed)*: Speed.
ASSISTANT DIRECTOR: Mark it.
CLAPPER *(holding up slate in front of camera)*: Scene one, take one. *(claps slate and quickly exits)*
DIRECTOR: Action.

Now the scene takes place. When it is over the director will call "Cut" and the camera operator and recordist will switch off their machines. What is important here is not the specific words or who says them, but the fact that a systematized procedure is developed to get the recorder and camera started, slated, and then stopped with a minimum of wasted film.

After each take, the director will usually ask the camera operator and recordist if there were any problems or mistakes. The script girl has constantly been making notes on every possible detail that, if changed, might spoil the continuity, such as the relative positions of all the fixtures, actors, and props; the lens focal length and the camera position; and the actions of the actors, such as how they picked up an object, in their right or left hand, etc. She makes notes as to whether the director wants the take printed ("P") or thought it was no good ("NG"). The script girl is sometimes aided by a Polaroid camera.

Professional camera crews also fill out camera report cards during the shooting. They partially duplicate the script girl's notes, indicating footage of each take, effects, the "P"/"NG" indication, etc. This information will later be transferred to a negative report sheet that will accompany the film to the lab.

231545

de luxe general ⊙⊙®

1418 NORTH WESTERN AVENUE, HOLLYWOOD, CALIFORNIA 90027 • TELEPHONE 466-8631
1546 NORTH ARGYLE AVE., HOLLYWOOD, CALIF. 90028 • PHONE DAY 462-6171 NITE 462-6349

camera report
sound report

DATE **2-22-71**   CUSTOMER ORDER NUMBER _____

COMPANY **TARNAWA Films**

DIRECTOR **Dunski**   CAMERAMAN **Plewa**   RECORDIST

PRODUCTION NUMBER OR TITLE **"Gidjet Gets a Hockey Puck"**

MAGAZINE NUMBER **4**   ROLL NUMBER **6**

35 MM COLOR   35 MM B/W   (16 MM COLOR)   16 MM B/W

☐ ONE LIGHT   ☐ TIMED DAILIES   ✗ ONE LIGHT   ☐ ONE LIGHT
☐ TIMED DAILIES   ☐ TIMED DAILIES   ☐ TIMED DAILIES

TYPE OF FILM/EMULSION **7252**   SPECIAL INSTRUCTIONS _____

PRINT CIRCLED TAKES ONLY:

SCENE NUMBER	TAKES				REMARKS		Dial
	1 ⁵	2 ⁶	3 ⁷	4 ⁸	DAY OR NIGHT	INTERIOR OR EXTERIOR	
5	(42)	13	(15)		Night	Int.	42
5 A	(10)				effect		55
5 B	35	(37)			↓	↓	70
8 C	24	(25)			Day	Ext.	80
17	(179)				↓	↓	115
							152
							176
							201
							380

All contracts with this company are accepted with the understanding that all film delivered to it is covered by the owner against loss. This company takes every necessary precaution for the safekeeping of the film, but assumes no responsibility for its loss.

NUMBER CANS TO LABORATORY _____   BALANCE NEGATIVES ON HAND _____

GOOD FOOTAGE **308**   RECEIVED _____

N.G. FOOTAGE **72**   EXPOSED _____

WASTE FOOTAGE **20**   ON HAND _____

TOTAL FOOTAGE **400**   EMULSION NUMBER **7252 20131-D**

TRACK SPECIFICATIONS

CAMERA REPORT CARD

CAMERAMAN **PLEWA**   DIRECTOR **DUNSKI**   PROD. NO. **1065**

CAMERA **Arri BL # 5712**   MAG. NO. **4**   FOOTAGE **400**

DATE LOADED **2-22-72**   LOADER **TONER**   FOOTAGE EXPOSED **380**

TYPE **7252**   EMUL. BATCH **7252 20131-D**   CAN NO. **6**

Scene No.	SHOT NUMBER Sound	SHOT NUMBER Silent	Dial Feet	REMARKS	Scene No.	SHOT NUMBER Sound	SHOT NUMBER Silent	Dial Feet	REMARKS
5		(42)	42	NIGHT INT. PRT FOR NITE	17	(179)		380	DAY EXT.
		13	55						
		(15)	70					GOOD	308'
5A		(10)	80	EFFECT				NG	72'
5B	35		115					WASTE	20'
		(37)	152	↓	↓				400
8C	24		176	DAY EXT.					
		(25)	201	↓	↓				

10-1 Camera report card.

Right:
10-2 Negative report sheet. (Courtesy of DeLuxe General, Inc.)

RYDER SOUND SERVICES, INC.

1161 NORTH VINE STREET   HOllywood 9-3511

Producer	Date 30 Nov 71
Production No. 128	Roll No. 1
Mixer Jackson	Sheet No. 1 of 1
Boom Man Smith	Recordist
Stage #	Recorder # 16
Location	Microphone # 815/0825

Print Circled Takes Only

Scene No.	Take	Footage	REMARKS
10	1	105	Sync S
	2	213	
	3	315	
	(4)	425	
52	1	456	
	(2)	490	
52A	(1)	698	
	2	757	
	3	820	
	4	892	
FS	—	901	False Start
End of Roll			

10-3 Sound recording report sheet. (Courtesy of Ryder Sound Services, Inc.)

POST-SHOOTING PROCEDURE

When the magazines are unloaded and prepared for the film lab, it is important to note what magazine each roll of film was shot with, in case that magazine is defective and, for example, is scratching the film or has a light leak. If possible, it is convenient to have one person doing all the paperwork involved, including the negative report sheets, etc.

A log sheet is also kept for the sound. It accompanies the original ¼-inch tape when it is sent to the sound department for transfer to magnetic film.

POST-PRODUCTION

Post-production expenses will primarily involve editing, sound mixing, music scoring and recording, optical effects, titles, negative cutting, and all the lab expenses along the way to the release print.

It is preferable to score a picture rather than "lift" the music from a record. Many excellent student and amateur films are not releasable because the producer cannot pay the price demanded for the rights to the music. Music libraries will sell the rights to "stock music" at fairly reasonable prices. However, stock music is never original and is often overused and dull. Having a picture especially scored is usually better. When music is composed for the picture, a likely expense is an additional work print for the composer to study and to use during the scoring and re-recording. It is sometimes better to print this from the editor's "fine cut" work print, rather than from the A-B rolls. Once the A-B rolls are prepared, they are difficult to change, so it is advisable to remain flexible as long as possible, leaving the negative cutting until after the mixing and dubbing. If, on the other hand, there are many optical effects, visible only in the print, the composer's print may *have* to be taken from the A-B rolls.

COPYRIGHT

To copyright a film, the first thing you have to do is to print the copyright symbol, ©, followed by your name and the year on the title credit of the film. For example "© William Shakespeare, 1984." This first step to copyright should always be taken. It signifies a claim to the right to the material.

To make the copyright truly binding in the United States, the film has then to be filed with the Registrar of Copyrights, Library of Congress, Washington, D.C. 20450. Write to this address and ask for form L-M and information regarding film copyrighting. Following the Library of Congress directions, you can copyright the film for 28 years. The copyright can be renewed once for another 28 years. The first time a film is copyrighted you are sometimes required to deposit two prints with the Library of Congress, or a blown-up still photo from each shot, whichever the copyright office recommends. Having your film copyrighted makes it illegal for someone to make copies of all or part of it. It unfortunately cannot prevent someone from taking the same idea and applying his own interpretation.

196

CHAPTER 11
FILM SCHOOL ORGANIZATION

The teaching of film can be approached in roughly two ways: the "course" system or the "project" system. The course system is modeled after the normal university course approach and consists of a series of lectures, followed by demonstrations and, toward the latter part of the program, group productions organized by the film department. The project system has as its core a workshop situation with a minimum of formal lectures and a great emphasis on film projects — the making of individual and group films. Today, in the era of everyone "doing his own thing," the second approach is naturally more popular with the students, and, indeed, many students feel that their projects should be theirs alone and are unwilling to share either the work or the credits with others. However, there are also students who at once grasp the obvious advantages of forming production crews of various sizes. Both approaches must be considered when planning a general policy for a film department.

Smaller schools with limited equipment and limited teaching staff quite obviously cannot permit the relative anarchy of students being given equipment and control for their own one-man projects, and so limitations must be established at the outset. Happily, larger schools may be able to afford both individual and group projects.

By their very nature, certain films are largely a one-man job. Others, using more involved sound systems and more complicated lighting, will always require a larger crew. To deal with these problems certain European film schools of high repute have departmentalized the film-making process into categories such as directing, cinematography, production management, screenwriting, and acting. In these schools, after a period of communal study students elect to study toward a degree in *one* of these departments. The advantage of such a system is that student films can simultaneously be directed by one student, filmed by another, the production overseen by a third, and so on. This structure can be followed in more generalized film courses, but usually it is profitable, in this case, to work in rotation so that each student may direct his own film, but work as cameraman on another student's film, as sound man on a third production, etc. In this relatively painless way the student can receive a grounding in the various techniques. This approach is also recommended for another reason: with the highly flexible film-making techniques of today, the film maker, more than ever before, must learn all the various sides of his craft.

Admission methods in practice are varied and necessarily imprecise. Because of geographical difficulties American film schools cannot rely on an extended interviewing system for candidates. So, students who have the potential to be film makers will be chosen after a consideration of all forms of submitted work, ranging from films, photographs, and scripts to paintings, drawings, and even poetry. Ideally, candidates should be selected after an interview and after taking a series of tests. These tests might consist of such things as asking the candidate to write a shooting script from a short story or showing him a film he had not previously seen and asking him for a full criticism of it. Have him compose frames on the ground glass of a camera viewfinder, or ask him to select certain pictures from a group of photographs and arrange them to explore and express a given theme or idea, such as "love," "peace," "jealousy," etc. Of course even after such interviews, it must be understood that the process of admission is in itself a value judgment. The personal tastes of the admissions panel will weigh heavily on the selection of candidates.

Once the student is admitted, a film school, like a driving school, should proceed with due caution but all possible speed. Before a student is entrusted with expensive equipment, he must know how to use it without destroying it. The satisfactory completion of a crash course in the operation of the equipment should be the first requisite in any film course. At the same time, practical experiments with camera angles and movements, lenses, and filters should be covered to give the student a chance to understand the basics of cinematography. This will save costly errors on beginning film projects.

If the student is to work in 16mm film, the early experiments should be done in 16mm. However, an 8mm or Super-8 camera is an economical "sketch book" with which to make the otherwise expensive mistakes that are usual at this stage of learning.

In some cases the crash course may be broken down into subjects — for example, camera, lighting, sound operations, projection, editing, lab practices, and basic direction. In the case of basic direction the use of videotape systems can prove of enormous value.

These crash courses should be aimed at speedily preparing the students for a project-oriented workshop situation. In some schools where facilities for workshop projects for each student are not available, the students could each write a script. A vote might be taken to decide which script will be used for the project. The author of the chosen script might direct it, with the other students working as his crew.

Workable ratios of students to equipment have been tested in practice. An excellent norm is five students to a camera, five students to an editing machine, and eight students to a professional motion-picture tape recorder. Ratios in video equipment depend entirely on the projects being undertaken. Fifteen students to one faculty member is a fair ratio, although ten to one is much better. If each faculty member has to carry more than fifteen students with projects, project output will be diminished and guidance will not be as good. To preserve and maintain valuable school equipment a professional technician is absolutely necessary.

A technical manual such as this cannot discuss film aesthetics, film history, and other important film subjects that are not immediately connected with film-production techniques. In addition to employing its own experts in screenwriting or direction, it is common for a film school to depend on other departments of the university, such as the English, art, and drama departments, for help in teaching the basics of other creative skills besides cinematography.

Glossary

A-B Rolls A method of preparing the original footage for printing from two rolls (A and B) onto a printing stock. Roll A may contain takes 1, 3, 5, . . . and roll B takes 2, 4, 6, ... The process requires two printer runs. This method prevents the splices from showing on the print and permits dissolves and other common optical effects without the use of an optical printer.

A-Wind, B-Wind Terms designating the position of sprocket holes and emulsion on rolls of a raw stock perforated along one edge only. See figure 2-15. In popular usage the terms could apply to single- or double-sprocketed film generations in the lab as well.

Academy Aperture A frame area enclosed by an Academy mask giving screen proportions of approximately 3:4.

Acceptance Angle A characteristic of an exposure meter describing the angle of the light cone reaching the photocell. Applies also to the camera-lens angle.

Acetate Base Also called "Safety base." A film base made of cellulose tri-acetate with slow-burning characteristics.

Aerial Perspective Perspective augmented by water and dirt particles in the air, which gradually obscure the view of distant objects.

Ambient Light Light surrounding the subject, generally of a soft, low-contrast quality.

Anamorphic Lens A lens used to produce a wide-screen image. It optically "squeezes" the picture, allowing a wider horizontal angle of acceptance, and then "unsqueezes" it during the projection.

Answer Print See **first trial composite print.**

Anti-Halation Backing or Layer An opaque layer on the back of the film base to prevent internal light reflections in the film base. It prevents or minimizes the halo effect around the images of strong lights such as car headlamps or street lights.

Aperture, Lens The opening through which light passes within the lens. Its diameter is adjustable by means of a lens iris (**diaphragm**).

Aperture Plate In camera: a plate with a rectangular opening that limits the area of a film frame being exposed. In projector: a plate that defines the frame being projected.

Apple Boxes Wooden boxes in three basic sizes (full, half, and quarter) used on the set in a variety of ways — to raise actors, furniture, lights, etc.

ASA Speed Film sensitivity to light as rated in numbers established by the American Standard Association (now American National Standards Institute, Inc.).

ASC American Society of Cinematographers.

Arc Light A powerful lamp in which the electric current flows between two electrodes. A carbon arc operates in the normal atmospheric pressure, while a mercury arc works with the current flowing through an enclosed mercury vapor, sometimes at a very high pressure. Arcs operate primarily on direct current.

Aspect Ratio The ratio of height to width of a film picture frame and of the projected image.

Assembly The first stage of editing, when all the shots are arranged in script order.

Baby Focusable studio lamp with a Fresnel lens and a 500-watt to 1000-watt bulb.

Baby Tripod, Baby Legs Very short tripod used when shooting low camera angles.

Backdrop Painted or photographed background used behind the set windows and doors.

Back Projection See **process projection.**

Barndoors Two or four metal shields hinged in front of a lamp to limit and shape the pattern of light.

Barney A padded camera cover, shaped to allow the camera operation. It reduces mechanical noise and sometimes contains electric heating elements.

Base, Film See **acetate base.**

Batch, Emulsion A quantity of raw stock with emulsion made at the same time and under the same conditions, therefore maintaining identical sensitometric and color characteristics.

BCU (Big Closeup) A single feature such as eyes, mouth, hand, etc., filling the screen. Also known as XCU (extreme closeup).

Belly Board A board for mounting a camera as low as possible.

Bin A boxlike or barrellike container with a frame from which to hang lengths of film during editing. It is usually lined with a disposable linen bag to prevent scratching.

Bi-pack Printing 1. Printing in contact with printing stock, using a contact printer. 2. Printing two bi-packed films, sandwiched together, onto the third film (printing stock), using an optical printer.

Bleaching A step in color-film processing when the metallic-silver image is converted into halides, which are later removed during fixing.

Bleeding A phenomenon in the developing process appearing on the border between high- and low-density areas, when vigorous development action spreads from the highlights into the shadows and degrades the sharp cutoff line between these areas. It is often noticeable around a figure silhouetted against the sky.

Blimp Soundproof camera housing to prevent mechanical noise from being picked up by the microphones. Many modern cameras are self-blimped, i.e., built to operate noiselessly.

Blocking the Scene Establishing the positions and movements of actors and/or camera in the scene.

Bloop 1. A noise caused by the splice in an optical sound track passing in front of the exciter lamp. 2. A patch or fogging mark covering the splice line to eliminate this noise. 3. A sound signal recorded on tape simultaneously with a light exposing a few frames of film to establish the synchronization between the two. Also called "clap." See **slate, electronic**. 4. Colloquial for **sync pop**.

Blue Coating Magnesium fluorite deposit on the glass-air surfaces of a lens. This anti-reflective coating greatly improves the light-transmitting power of the lens and therefore prevents reflected and scattered light from flaring the image.

Boom, Microphone A sound dolly with a long extendable arm enabling the operator to position the microphone and move it silently around the set, following the actors.

Booster Light Usually an arc lamp or cluster-type quartz lamps used on exterior locations for boosting the daylight, especially when filling the shadows.

Breaking Down Separating individual shots from a roll of rushes in the early stage of editing.

Brightness Ability of a surface to reflect or emit light in the direction of the viewer.

Broad A single or double lamp designed to provide even, soft illumination over a relatively wide area. Used as a general fill light.

Brute A type of arc lamp that draws 225 amps. "Mini-Brute" and "Maxi-Brute" are trade names of cluster-type quartz lighting instruments produced by Berkey-Colortran, Inc.

Buckle-Trip or Buckle Switch A circuit breaker in the film path of many modern cameras, which acts as a safety device in case of a camera jam.

Butterfly A net sometimes stretched over an outdoor scene to soften the sunlight.

B & W Black-and-white.

Candela A unit of light intensity. The luminance of a light source is often expressed in candelas per square meter.

Candle Per Square Foot Brightness unit used less commonly than **foot-lambert**.

Capstan A spindle that drives the tape in a sound recorder at a constant speed.

CC Filters Color-compensating filters. A series of filters in yellow, cyan, magenta, blue, green, and red, growing in density by small steps. Used for precise color correction at the printing stage, but sometimes also when filming, especially in scientific cinematography.

Cement, Film An acetone-based solution used for splicing films by partially dissolving the base and thus welding them together.

Century Stand A metal stand for positioning a lighting accessory such as a **flag, cookie, scrim**, etc.

Cinch Marks Scratch marks on film, chiefly caused by pressing on the edges of an unevenly wound roll of film, or by pulling on the end of a loosely wound roll.

Cinema Vérité Style of documentary filming when maximum authenticity of the photographed real action and dialog is preserved, without narration, optical effects, or added music.

Cinemascope A wide-screen system utilizing an **anamorphic lens**.

Cinex Printer An instrument for printing a strip of adjacent frames using a series of standard printer lights.

Cinex Strip A strip of positive film printed on the cinex printer, which allows the cameraman to judge the original as printed at different printer lights.

Circle of Confusion A circle representing on film an image point formed by a lens. .001 inch is the largest acceptable circle of confusion in 16mm cinematography.

Clapper Board Also called "clapstick" or "clapper." Two short boards hinged together and painted in a matching design. When sharply closed, they provide an audible and visible clue which is recorded on film and sound tape simultaneously. This helps to synchronize the picture film with the magnetic film in the editing process. A slate with relevant information, like scene and take number, is usually attached to a clapper board. Modern cameras are often equipped with an electronic slate. See **slate, electronic**.

Claw Part of the camera pull-down mechanism; a metal tooth that engages film perforations and moves the film down one frame at a time.

Code Numbers Progressing ink numbers printed at one-half-foot intervals on the edges of both picture and sound **dailies** to help the syncing-up process in editing.

Coding Machine A machine used for printing code numbers.

Colorblind Film Black-and-white emulsion sensitive to only one color, usually blue. See also **orthochromatic film**.

Color Chart A test chart representing the colors of the spectrum. Sometimes the color steps are parallel with the fields of gray that have the same visual luminosities as the corresponding steps of the colored half, as on the Illford Test Chart. Other test charts may have gray steps from white to black growing in logarithmic progression of blackening and independent of the color fields.

Color Sensitivity Corresponding photochemical reaction of film emulsion to different wavelengths, representing colors in the visible spectrum.

Color Temperature A system of evaluating the color of a light source by comparing it to a theoretically perfect temperature radiator called a "black body." At lower temperatures a black body emits reddish light, and when heated to high temperatures its light changes to bluish. Color temperature is measured in degrees Kelvin. A degree Kelvin is the same as a degree Centigrade, but the two scales have different starting points, 0° K = −273° Centigrade.

Complementary Colors Colors obtained by removing the **primary colors** from the visible spectrum. Minus-blue (yellow), minus-red (cyan), minus-green (magenta).

Composite Master Positive A composite print made to generate picture-and-sound duplicate negatives, which are in turn used for printing release prints.

Composite Print (Married Print) Positive print with picture and sound in **projection sync**.

Conforming Cutting the original footage to match the finished **work print**.

Contact Printer A printing machine in which the printing stock and the film being printed are in contact, emulsion to emulsion.

Contrast Scene contrast refers to the brightness range of a scene. Lighting contrast refers to the light-intensity differences between the sources. Emulsion and/or development contrast refers to the density range of the developed original and/or any subsequent generations, as compared with the scene contrast.

Cookie Also called "kukaloris" or "cucaloris." An irregularly perforated shadow-forming **flag**, opaque or translucent, made of plywood, plastic, etc.

Core A centerpiece around which a film is wound. Made of plastic, metal, or wood.

Covering Power A lens characteristic denoting the capacity to produce a sharp image over a film frame of a given size.

Crab Dolly A camera-mounting device with wheels that can be steered in any direction. Usually fitted with an adjustable-height column.

Cradle A lens support for heavy lenses, used to improve steadiness and protect the lens mount from damage.

Crane A large camera-mounting vehicle with a rotating and high-rising arm, operated electrically or manually.

Crystal Motor Also called "crystal-controlled motor." A motor operating at a precise synchronous speed, regulated by reference to an accurate crystal frequency source.

Crystal Sync System A double system of synchronous filming not requiring connecting cables between the camera and the recorder. Both mechanisms are regulated by very precise crystal-control systems.

CS (Close Shot) Head and torso down to the waist line filling the frame.

CU (Closeup) Head and shoulders filling the frame.

Cucaloris, Kukaloris See **cookie.**

Cut The point of joining two shots by splicing, thus creating an immediate transition, as opposed to **fade** or **dissolve.**

Cutter 1. Term used either interchangeably with "editor" or to define a person who is responsible for the mechanical rather than the creative elements of editing. 2. Shadow-forming device, usually rectangular in shape; a type of **flag.**

Cutting Copy See **work print.**

Cyclorama (Cyc) Stage background, usually white, with rounded corners, to create a limbo or sky effect. Made of plaster or stretched plastic.

Cyc Strip Lighting instrument shaped like a trough with up to 12 bulbs for even illumination of a cyclorama.

D Log E Curve Also called sensitometric curve, characteristic curve, H&D curve, or gamma curve. The graph curve representing a relationship between the film density and the logarithm of exposure. Its shape changes depending on the time and temperature of development. It enables the cameraman and the lab technicians to evaluate the photographic characteristics of a given film emulsion.

Dailies Also called "rushes." The first print from original footage, with or without synchronous sound tracks, delivered from the lab daily during the shooting period, for viewing by the director, cameramen, etc.

Daylight Loading Spool Metal spool with full flanges to protect the film stock from exposure to light during the loading and unloading of camera or magazines.

Definition Ability of an emulsion to separate fine detail, depending on several factors, such as graininess and subject contrast.

Degausser An instrument used for the process of demagnetizing. See also **erasing.**

Densitometer An instrument for measuring the density of a processed photographic emulsion.

Density The light-stopping power of silver deposit in the processed photographic emulsion.

Depth of Field The distance through which objects will appear sharp in front of and behind the point at which the camera is focused.

Depth of Focus The distance through which the film can be moved backward and forward behind the lens, before the image of a flat object becomes unsharp. Has little application in cinematography, as the film is held at a fixed distance from the lens by the **gate.**

Dialog Replacement Technique of recording dialog under the acoustically perfect conditions of the dubbing studio, to replace the poor dialog of scenes already shot on location. Actors time the delivery of their lines so as to match their lip

movement as viewed on the screen.

Diaphragm, Lens Also called "iris." An adjustable opening that controls the amount of light reaching the film through the lens. Calibrated in f-stops or T-stops.

Dichroic Filter A filter used on tungsten lamps to convert their color temperature to that of daylight. The filter reflects excessive red and transmits light that is bluer than originally.

Differential Focus Also called "split focus." Focusing at a point between two subjects in depth, to accommodate them both in the depth-of-field range, i.e. both in sharp focus.

Diffused Light Light originating from a physically large source. It is either reflected or directed through a diffusing medium.

Diffusers For lenses: Fine nets, muslin, granulated or grooved glass, positioned in front of the lens. For lamps: Cellular diffusing materials like tight nets, spun glass, etc., placed in front of the lamp.

Dimmer An instrument used to change the voltage of lights on the set, regulating in this way their intensity. Not recommended for color cinematography, as the color temperature of the lights will also change.

Discontinuous Spectrum Characteristic of light sources such as fluorescent tubes, which emit energy only in a few wavelength bands of the spectrum. Some colors are not represented in the discontinuous spectrum.

Dissolve Also called "lap dissolve." An optical effect representing a transition through a superimposed disappearance of one scene and appearance of the next.

Dolly A wheeled vehicle for mounting a camera and accommodating a camera operator and assistant. Often equipped with a boom on which the camera is mounted.

Dot Shadow-forming device in the form of a small round **scrim.**

Double Exposure Two pictures exposed on the same frame of film, resulting in **superimposition.**

Double-Headed Projection A synchronous projection of separate picture and sound tracks, which are run in **interlock.** Done on a double-system projector.

Double-System Sound Recording Synchronous shooting system in which the sound is recorded on a tape or film separate from the film in the camera. See also **single-system sound recording.**

Dubbing 1. See **dialog replacement.** 2. Another term for **re-recording.**

Dupe Negative See **picture duplicate negative.**

Dynamic Range The difference in decibels between the noise level and the overload level of a sound system.

Edge Fogging Unwanted exposure on the film edges caused by light leaks in the camera, film magazines, or film cans if faulty or misused.

Edge Numbers Also called "key numbers," or "negative numbers." Numbers and key lettering exposed every half foot on the edge of the raw stock

and consequently reprinted on the printing stock. These numbers make it possible to synchronize the original footage and the work print at the **conforming** stage.

Editing Machine Vertical or horizontal viewing machine for running separate picture films and sound tracks in sync or independently. Modern designs achieve high levels of sophistication in the range of available operations.

Editorial Synchronism (Edit Sync) Picture and sound track on separate films arranged and marked in synchronous relationship for editing purposes in parallel alignment, i.e., corresponding frames of picture and sound are opposite each other in the editing equipment. See also **projection synchronism.**

Effects Track A sound track containing sound effects as opposed to dialog, narration, and music tracks.

Electronic Clapper See **slate, electronic.**

Electroprint An electroprint process of transferring sound directly from the magnetic track to the optical track of the release print.

Emulsion A light-sensitive coating composed of silver halides suspended in gelatin, which is spread over a film base.

Erasing Removing of the magnetic pattern from a tape or film by passing the tape through a magnetic field that is alternating at a high frequency.

Establishing Shot A shot usually close to the beginning of a scene defining the place, time, and other important elements of the action.

Exciter Lamp Part of the optical sound recording and reading system; it excites a current in a phototube. This current is modulated by an optical sound track moving between the lamp and the phototube, resulting in sound reproduction through amplifiers and loudspeakers.

Exposure A process of subjecting a photographic film to any light intensity for a given time, resulting in a **latent image.**

Exposure Index A series of numbers, such as ASA ratings, that enables one to determine the correct exposure when using a light meter, exposure tables, or even experience.

Exposure Meter An instrument for measuring the light intensity, either incident upon or reflected from a photographic subject.

Fade-Out, Fade-In An optical effect consisting of the picture's gradual disappearance into blackness (fade-out), or appearance from the blackness (fade-in).

Fall-Off 1. A gradual diminishing of light falling on the set obtained by the use of barndoors, flags, etc. 2. Weakening of light intensity when the distance from the light source increases.

Fast Lens See **speed.**

Fill Leader Film leader, usually white or yellow, used to fill those parts of a sound roll where sound does not occur, when preparing separate rolls bearing different sounds such as dialog, music, effects, etc., for a sound **mixing** session.

Fill Light Light coming from the camera direction

and illuminating the shadows caused by the **key light**.

Film Chain Also called "telecine." Technical process of showing film materials on the television screen.

Film Plane Plane in which film is held during exposure. It is often marked on the outside of camera body to facilitate the tape measurement to the photographed subject for focusing purposes.

Filter Factor A number by which the exposure must be multiplied to allow for the light absorption of an optical filter.

Final Trial Composite A composite print with all required corrections accomplished and therefore ready for release.

Fine Cut The work print at an advanced stage of editing.

Finger Narrow rectangular shadow-casting device. See also **flag**.

First Trial Composite First composite print, usually showing the necessity for further corrections in color, density, sound quality, etc.

Fishpole A long lightweight hand-held rod on which a microphone can be mounted in situations where the **boom** is not practical.

Fixing Film-processing stage after development, when the unexposed silver halides are converted into soluble silver salts, to be removed by rinsing in water. Fixing terminates the film's sensitivity to light.

Flag Shadow-casting device made of plywood or cloth stretched on a metal frame. Specific types of flag include the **cutter, finger, gobo,** and **target**.

Flange A disk used on a rewinder, against which the film is wound on a core.

Flare 1. Spots and streaks on film caused by strong directional light reflected off the lens components or filters. Also caused by leaks in the magazines and camera body. 2. Uniform, overall fog caused by reflections in some lenses.

Flat A section of a studio set, usually modular, 8 to 10 feet high and 6 inches to 12 feet wide. Constructed on a wooden frame covered with a variety of materials like plywood, fireproof hessian, etc. Surface treatments vary from paints to wallpapers, papier-mâché, fabrics, metals, etc.

Flat Light Shadowless frontal light, usually from soft-light sources.

Flip-Over An optical effect of the picture on the screen turning over in the horizontal or vertical axis and revealing another image.

Fluid Head A type of tripod head in which the slowing effect of a fluid being pushed through narrow channels is employed to cushion any jerky movements and smooth out horizontal and vertical rotations.

Flutter, Picture Also called "breathing." Picture unsteadiness caused by an unwanted film movement in the optical axis of camera, printer, or projector.

Flutter, Sound See **wow and flutter**.

F-Number Also called f-stop. A number obtained by dividing the focal length of the lens by its effective **aperture**. F-numbers represent the **speed** of the lens at any given **diaphragm** setting.

Focal Length The distance between the principal point (effective optical center) of the lens and the focal point (film plane), when the lens is focused at infinity.

Focal Plane A plane in which the image of a distant object is sharply formed by a lens focused on infinity. It should coincide with the **film plane**.

Focal Point, Principal Point at the intersection of the lens's optical axis and the focal plane.

Focus 1. See **focal point**. 2. Colloquially, the position of an object at the exact distance at which the lens is focused.

Fog Density The density of a developed piece of film caused by factors other than light, such as age, temperature, etc.

Fogging, Chemical Film density caused during processing by certain chemicals in the developer or by excessive exposure to air during development.

Fogging, Light Film density caused by unwanted exposure to light.

Follow Focus A technique of continuous refocusing of a lens during the shot in which the distance between the camera and the subject changes more than can be accommodated by the depth of field.

Follow Shot Shot in which the camera is moved to follow the action.

Foot-Candle International unit of illumination. The intensity of light falling on a sphere placed one foot away from a point source of light of one candlepower, i.e., one **candela**.

Foot-Lambert International unit of brightness. Equal to the uniform brightness of a perfectly diffusing surface emitting or reflecting light at the rate of one **lumen** per square foot.

Frame One individual picture on a strip of film.

Freeze-Frame An optical effect of arresting the film action by printing one frame several consecutive times.

Frequency The rate of vibration, measured by the number of complete cycles executed in one second. The unit of frequency is a cycle per second, called a Hertz (Hz).

Fresnel Lens A type of lens used on spotlights. The convex surface is reduced to concentric ridges, to avoid overheating and to reduce weight. Lamps equipped with this lens are called Fresnels in popular usage.

Friction Head A type of tripod head in which a smoothly sliding friction mechanism regulates the camera pan and tilt movements. The amount of friction required can be adjusted.

Front Projection See **process projection**.

FX Abbreviation for "effects," such as sound effects or special effects.

Gaffer The chief electrician on the film crew.

Gaffer's Tape Wide and strong adhesive tape used for securing the lighting instruments, stands, cables, etc., on the set.

Gamma A degree of photographic contrast arrived at by measuring a slope of the straight-line portion of the **D log E curve** of a photographic emulsion.

Gang, Synchronizer A term describing the accommodation of each film in a synchronizer. Synchronizers are rated as 2-gang, 3-gang, 4-gang, etc.

Gate The aperture and pressure-plate unit in cameras and projectors.

Gator Grip An alligator-type grip used to attach lightweight lamps to sets, furniture, pipes, etc., mainly on location. A stronger variety is called a gaffer grip.

Geared Head A type of tripod head in which the pan and tilt movements are operated by crank handles through a gear system. These gears can be regulated.

Generation A term used in describing how many printing stages separate a given film from the original.

Geometry, Film The print emulsion position (**wind**) in relation to the left-right picture orientation. Geometry changes in successive printing generations.

Ghost See **halation**.

Gobo A black wooden or cloth screen (a large **flag**) used on a stand or a clamp to protect the lens from direct strong light that could cause **flare**.

Grading A lab operation before printing to select printer lights and color filters to correct the densities and color rendition of the original footage and thus obtain a visually more satisfactory print. The technician in charge is called a timer or grader.

Grain Fine silver particles embedded in the gelatin of a film emulsion.

Graininess Impression of nonuniformity in the photographic image caused by silver particles (grains) suspended in random fashion in many layers. The depth of these layers depends on the density of the image.

Green Print A print that, because of improper lab handling during hardening or drying, does not go smoothly through the projector gate.

Gray Scale Chart representing a series of gray fields from white to black in definite steps.

Grip A member of a film crew responsible for laying camera tracks, erecting scaffolds, helping with set construction, etc.

Ground Glass A finely ground glass on which an image is formed in the camera viewfinder system.

Guide Track A sound track recorded synchronously with the picture in acoustically poor conditions to be used as a guide during the post-synchronizing session.

H&D Curve See **D log E curve**.

Halation Also called "ghost image." A halolike, blurred flare surrounding the outlines of bright objects caused by light reflected from the film base. Almost eliminated in modern emulsions.

Halogen Elements such as iodine, chlorine, bromine, fluorine, and astatine are classified as halogens. They are used in manufacturing tungsten halogen lamps, such as quartz-iodine bulbs.

Head, Camera Also called "tripod head." A device for mounting the camera on a tripod or other supports. It allows for vertical and horizontal camera movements, called tilting and panning respectively. See also **friction head, gear head, fluid head.**

Hertz (Hz) Unit of frequency. One Hertz equals one cycle per second. 1000 Hz equals 1 KHz (kiloHertz).

High-Key A lighting style in which the majority of the scene is in highlights. Usually enhanced by bright costumes and sets. Low ratio of key plus fill light to fill light lowers the contrast, helping to obtain this effect.

High-Hat Low camera support of fixed height.

Highlights The brightest parts of a photographed subject, represented as the heaviest densities on the negative and as the most transparent on the positive.

Horse A simple cutting-room device for dispensing film. Often used for supplying the **leader.**

Hot Spot A very bright area in the scene, caused by excessive light or a strong reflection.

Hue A scientific term for color.

Hyperfocal Distance Distance at which a lens must be focused to give the greatest depth of field. Then all objects from infinity down to half the hyperfocal distance will be in acceptable focus.

Incandescent Light Electric light produced by the glowing of a metallic filament such as tungsten. Modern quartz-type lamps, better called tungsten-halogen lamps, are incandescent.

Incident Light Light coming directly from the source toward the object and the light meter, as opposed to light reflected from the photographed subject toward the light meter. See also **exposure meter.**

Infrared A range of wavelengths slightly longer than those in the visible spectrum.

Inky-Dink The smallest focusable studio lamp, with Fresnel lens and a bulb up to 200 watts.

Insert A shot inserted to explain the action, e.g. a closeup of a letter, newspaper headline, calendar, gun, etc.

Interlock System Electrical or mechanical system in which two mechanisms will start, stop, and run in synchronization. Used for cameras, sound systems, and projectors.

Intermittent Movement The stop-and-go movement of the film-transport mechanism in the projector or camera, making it possible for each individual frame to be stationary during the moment of exposure or projection.

Intermittent Pressure Pressure applied on film in the camera gate during the periods of rest in the intermittent-movement cycle.

Internegative A negative printed from a color reversal original.

Iris See **diaphragm.**

Jam, Camera Also called "salad." A camera trouble when film piles up inside the camera body, sometimes caught up between the sprocket wheels and the guide rollers.

Jellies, Color Color gelatin filters used in front of the lamps.

Junior (2K) A studio lamp, focusable, with Fresnel lens and 2000-watt bulb. Perhaps the most used studio lighting instrument.

Kelvin Scale A temperature scale used in expressing the color temperature. Kelvin degrees have the same intervals as the Centigrade scale, but $0°$ K $= -273°$ C.

Key Light The main source used to light the subject. Its direction and amount relative to fill light establishes the mood of the illumination.

Key Numbers See **edge numbers.**

Kinescope Recording Process of recording on a motion-picture film pictures that originated in a television camera.

Lamp A term basically used for the light bulbs of various designs, but also employed to describe the lighting instrument as a whole.

Lap Dissolve See **dissolve.**

Latent Image An invisible image formed in the photographic emulsion when it is exposed to light. Latent image becomes visible after the development.

Latitude, Exposure An emulsion's ability to accommodate a certain range of exposures and produce satisfactory pictures.

Leader Uniformly black, white, colored, or transparent film used in editing processes, such as preparing sound tracks or A-B rolls, or for head and tail protection of film rolls. See also **SMPTE universal leader.**

Lekolite An ellipsoidal spotlight with pattern-forming capability manufactured by Century Strand, Inc. Very popular in theater lighting but also used in film and TV as effect light.

Lighting Instruments The proper term in the film industry for lighting sources (luminaries) of different designs. Sometimes they are popularly called "lamps," but strictly speaking, a lamp is just the electric bulb in the lighting instrument.

Logging, Film Entering in a logbook all the printed shots itemized by scene and take number, length in feet and frames, and edge numbers. A description of the action is also included.

Long Pitch Specific distance between film perforations designed for original camera stocks, which could also be used in projection (such as some reversal stocks), and for films used in high-speed cameras.

Loop, Film Slack loop formed before and after the gate in cameras and projectors to accommodate the transition from continuous to intermittent movement.

Low-Key Lighting style in which the majority of a scene is scarcely lit. Usually enhanced by dark costumes and sets. High ratio of key light to key plus fill light is employed for this effect.

LS (Long Shot) Full figure filling the frame.

Lumen The light emitted by a source of power of one **candela** which falls on one square unit of surface at one unit of distance from the source.

Lux An international unit of light intensity. One lux equals an illumination of a surface, all points of which are 1 meter distant from a point source of 1 **candela.** One **foot-candle** = 10.764 lux.

Macrocinematography Filming of small objects, often requiring lens extension with bellows or extension rings, but not so small as to necessitate filming through a microscope.

Magnetic Film Magnetic recording materials in one of the standard film gauges, with sprocket holes on one side in 16mm or on both sides for 35mm and wider gauges.

Magnetic Head Electromagnet containing a coil or coils of wire wound over an iron ring broken to create an air gap. Used to record electromagnetic variations on recording materials.

Magnetic Master A final edited or re-recorded magnetic track used for transfer to magnetic or optical release prints or to produce another master.

Magnetic Tape Thin plastic base, like PVC or polyester, coated with magnetic iron oxide dispersed in a binder.

Magnetic Recording Recording sound or picture by introducing magnetic changes in a ferromagnetic medium, such as the coating on magnetic tapes and films.

Married Print See **composite print.**

Master Positive See **picture master positive.**

Mask Opaque shape, often in contact with film, preventing the exposure of certain parts of the frame. Can either be in the form of a film strip traveling in contact with the film stock to be exposed, or as a plate in a camera, projector, or printer aperture to regulate the size and shape of the picture frame. Sometimes means a light-obstructing device of desired shape in front of the lens.

Matte See **mask.**

Matte Box A combination of filter and/or matte holder and sun shade mounted in front of the camera lens.

Meat Axe A colloquial term for a small **flag** or **scrim** holder.

Microcinematography Cinematography through the microscope.

Mixing Creatively combining the sound signals coming from several microphones, or several tapes, and re-recording them onto a single track.

Molefays Lighting instruments manufactured by Mole-Richardson Co. in the range from one-bulb to twelve-bulb clusters, employing usually the FAY type (650-watt) bulbs. Used for an even illumination of large areas, often to provide a fill light in outdoor filming. FAY bulb has a color temperature of 5000° K, but can be replaced by bulbs of other color temperatures.

Molepars Lighting instruments manufactured by Mole-Richardson Co. in the range from one-bulb to nine-bulb clusters, employing the 1000-watt PAR lamps.

MOS Filming without sound (silent). A humorous coinage from the early days of cinema, when immigrant German technicians spoke of shooting "mit out sound."

Moviola A trade name of an editing machine that allows viewing picture film or films synchronously, with one or more sound films. Often used as a generic term in referring to editing machines in general.

MS (Medium Shot) Frame composition in which a three-quarter-length figure fills the screen.

Negative Numbers See **edge numbers.**

NG "No good," notation for picture and sound takes that will not be used in the final edited film.

Negative Image A photographic picture with reversed brightnesses of the photographed scene. What was bright in the scene is dark (dense) in negative and vice versa.

Neutral Density (ND) Filters Colorless filters in range of densities, used to cut down the amount of light entering the lens. Employed on the camera or on the windows. ND filters do not affect the color rendition of the lens. Used when the light is too intense for a given film, or a required f-stop.

Newton Rings Ring patterns on film print caused by optical interference when light passes through two film surfaces slightly separated by the imperfect contact in a contact printer.

Nitrate Base Film base made of cellulose nitrate, highly inflammable and self-igniting under certain conditions. Used up to 1951, when it was superseded by the tri-acetate safety base.

Noise An unwanted sound or signal generated in the sound or video system or transferred by these systems from other sources, such as the power supply.

Opacity A ratio of the light incident upon the measured portion of film frame to the light transmitted. The logarithm of the opacity equals the density.

Optical Effects Special effects such as fades, dissolves, superimpositions, freeze-frames, split screens, wipes, etc., usually created at the printing stage.

Optical Negative Track See **sound release negative.**

Optical Sound Recording Process of converting electrical sound signals into light-beam intensity or width, in order to record these signals on light-sensitive emulsion, creating in this fashion an optical sound track of variable density or variable area, respectively. Today used mainly in the preparation of release prints.

Original (Negative or Reversal) Film stock that was exposed and processed to produce either a negative or a reversal picture.

Orthochromatic Film Black-and-white film emulsion sensitive only to blue and green.

Out-Takes (Out) Shots or takes that will not be used in the final version of the film.

Overload An amplitude distortion in sound recording when the system receives a signal of higher amplitude than it can carry.

Panchromatic Film Black-and-white film with an emulsion sensitive to all colors of the visible spectrum.

Pan, Panning Camera pivotal movement in a horizontal plane. Sometimes used when describing pivotal camera movements in other planes.

Parallax A displacement of an image as seen by the independent viewfinder in relation to the image as seen through the lens. Especially evident in closeups. Independent viewfinders are usually adjustable to match the view area of the lens but not the lens's perspective.

Parallel A wheeled scaffolding with raised platform to accommodate the camera crew for high-angle shots, or the lamps and electricians.

Perforations, Film Accurately spaced holes along one or both edges of the film, used to position and move the film through various mechanisms, such as cameras, printers, and projectors.

Persistence of Vision The phenomenon of the eye retaining for a short period of time the image just seen. Therefore a stream of images of short duration (such as projected frames of film) are seen as a continuous picture without flicker.

Photoflood Type of light bulb in which a very high voltage reaches the filament, boosting the light output and color temperature, but shortening the life of the bulb itself.

Picture Duplicate Negative (Dupe) Negative printed from a master positive, or a reversal printed straight from the picture negative.

Picture Master Positive Special print made as an intermediate step in producing a picture duplicate negative.

Picture Print Film print bearing positive images.

Picture Release Negative Edited picture negative from which the picture part of release prints will be printed.

Pilot Pin See **registration pin.**

Pilot Print A color test strip provided by the lab with the black-and-white rushes printed for economy reasons from a color original. A pilot print gives the cameraman an indication of how his shots will look when printed in color through various filter combinations.

Pitch The distance between the leading edge of one perforation and the leading edge of the next along the length of the film.

Plate, or Process Plate Background materials (still or motion picture) shot to be used in back or front projection. See also **process projection.**

Playback Instant playback of recorded materials to check the quality of recording. Playback also means a reproduction of previously recorded music, vocals, etc., when filming the performers in acoustically adverse conditions. In this technique the sound is recorded (pre-scored) in the sound studio and the picture is filmed on a visually desirable location while playing back the previously recorded sound.

Polarity Correct polarity in connecting the batteries or other power sources means that the plus terminal on the power source is connected to the plus terminal on the equipment, and the minus terminals are connected accordingly. Plus is usually marked red.

Polecats Extensible metal tubes to erect a lamp support in the form of a pipe wedged between the walls, or floor and ceiling, of a room, or used in conjunction with other tubes to form a more elaborate scaffolding for holding lamps. Pole Kings manufactured by Berkey Colortran, Inc. are a good example of this equipment.

Post-Flashing, Post-Fogging A method of reducing contrast of some films (mainly Ektachrome EF) by additional exposure of the already exposed but not developed film, by a weak and even light. This procedure causes a slight overall fogging, which affects the shadows more than the highlights of the picture, hence reduces the contrast.

Post-Synchronization See **dialog replacement.**

Practical A lamp or other prop on the set that is rigged to be operational during the scene action.

Pre-Scoring Recording of sound track to accompany the action, which is shot to the playback of this sound track. Used often when filming singers or musicians performing in acoustically inferior locations.

Pressure Plate A part of film gate in the camera, optical printer, or projector that presses the film, keeping it flat against the aperture plate during the exposure.

Primary Colors Blue, green, and red. By mixing these three colors of light, all others hues can be obtained.

Print, Picture See **picture print.**

Print, Reversal See **reversal print.**

Printer Machine for printing from one strip of film (exposed and processed) to another strip of film (raw stock), by moving both these films in front of an aperture with regulated illumination. There are continuous and step printers, depending on the mode in which the film moves. Another division, mainly among step printers, distinguishes the contact printer, in which two strips of film touch each other emulsion to emulsion, and the optical printer, in which the picture is exposed on the raw stock via an optical system. This allows for picture modifications such as change in frame size and shape, zoom effect, freeze-frame, flip-over, wipe, rotation, etc.

Printer Light Scale A scale of variations in printing-light intensity, allowing one to print the original images brighter or darker, to obtain an evenly exposed print from an original with uneven exposures. The light scale is also used when executing optical effects such as fades and dissolves.

Print-Through A condition where the signals recorded on tightly wound magnetic tape affect the coating of adjacent layers, causing an echo effect when the tape is played. High recording levels and high temperature in storage will augment the print-through effect.

Processing All the chemical and physical operations necessary to convert a latent image into a satisfactory picture on film.

Process Projection A technique of filming live action staged in front of the screen on which the background view is projected. This background plate can be projected either from behind the translucent screen (back projection), or from the front on a highly reflective screen (front projection).

Process Shot A shot of live action in front of a

process projection.

Projection Synchronism (Projection Sync) A 26-frame displacement between the optical sound track and the 16mm picture on the **composite print**, to accommodate the distance between a film gate and an exciter lamp on the 16mm projectors.

Props Short for "properties," i.e., movable objects used on the set in the filmed scenes.

Protection Print (Protective Master) A master positive print made from the assembled original (A-B rolls) and kept as a protection in case the original is damaged or lost.

Pull-Down The action of moving the film one frame at a time for exposure or projection by the intermittent mechanism of the camera, printer, or projector. See also **intermittent movement**.

Pup Light See **baby light**.

PVC Base Tape or film base made of polyvinyl chloride.

Quartz Lights Popular name for tungsten-halogen lamps. Tungsten filament and halogen gas are sealed in an envelope made of quartz or other materials that permit bulb temperature up to 600° C. The particles evaporating from the filament combine with the halogen gas and are redeposited back on the filament. This recycling process prevents the darkening of the bulb so that the color temperature stays fairly constant during the lamp's life.

Radio Microphone A microphone with a miniature transmitter and a piece of wire as an aerial. The receiving station can amplify the signal and transmit it to a recorder located even farther away.

Raw Stock A film that has not yet been exposed and/or processed.

Rectifier An instrument to convert alternating current into direct current.

Reduction Printing Optical printing of a film onto a raw stock of a smaller gauge.

Reflector A board with a light-reflecting surface, hard or soft depending on the texture of the surface, used mainly for redirecting the sunlight to fill light into the shadows in the scene.

Registration The positioning of film in the aperture gate of a camera, printer, or projector in precisely the same place for each consecutive frame.

Registration Pin A part of the intermittent mechanism in more elaborate cameras. It secures the steadiness of the film by engaging the perforation during the period of exposure.

Release Negative See **picture release negative**.

Release Print A composite print made in projection synchronism for general distribution, after an approval of the **final trial composite print**.

Re-Recording Transferring several sound tracks, e.g. dialog, music, and effects, onto a single track, creatively mixing sounds by controlling levels and other characteristics.

Reticulation A phenomenon of emulsion cracking in a leather-grain pattern, caused by too high a temperature in processing.

Reversal Print A print made on a reversal material.

Reversal Master Print 16mm reversal print used to make other prints.

Retrofocal Lens (Inverted Telephoto Lens) A lens of a special optical design that allows a longer physical distance between the rear end of the lens and the film plane. Convenient in the design of lenses with nominally extremely short focal length; the retrofocal design increases physical size and facilitates mounting and operating.

Rewinds Geared devices for rewinding film. Manual rewinds are usually used in editing rooms, and electric ones in projection rooms and libraries.

Rigging Positioning lamps in the studio according to the preliminary lighting plot.

Riser A low platform to raise an actor, camera, or furniture a few inches off the ground.

Rough Cut Roughly edited film at the work-print stage with finer changes to be made before the **fine cut**.

Rushes See **dailies**.

Safety Base See **acetate base**.

Salad See **jam**.

Sample Print See **final trial composite print**.

Saturation The criterion of the purity of a color. It indicates the distinctness and vividness of hue. Color is most saturated when it appears the strongest and most brilliant, least saturated when a color is approaching a neutral gray.

Scoop A studio lamp of a soft, wide, round pattern; 500 to 1500 watts.

Scratch Print (Slash Print) A print made from an assembled original (A-B rolls), but without the printer-light corrections. Used for music or narration recording and similar applications where the visual quality is of little importance.

Scratch Track See **guide track**.

Scribe Sharp, pointed instrument to scratch the emulsion when marking film edges in preparation for **conforming** original footage for splicing.

Scrim Lighting accessory made of wire mesh, silk, spun glass, or plastic translucent materials, positioned in front of a light source when attenuation or diffusion of light is required.

Script A written screenplay that undergoes several phases from an outline and rough treatment to the final shooting script where all the scenes are described in detail.

Secondary Colors See **complementary colors**.

Senior (5K) Focusable studio lamp with a Fresnel lens and 5000-watt bulb.

Sensitometer An instrument in which a strip of film is exposed to a series of light intensities in logarithmic steps, which will produce corresponding densities when the film strip is developed.

Sensitometry The science of measuring a film emulsion's sensitivity to light and of evaluating the related processes, such as development.

Sensitometric Strip Film strip exposed to a series of logarithmically growing light intensities in a sensitometer, developed and measured for densities to establish a proper developing time for the given emulsion.

Shooting Script See **script**.

Shot A homogeneous element of the film structure between two cuts or two optical transitions.

Shutter A mechanism for covering the aperture of a camera during the period in which the film is moved between exposures.

Silver Halide Light-sensitive silver compound such as silver bromide, silver chloride, silver fluoride, or silver iodide, used in photographic emulsions.

Single-System Sound Recording A technique of recording synchronous sound simultaneously with the picture on the magnetic track adhering to the edge of a picture film.

Sky Light (Sky Pan) A nonfocusable studio lamp with a 5000-watt to 10,000-watt bulb providing illumination over a broad area, such as set backdrops.

Slate Board A board with written information such as production title and number, scene and take number, and director's and cameraman's names, photographed at the beginning or end of each take as identification. See also **clapper board** and **slate, electronic**.

Slate, Electronic An electrical device synchronously exposing a few frames in the camera and providing an electric signal that is recorded on the magnetic tape, so that the two can later be matched in editing.

Slip Focus See **differential focus**.

SMPTE Society of Motion Picture and Television Engineers.

SMPTE Universal Leader (Society Leader) Film leader introduced in 1965 with numbers from 8 to 2, each printed over 24 frames, i.e., one second at standard projection speed. A rotating line covers a full circle in each second.

Snoot A funnel-shaped light-controlling device used on lamps in place of barndoors for more exact light-beam pattern.

Sound Boom See **boom**.

Sound Displacement See **projection sync**.

Sound Master Positive Special sound print made from a sound release negative in order to produce sound duplicate negatives used for making release prints.

Sound Print A positive print with sound only, made from (1) a sound negative; (2) sound positive through reversal process; (3) direct from magnetic tape, as positive recording.

Sound Release Negative An optical sound negative from which final sound printing onto the release print will be made.

Sound Speed Standardized speed of filming and projecting at 24 frames per second, when picture is synchronized with a sound track. Applies to films of all gauges.

Sound Track An optical or magnetic band carrying the sound record alongside the picture frames on a motion-picture film. Also any magnetic or optical sound film at the stage of editing and mixing.

Spectrum, Visible A narrow band of electromagnetic waves from approximately 400 to about 700 millimicrons, which produce in the human brain a sensation of light.

Speed 1. Camera speed is the rate of film advancement, expressed in frames per second (fps). 2. Lens speed is the full amount of light a lens is capable of transmitting, expressed as a lowest f-stop (purely geometrical computation), or as a lowest T-stop (real-light transmission as measured individually for the given lens). 3. Emulsion speed is the emulsion sensitivity to light, expressed as an index of exposure.

Splicer A machine for joining pieces of film together. Depending on the method used, there are tape splicers and cement splicers. Cement splicers can be cold or hot (heated for faster splices), negative or positive (making narrower or wider splices respectively), and hand- or foot-operated, the latter being much faster in operation.

Splicing Technique of joining separate film pieces into a continuous film strip. At the work-print stage, transparent tape splices are the most common, as the tape can easily be removed for changes in editing. Originals or damaged release prints are joined with a cement splice, which welds together the two pieces of film in a more permanent way. A negative splice, used for joining original footage, is narrow and therefore less visible, and the positive splice, used to repair broken prints, is wider.

Split Reel A reel with a removable side, so that the film on a core can be placed in or removed from the reel without rewinding.

Spotlamp A general name for many studio lamps of similar design but different in size, such as the **baby, junior,** and **senior.** Equipped with Fresnel lens and focusable from spot to flood beam pattern.

Static Marks Unwanted exposures in the form of random lines caused by discharges of static electricity. They occur when unexposed film stock is rewound, especially at an uneven speed, or when the rewinds are not grounded. They may also happen in the camera through too much friction, particularly in low temperatures and low humidity.

Step Printer See **printer.**

Still A static photograph as opposed to the motion picture.

Stock Footage Film-library footage of famous or typical places and situations, historical events, and the like, which can be used more than once in different film productions.

Story Board A series of drawings as visual representation of the shooting script. Sketches represent the key situations (shots) in the scripted scenes. Dialog or indication of music, effects, etc. appear below the pictures.

Superimposition (Super) Two scenes exposed on the same piece of raw film stock, one on top of the other. Superimposition is usually done in the printer, but can be performed in the camera, although this offers less control of the operation.

Swish Pan A very fast panoramic movement of the camera, resulting in a blurred image. Used sometimes as a transition between sequences or scenes.

Sync Motor (Synchronous Motor) Constant-speed motor for camera or projector that can be electrically or mechanically synchronized, i.e. run at the same speed along with the sound-recording and/or sound-reproducing machines.

Sync Pop One-frame sound signal placed near the heads of the edited sound tracks to confirm proper synchronization during mixing operation.

Sync Tone Oscillator Small oscillator in the camera producing electrical signals that indicate exactly the speed of the camera motor. These signals are transmitted to the sound recorder and recorded on magnetic tape as a guide enabling precise synchronization of sound and picture at the later stage. Sync pulses are inaudible on normal playback and do not interfere with the sound recording on tape.

Synchronism Coordination of picture and sound. See **editorial synchronism, projection synchronism.**

Synchronous Speed Camera speed of exactly 24 frames per second synchronized with the sound recording.

T-Stop Calibration of the lens light-transmitting power arrived at by an actual measurement of the transmitted light for each lens and each stop individually. T-stops are considered more accurate than f-stops (**f-numbers**).

Tachometer A meter indicating the camera speed in frames per second.

Take A scene or part of a scene recorded on film and/or sound tape from each start to each stop of a camera and/or recorder. Each **shot** may be repeated in several takes, until a satisfactory result is achieved.

Target A black disk, up to 10 inches in diameter, used to control the lamp beam and create desirable shadows. A type of **flag.**

Telecine See **film chain.**

Tenner (10 K) A studio focusable lamp with Fresnel lens and 10,000-watt bulb.

Test Strip Several feet of film left at the beginning or end of the roll for lab tests before the rest of the roll is developed. Test strip can be of unexposed footage to be used as a **sensitometric strip,** or of footage exposed in the same manner as the rest of the roll to be tested for the optimal development time necessary to obtain the most pleasing picture. This second method may be used when the cameraman has some doubts about the correctness of his exposure calculations.

Threading Also called "lacing." Placing film in a proper way for correct passage through all the film-transport mechanisms of camera, printer, projector, or other film-handling machine.

Tilt, Tilting Camera pivotal movement in a vertical plane. Sometimes called vertical **panning.**

Timing See **grading.**

Timing Card Listing of **printer** lights to be used for printing from the given original. This card is then kept for future reference.

Tracking See **dolly.**

Transfer, Sound Process of duplicating sound recording, e.g. from ¼-inch magnetic tape to 16mm magnetic film for editing, or from 16mm or 35mm magnetic master to 16mm optical track in the preparation of a composite print.

Treatment A literary presentation of an idea for a future film before a proper script is developed.

Trial Composite Print See **first trial composite print.**

Triangle A triangular device made of metal or wood and used as a tripod base to prevent the tripod legs from slipping.

Trim Bin See **bin.**

Trims Leftover pieces of film from the shots that were incorporated into the work print and the final composite print. These unused trims are filed in case the editor changes his mind.

Trombone A tubular device for hanging small studio lamps from the top of set walls.

Tungsten Light Light generated by an incandescent lamp with a tungsten filament.

Turret, Lens A revolving lens mount for two to four lenses, enabling the cameraman to make a fast choice of lens for the next shot.

Ultraviolet A range of wavelengths shorter than those in the visible spectrum but detected by film emulsions unless an ultraviolet (UV) filter is used to stop this radiation.

Universal Leader See **SMPTE universal leader.**

Variable-Area Track An optical sound track on which the electrical signals are recorded as the varying width of a constant-density image.

Variable-Density Track An optical sound track on which the electrical signals are recorded as the varying density of the image.

Variable-Focus Lens See **zoom lens.**

Variable-Speed Motor See **wild motor.**

Vignetting Blurring of the photographic image on the sides of the frame, caused by close-range objects obscuring the view. Unintentional vignetting is sometimes caused by a sun shade extended too far in front of the lens or a badly positioned flag to protect the lens from flare. In some camera designs a long lens mounted in an adjacent turret socket can cause vignetting.

VO (Voice-Over) Indication in the script that the shot, scene, etc., will be accompanied by a voice not visibly originating in the picture. Voice-over can be in the form of narration, inner monologue, "voice from the past," etc.

VU Meter Volume-unit meter, indicating the recording level on sound recording equipment.

Walk-Through First rehearsal on the set, for camera positions, lighting, sound, etc., when the director describes the scene in detail to the crew and the actors. Sometimes stand-ins are used instead of actors for this operation.

Waxing Applying wax to the edges of film to improve the film passage through the projector and prevent the piling up of emulsion, which is likely if the film has been incorrectly dried during processing.

Weave Undesirable sideward movement of film in the camera or projector.

Wild Motor Camera motor that does not run at an exact synchronous speed. Usually adjustable for different speeds.

Wild Recording Sound recording not synchronized with the picture, such as many sound effects, and background noise. This recording results in a wild track.

Wind Film wind refers to the emulsion position on the roll of a single sprocket film. See **A-wind, B-wind.**

Work print A print built up from dailies. It undergoes editorial improvements from the assembly stage through **rough cut** to a **fine cut.** Finally it is used to guide the negative cutter when **conforming** the original.

Wow and Flutter Sound distortions in recording or playback caused by speed variations in the tape movement.

XLS (Extreme Long Shot) Distant landscape or vast interior shot in which the human figures appear relatively small.

Zoom, Zooming The magnification of a certain area of the frame by bringing it optically to the full screen size and excluding the rest of the frame in the process.

Zoom Lens A lens with a continuously variable focal length over a certain range allowing the change of subject magnification during the shot. On many modern cameras zoom lenses substitute for the standard complement of primary lenses.

Bibliography

GENERAL BOOKS ON FILM TECHNIQUES AND PRODUCTION

Baddeley, W. Hugh. *The Technique of Documentary Film Production.* New York: Hastings House, 1969. A practical and well-written book on various aspects of documentary film work.

The Focal Encyclopedia of Film and Television Techniques. New York: Hastings House, 1969. A major reference book with 1,600 entries and a compact overall view titled "Film and Television: A Basic Anatomy" at the end of the book. Expensive.

Happe, L. Bernard. *Basic Motion Picture Technology.* New York: Hastings House, 1971. A comprehensive survey of film technology written in a remarkably clear manner and full of precise information. Well illustrated. To be recommended.

Lipton, Lenny. *Independent Filmmaking.* Hardcover and paperback. San Francisco: Straight Arrow Books, 1972. Well-written, extensive book on film techniques in 16mm and all 8mm formats. Mainly for film makers working outside a studio situation, and therefore does not cover studio lighting techniques.

Mercer, John. *An Introduction to Cinematography.* Paperback. Champaign, Ill.: Stipes Publishing Company, 1971. A basic textbook of film production recommended in many college film courses. Concise and practical.

Pincus, Edward. *Guide to Filmmaking.* Revised edition. Chicago: Regnery, 1972. Very practical approach to all technical phases of film production. Easy to read.

Roberts, Kenneth H., and Sharples, Win, Jr. *A Primer for Film-Making.* New York: Pegasus (Bobbs-Merrill), 1971. A large book on many aspects of film production. Good survey of camera aesthetics and creative film editing. Important.

Smallman, Kirk. *Creative Film-Making.* Paperback. London and New York: Collier-Macmillan, 1969. Film techniques described in relation to creative process. Low-budget-oriented.

Spottiswoode, Raymond. *Film and Its Techniques.* Berkeley, Calif.: University of California Press, 1963. An early textbook by the chief editor of the *Focal Encyclopedia of Film and Television Techniques.* Needs updating, but still useful reading.

Wheeler, Leslie J. *Principles of Cinematography.* New York: Macmillan, 1969. The book deals mainly with lab technology and operations. Also has informative chapters on camera principle, projection, and sound reproduction. Technical and very thorough.

CAMERA TECHNIQUES, FILMS, FILTERS, LIGHTING

Applied Infrared Photography. Kodak Technical Publication M-28. Rochester, N.Y.: Eastman Kodak Company, 1970. Very useful.

Campbell, Russell. *Photographic Theory for the Motion Picture Cameraman.* Paperback. London: Screen Textbooks, A. Zwemmer Ltd., 1970. New York: A.S. Barnes, 1970. A thorough technical explanation of film emulsion characteristics in black-and-white and color materials.

———. *Practical Motion Picture Photography.* Paperback. London: Screen Textbooks, A. Zwemmer Ltd., 1970. New York: A.S. Barnes, 1970. Very practical approach with key technical questions answered by a score of leading British cinematographers. Includes chapters on underwater and aerial photography.

Carlson, Verne and Sylvia. *Professional 16/35mm Cameraman's Handbook.* New York: AMPHOTO, 1970. Detailed operational instruction in the use of many professional cameras and related procedures. Excellent manual to have with you on the job.

Clarke, Charles G. *Professional Cinematography*. Hollywood: American Society of Cinematographers, 1968. Well-written book with special interest in Hollywood studio lighting techniques.

Clauss, Hans, and Meusel, Heinz. *Filter Practice*. London and New York: Focal Press, 1965. Very clear explanation of filters for black-and-white and color photography in everyday language. To be recommended.

Cox, A. *Photographic Optics*. London and New York: Focal Press, 1971. Fundamental work on the subject.

Feininger, Andreas. *Successful Color Photography*. New York: Prentice-Hall, 1969. A very clear introduction to the technical problems of color for still photographers, but useful also to film makers.

Fielding, Raymond. *The Technique of Special-Effects Cinematography*. New York: Hastings House, 1969. Extensive textbook on all major special effects used in films.

Lighting Handbook for Television, Theater, Professional Photography, Danver, Mass.: GTE Sylvania Inc., 1971. A manufacturer's publication, containing technical information on lamps, light characteristics, and electricity and helpful lighting hints.

Mascelli, Joseph V., ed. *American Cinematographer Manual*. Hollywood: American Society of Cinematographers, 1969. Known as the "bible," this is a compact reference book giving data and short descriptions of techniques in all aspects of cinematography.

Ross, Rodger J. *Color Film for Color Television*. New York: Hastings House, 1970. Explains the technology of color film and its use in television application. Very useful.

————. *Television Film Engineering*. New York: Wiley, 1966. Describes principles and procedures of achieving high-quality film image and sound for television transmission. Important.

Souto, H. Mario Raimondo. *The Technique of the Motion Picture Camera*. New York: Hastings House, 1969. Comprehensive survey of many modern cameras, plus a chapter on shooting techniques, trouble shooting charts, and other useful charts and information.

EDITING TECHNIQUES

Burder, John. *The Technique of Editing 16mm Films*. Revised edition. New York: Hastings House, 1971. Description of 16mm editing mechanics in clear, down-to-earth language.

Reisz, Karel, and Millar, Gavin. *The Technique of Film Editing: Basic Principles for TV*. New York: Hastings House, 1968. A classic book on the aesthetics of editing technique. Important.

Walter, Ernest. *The Technique of the Film Cutting Room*. New York: Hastings House, 1969. Probably the best book on 35mm cutting techniques, also largely applicable to 16mm production cutting.

SOUND TECHNIQUES

Huntley, John, and Manvell, Roger. *The Technique of Film Music*. New York: Hastings House, 1957. The use of film music shown in relation to the development of film art, and description of music functions in film today.

Mackenzie, G.W. *Acoustics*. London and New York: Focal Press, 1964. Combines practical aspects and scientific explanations of speech and music characteristics, microphones, room acoustics, sound insulation, and other related problems.

McWilliams, A.A. *Tape Recording and Reproduction*. London and New York: Focal Press, 1964. Thorough but probably too scientific for a beginner without the basic understanding of electronics.

Tremaine, Howard M. *The Audio Cyclopedia*. Indianapolis: H.W. Sams, 1969. Considered to be the best reference book on sound techniques in existence.

AESTHETIC AND PSYCHOLOGICAL ASPECTS OF CINEMATOGRAPHY

Evans, Ralph M. *Eye, Film, and Camera in Color Photography*. New York and London: Wiley, 1960. Basically for still photographers, but dealing with psychology of vision and other problems of importance to film makers as well.

Mascelli, J.V. *The Five C's of Cinematography*. Hollywood: Cine/Graphics Publications, 1965. Covers camera angles, continuity, cutting, closeups, composition. Useful for beginners.

Nilsen, Vladimir. *The Cinema as Graphic Art*. New York: Hill and Wang, 1959. An important classic on the aesthetics of film, written by a Russian cameraman who analyzes the theory of representation, giving many examples from the Russian silent cinema.

PRODUCTION PLANNING AND BUDGETING

Brown, William O. *Low Budget Features*. William O. Brown Co. Motion Picture Production Services, Hollywood: 1971. Excellent book for film budgeting and production planning. Very thorough. Expensive.

MONTHLY JOURNALS

American Cinematographer, International Journal of Motion Picture Photography and Production Techniques. Published by the ASC Holding Corporation, Hollywood. Very informative and easy-to-read cameraman's journal.

Journal of the Society of Motion Picture and Television Engineers. Published by the Society of Motion Picture and Television Engineers, New York. A scientific publication presenting technical developments in the field of film and television.

INDEX